A CELEBRATION OF POETS

ATLANTIC
GRADES 4-12
SPRING 2012

creativeCOMMUNICATION
A CELEBRATION OF TODAY'S WRITERS

A CELEBRATION OF POETS
ATLANTIC
GRADES 4-12
SPRING 2012

AN ANTHOLOGY COMPILED BY CREATIVE COMMUNICATION, INC.

Published by:

PO BOX 303 • SMITHFIELD, UTAH 84335
TEL. 435-713-4411 • WWW.POETICPOWER.COM

Authors are responsible for the originality of the writing submitted.

Copyright © 2012 by Creative Communication, Inc.
Printed in the United States of America

ISBN: 978-1-60050-499-0

FOREWORD

Dear Reader:

Is writing meaningful to your life? The greatest gift that my mother ever gave me was her writing. For over 70 years, she kept a record of every moment that was meaningful in her life. Taking these stories, she created several books which allow me to remember and relive moments in my childhood and the life my mother had as she grew up. She got into the habit of writing and has now left a great legacy.

As a parent, I know that my children bring home samples of their writing from school assignments each week. However, after a few days on the school bulletin board or fridge at home, these slices of their lives often get thrown away.

The books we publish create a legacy for each of these students. Their work is recorded to show friends, family and future generations. We are glad to be part of capturing their thoughts, hopes and dreams.

The students that are published have shared a bit of themselves with us. Thank you for being part of this process, as every writer needs a reader. We hope that by recognizing these students, writing will become a part of their life and bring meaning to others.

Sincerely,

Thomas Worthen, Ph.D.
Editor
Creative Communication

WRITING CONTESTS!

Enter our next POETRY contest!
Enter our next ESSAY contest!

Why should I enter?
Win prizes and get published! Each year thousands of dollars in prizes are awarded throughout North America. The top writers in each division receive a monetary award and a free book that includes their published poem or essay. Entries of merit are also selected to be published in our anthology.

Who may enter?
There are four divisions in the poetry contest. The poetry divisions are grades K-3, 4-6, 7-9, and 10-12. There are three divisions in the essay contest. The essay divisions are grades 3-6, 7-9, and 10-12.

What is needed to enter the contest?
To enter the poetry contest send in one original poem, 21 lines or less. To enter the essay contest send in one original non-fiction essay, 250 words or less, on any topic. Please submit each poem and essay with a title, and the following information clearly printed: the writer's name, current grade, home address (optional), school name, school address, teacher's name and teacher's email address (optional). Contact information will only be used to provide information about the contest. For complete contest information go to www.poeticpower.com.

How do I enter?
Enter a poem online at:
www.poeticpower.com
or
Mail your poem to:
Poetry Contest
PO Box 303
Smithfield UT 84335

Enter an essay online at:
www.poeticpower.com
or
Mail your essay to:
Essay Contest
PO Box 303
Smithfield UT 84335

When is the deadline?
Poetry contest deadlines are August 16th, December 6th and April 9th. Essay contest deadlines are July 19th, October 18th and February 19th. Students can enter one poem and one essay for each spring, summer, and fall contest deadline.

Are there benefits for my school?
Yes. We award $12,500 each year in grants to help with Language Arts programs. Schools qualify to apply for a grant by having 15 or more accepted entries.

Are there benefits for my teacher?
Yes. Teachers with five or more students published receive a free anthology that includes their students' writing.

For more information please go to our website at **www.poeticpower.com**, email us at editor@poeticpower.com or call 435-713-4411.

TABLE OF CONTENTS

STATES INCLUDED IN THIS EDITION:

DELAWARE
DISTRICT OF COLUMBIA
MAINE
MARYLAND
RHODE ISLAND
VIRGINIA

Spring 2012 Poetic Achievement Honor Schools

Teachers who had fifteen or more poets accepted to be published

The following schools are recognized as receiving a "Poetic Achievement Award." This award is given to schools who have a large number of entries of which over fifty percent are accepted for publication. With hundreds of schools entering our contest, only a small percent of these schools are honored with this award. The purpose of this award is to recognize schools with excellent Language Arts programs. This award qualifies these schools to receive a complimentary copy of this anthology. In addition, these schools are eligible to apply for a Creative Communication Language Arts Grant. Grants of two hundred and fifty dollars each are awarded to further develop writing in our schools.

Appomattox Regional Governor's School for Arts and Technology
Petersburg, VA
Sara Artley
Dr. Cindy Cunningham*
Ms. Padden
Patty Smith

Blacksburg Middle School
Christiansburg, VA
Sandra Sim*

Bladensburg High School
Bladensburg, MD
Mrs. Rankin
Mrs. White-Dashiell*

Cedar Bluff Elementary School
Cedar Bluff, VA
Kathleen Osborne*

Church of the Redeemer Christian School
Gaithersburg, MD
Toni Morris*

Corkran Middle School
Glen Burnie, MD
Ms. Blanco
Denise Calabrese*
Margaret Turnblacer

Courthouse Road Elementary School
Spotsylvania, VA
Brenda Nettles
Michelle Sims

Delaware Military Academy
Wilmington, DE
Colleen Bradley
Brittany Carson*
Tara Dick

Featherbed Lane Elementary School
Baltimore, MD
Cassandra Collins*
Alicia London
Erin Lundberg*

Floyd T Binns Middle School
Culpeper, VA
Gina Burke*
Charissa Hollyfield*

Forest Park High School
Woodbridge, VA
Tori Dingley
Laura Dowling*

Gaithersburg Elementary School
Gaithersburg, MD
Jaclynn Fowle
Ms. Giles
Ms. Sonner

Greenville Elementary School
Nokesville, VA
Susan Robertson*

Hardin Reynolds Memorial School
Critz, VA
Amy Conner*

Hebbville Elementary School
Baltimore, MD
Darnell Peaker*

Holy Cross Regional School
Lynchburg, VA
Pam St. Angelo*

Homeschool Plus
Norfolk, VA
Carol Martin-Gregory*

Kilmer Middle School
Vienna, VA
Barbara E. Appling
Mary Kay Folk*

Magnolia Elementary School
Lanham, MD
Robert Allen*

Mary Walter Elementary School
Bealeton, VA
Patricia Baker*

Massabesic Middle School
East Waterboro, ME
Kelly Grantham
Ms. Kerry
Mrs. Swett
Monica Wardwell

McLean School of Maryland
Potomac, MD
Joan Koss*
Joanne Levin

Monelison Middle School
Madison Heights, VA
Melissa Ragland*
Lynette Smith*

Mount St Charles Academy
Woonsocket, RI
Donald Hogue
Ms. Tessier
Denise Turcotte*

Norfolk Christian Middle School
Norfolk, VA
Paula Ross*

Norfolk Collegiate Middle/Upper School
Norfolk, VA
Ms. Arnold
Lindsay Belle*
Charles E. Cook*
Judy Davis
Anton Pav

Ocean Lakes High School
Virginia Beach, VA
Lora Molodow*

Rachel Carson Middle School
Herndon, VA
 Barbara S. Adams
 Kathryn Balderston
 Tiffany Estrella
 Carla Gibson
 Susan Miles
 Theresa Palmer
 Barbara Poole
 Leigh C. Toweson

Riderwood Elementary School
Towson, MD
 Gene Monahan*
 Mrs. Sussman

Rockbridge Middle School
Fairfield, VA
 Megan Ziegler*

Rosemont Forest Elementary School
Virginia Beach, VA
 Beverly Wooddell*

St Brigid School
Portland, ME
 Lorilee A. Newman*

St Christopher's School
Richmond, VA
 Cynthia Brown
 Linda DiLucente
 Deborah Epes
 Renee Fraine
 Teresa Gordon
 Marion Halladay
 Kim Harley
 Margaret Hunter
 Glorietta Jones
 Paula Jones
 Scott Mayer
 Jim Morgan
 Jen O'Ferrall
 Sandra Oakley
 Alisa Pava
 Dorothy Suskind

St Christopher's School (cont.)
Richmond, VA
 Betsy Tyson
 Christie Wilson
 Nancy Young

St Clement Mary Hofbauer School
Baltimore, MD
 Gerianne Dilks
 Christine Godlewski
 Megan Gray
 Linda House*
 Julie Mullen
 Wendy Parker
 Catherine Urban

St John Neumann Academy
Blacksburg, VA
 Rachael Beach*
 Patricia Kesler
 Laura Minnis
 Jenny Mishoe
 Sarah Pickeral
 Betsy Roberson

St Joseph School-Fullerton
Baltimore, MD
 J. Delores Keefer*

St Mary School
Cranston, RI
 Jane Bowry*

St Rocco School
Johnston, RI
 Judy Carroccio*

Stearns High School
Millinocket, ME
 Linda Wasilauskis*

Stevensville Middle School
Stevensville, MD
 Kelly N. Sell*

The School of the Cathedral Mary Our Queen
Baltimore, MD
David Bentzley*

Tilghman Elementary School
Tilghman, MD
Daniel Bieber*

Trinity School
Ellicott City, MD
Debby Moulding*
Lisa Slaton

Tunstall High School
Dry Fork, VA
Mariah Sells*

Western Heights Middle School
Hagerstown, MD
Natasha Whetsell*

William S Cohen Middle School
Bangor, ME
Trisha Smith*

Woodbridge Sr High School
Woodbridge, VA
Catherine Hailey*
Vitali Kopylov
Melissa Morse
Ann Ragsdale
Emily Robinson

Language Arts Grant Recipients 2011-2012

After receiving a "Poetic Achievement Award" schools are encouraged to apply for a Creative Communication Language Arts Grant. The following is a list of schools who received a two hundred and fifty dollar grant for the 2011-2012 school year.

Annapolis Royal Regional Academy, Annapolis Royal, NS
Bear Creek Elementary School, Monument, CO
Bellarmine Preparatory School, Tacoma, WA
Birchwood School, Cleveland, OH
Bluffton Middle School, Bluffton, SC
Brookville Intermediate School, Brookville, OH
Butler High School, Augusta, GA
Carmi-White County High School, Carmi, IL
Classical Studies Academy, Bridgeport, CT
Coffee County Central High School, Manchester, TN
Country Hills Elementary School, Coral Springs, FL
Coyote Valley Elementary School, Middletown, CA
Emmanuel-St Michael Lutheran School, Fort Wayne, IN
Excelsior Academy, Tooele, UT
Great Meadows Middle School, Great Meadows, NJ
Holy Cross High School, Delran, NJ
Kootenay Christian Academy, Cranbrook, BC
LaBrae Middle School, Leavittsburg, OH
Ladoga Elementary School, Ladoga, IN
Mater Dei High School, Evansville, IN
Palmer Catholic Academy, Ponte Vedra Beach, FL
Pine View School, Osprey, FL
Plato High School, Plato, MO
Rivelon Elementary School, Orangeburg, SC
Round Lake High School, Round Lake, MN
Sacred Heart School, Oxford, PA
Shadowlawn Elementary School, Green Cove Springs, FL
Starmount High School, Boonville, NC
Stevensville Middle School, Stevensville, MD
Tadmore Elementary School, Gainesville, GA
Trask River High School, Tillamook, OR
Vacaville Christian Schools, Vacaville, CA
Wattsburg Area Middle School, Erie, PA
William Dunbar Public School, Pickering, ON
Woods Cross High School, Woods Cross, UT

Grades 10-11-12 Top Ten Winners

List of Top Ten Winners for Grades 10-12; listed alphabetically

Elisa Barguil, Grade 11
Townsend Harris High School, NY

Cailey Horn, Grade 11
Rabun County High School, GA

Kevin Maerten, Grade 11
Holy Cross High School, NJ

Garrett Massey, Grade 11
Animas High School, NM

Ryan Miller, Grade 12
Upper St Clair High School, PA

Miranda Paul, Grade 12
Menaul School, NM

Kimberly Paulsen, Grade 11
Viewmont High School, UT

Mia Tannoia, Grade 10
Bradshaw Christian High School, CA

Felicia Thornton, Grade 11
Science & Math Institute, WA

Emily Wiseberg, Grade 11
Collège catholique Franco-Ouest, ON

All Top Ten Poems can be read at www.poeticpower.com

Note: The Top Ten poems were finalized through an online voting system. Creative Communication's judges first picked out the top poems. These poems were then posted online. The final step involved thousands of students and teachers who registered as the online judges and voted for the Top Ten poems. We hope you enjoy these selections.

Water

The beat,
The rhymes
I'm looking for the words to say
to tell you how I felt that day at the river
When we walked together
and sat by the creek,
and threw stones in the lake.
And I don't know what to do
'cause I wanna be THERE:
back on that day
when the world was mine and
I was yours
and you told me you loved me
while the ocean washed over our feet
and we kicked and splashed in the rain and the puddles
like little kids in our kiddie pool
while the fish swam 'round in their dentist-office tank
and the tears poured down my face
'til salt stings and feels like blood
but when I touch my face all I feel is
Water.

Rachuel Hanley, Grade 10
Woodbridge Sr High School, VA

Scattered Energy

There was a point where I almost felt,
Like I'd lost my mind, somewhere in-between
Time and space, without any concept —
As to what I was doing.

The more I pulled, the more it pushed me,
And I became angry at the helplessness…
The fear I couldn't separate from inside somewhere…
That tangled space of energy…
Scattered on different plains of thought.

Sometimes they feel like two people,
In others like one, but I'm losing track…
Having their own voices and opinions, I struggle
To find some kind of balance —
And blame it on the ignorance of others…

The diagnoses, the misdiagnoses…
Who am I anymore? Am I just energy?
Pieces of me left on the grounds I've traveled on?
Scattered on different plains of reason?

Aisha McClendon, Grade 11
Woodbridge Sr High School, VA

Lovely Storms

Lightning strikes the ocean,
The wind pushes my home,
I listen to the rain,
This melody is not unknown.

Sydney Seerden, Grade 10
Norfolk Collegiate Middle/Upper School, VA

A Letter from the Troposphere

The layer between me and the rest of the world is
26,000+ feet of compression.
At least that's what the monitor says,
so far down the aisle
I have to squint to make out the +.
Here I am, At-most-fear.
Although, I wouldn't say I'm afraid.
I'd say I'm lonely.
More than usual.
It's funny that when I can hold the whole lives,
the daily weavings of bunches of people between my fingers
I feel the most alone.
Blame it on the deep layer of glass
that envelopes me.
It's like they're in the fish bowl,
but I'm the fish.
All I know is that from up here,
the condos layer into eerie mandalas,
but the playgrounds are just primary colors.
And I couldn't tell you apart
from a lamp that needed a bulb change.

Lily Brinker, Grade 11
Greely High School, ME

Relate

I'm going to lay down some scenarios and let's hope you relate
Can you imagine being a dreamer who dreams of being great?
And the pain that you feel because you're not yet there?
And the rage you conceive when they laugh and don't care?
So your mottos keep faith stay strong be prosperous
And your attitude is screw everything that tries to say opposite
Can you imagine everyday living with a bad heartache?
But it's not from your break up; it's from not being yet great.
Just nod to yourself if you can relate
Can you imagine yourself being ahead of your time?
And you're not like the others you have a new state of mind
And you walk the earth alone you're the last of your kind
And you love only the sounds because they feed your rhyme
You don't even cry for attention you just want the respect
The only cancer that will murder everything it infects
Can you imagine the feeling you get when you get played
Then stopped paused and reset like a video game
And there is no one like you; you're just not the same
You just need the understanding and don't need the pain
Just nod to yourself if you can relate

Aaron Brown, Grade 11
Forest Park High School, VA

Life Is Hard When Love Is Involved

What would it be like
If loving wasn't easy.
What would people say
If hearts were broken every day.
Life wouldn't be easy.

Skylar Kissam, Grade 10
Norfolk Collegiate Middle/Upper School, VA

Brainwaves

My mind is filled with overachieving ideas
And melodramatic realizations

My thoughts in overdrive
Excite me beyond explanation
Simple conclusions enlighten me
Of a place where there's no such thing
As devastating

Jittered and overworked
All I can do is stride back and forth
While I imagine what my entire day would be
If my mind was constantly this awake
As it is long after the sun has set

Now, I am so ready and willing
To weigh situations and draw conclusions

So I make a promise to myself
As I tuck the covers over me
That when I wake up in the morning
I'll renew this feeling

The next day — nothing
Until night time
Again, when my brain is alive

Mikayla Thompson, Grade 10
Woodbridge Sr High School, VA

Disarray of Society

All the world has to live with you
All the world cannot have peace without you
Making a contrast between war and peace
Making a contrast for our love and hate

Oh disarray, how we hate you
Oh disarray how we can't see love without you
Making us all crazy
Making us want you more

Manifested in our lives
Manifested in our ideas
You raise global powers up
You rise up and put them down

Disarray is in our minds
Disarray is part of the world
Connecting us to fight against
Connecting us to make peace

Disarray, you bring chaos
Disarray, you spawn order
From you, the world is in darkness
From you, the world strives for light

Patrick Rigor, Grade 10
Delaware Military Academy, DE

Heroic Instinct

My thoughts flicker to the dying ones inside;
I must learn to cope.
My job, my duty, my love, my hope.
I clear my head of thoughts
and follow my instincts kick.
I know these images are the ones that stick.
I hear the sirens buzz around me.
The screams and cries and moans,
and cackling of bones.
The buildings in which we trust
falling to the ground.
Unbelievable thoughts: the only sound.
A mother with her child,
staring up at the sky,
"Mommy, why did daddy have to die?"
I turn my head for a second;
my eyes can't stand those tears
for this is what every American fears.
What is wrong in this world when someone kills another?
You may call me a hero, saving lives on this day of history,
which to me will always be a mystery.

Kayleigh Murphy, Grade 11
Spotsylvania High School, VA

Dipped in Desire

You are my treasure,
my nearest and dearest possession.
Your sparkle reflects upon me.
But much like gold or silver, do I really need you?
No.
Do I desire all the luxurious feelings and indulgences you supply?
Yes!
My self-confidence expands
as I twist you around my finger like an expensive engagement ring.
Envious peers creep down my spine
luring me into becoming something I am not.
Diamonds are a girl's best friend,
but you will never be my friend,
nor my enemy —
just a lonely prisoner
in my jewelry box.

Renee Ordoobadi, Grade 10
Woodbridge Sr High School, VA

In the Wilderness

As I travel I ask my Savior to speak
Not knowing I have fallen so deep
Strayed away like a long, lost sheep
Where is the rest of the herd that came with me?
Speak, Savior, speak!
Am I not doing enough?
Not knowing I've fallen so deep
Down in the wilderness where there are no sheep
Speak, Savior, speak

Tearrah Matthews, Grade 12
New Directions Alternative Education Center, VA

2K

Today is the day everyone on the team has been preparing for, for the last two weeks.

A 2K. It's the hardest workout in rowing. 2000 meters as hard as you can row on the erg.

It's not just a physical test but a mental one also. You have to push yourself, no one else can make you go faster or slower. Only you.

The coach says, "Strap in to the ergs. Set it for 2000." It's even painful to punch in the numbers, knowing how painful this will be.

My heart races as we're all ready and I'm sure the rest of my team is nervous too.

Coach turns on the music and puts it on full blast. We listen to dubstep as we work out.

The beats are strong and fast. Just like us.

We're all set. Coach calls out the commands.

Sit ready.

Attention! Row!

I'm off. The first 100 meters is a sprint. And I know the next seven minutes are going to be hell.

I'm holding my score of my last personal record. Adrenaline and blood are rushing through my body a mile a minute.

Breathing is now heavy and fast. Sweat is pouring down my face. I'm reaching 1000 meters.

And every rower knows the last 1000 are painful and slow. Time for another sprint as I meet the halfway point.

I listen to the music as the electronic beats pass through my body. 500 to go.

I'm getting ready for my final sprint at 250. I start to black in and out at this point in every 2K.

It's time to move as I start my sprint. It's all me as I use the last amount of energy in my body. It hurts but it's worth it.

I row as hard as I can until the meters say 0. It's all over now. I got a new personal record. I'm happy with how I did.

It's not about the size of the athlete but how far you're willing to push yourself. I broke those limits today.

All that work and it only took seven minutes.

Tyler Quick, Grade 10
Delaware Military Academy, DE

Secrets

When I told you that I loved you, the words I spoke were true.
Although at the time you weren't ready and maybe didn't understand my love,
In my heart I still do and always will love you.
When you asked me to wait because you weren't ready to be in a relationship
I think maybe I should have.
I mean I didn't want to, I didn't like the idea of not fully having you.
Truthfully to the closed eye and unknowing seeker, I'm still waiting till this day.
Maybe I was too overbearing and also childish in how I was afraid to talk to you to express my feelings.
Now I see that talking to you is the most natural thing ever.
Hugging you feels like where I was supposed to be.
It's funny how when people joke about what was and what should still be,
I immediately jump to defend myself and insist that we never were…but in reality we really were.
So, here they are…my unspoken words, my vow of love that remains unknown.

Matthieu Petit-Homme and Jalilah Marie, Grade 11
Eleanor Roosevelt High School, MD

Lonely Imagination

Sounds all around as demons are lurking around underground. Happiness surrounds me but none consumes me. Every breath I breathe takes more life out of me. Every beat my heart pounds the easier it is to break down. Chattering and the living fill the dead hallways with sound and adventure. Many voices bounce from hall to hall, but only one takes my ears captive. As the many voices fade away and double doors slam. The halls are dead quiet again, everything seems normal but for only a moment. My mind begins to wonder, my sight sees nothing but haze. I would fear I am deaf for I hear nothing but soft distance ringing. Until once again my ears are taken hostage by a single voice. Then three others join. They fill the hallway with laughter. When people pass an open door my eyes are too blurry to see who they are until I hear that voice again, voice from the past, locked away inside. With no sign of my own life living, only those around me, see my body functioning. I move and breathe just like everyone else this you can see. Silence again. Laughter has left these halls, sucked bone dry out of all of us, one by one. I see the hallways are dark again, no power for the lights, or somewhere in a ditch on the outside of town. Distant ringing in my ears again, can she save me from this living hell or am I truly going mad, slowly, but daily. Do you see her too? Or did my brain make her up to give my life meaning. Is she really around or just a figment of my imagination, created by my own true loneliness…?

Ryanne Good, Grade 11
Gloucester High School, VA

Outcast Knight

Towering, gleaming,
A wall of forged steel,

Resilient, and stout,
Trained not to kneel,

Forever remembering their sins…

Skilled, powerful,
They cannot, the pain, feel…

Grieving, Silently,
Hoping the world healed,

Remembering, the high paradise…

Having hardened with time,
Inner strength, armor,

Upholding good virtues,
Evils of mankind —

Remember…

Shain Bannowsky, Grade 10
Delaware Military Academy, DE

Family

Forever together
Permanently entwined
Spiritually and physically surrounding you
Everyone in the family coming together
The successes
The failures
The pessimists
The realists
All share one common thing
Undying love for each other
Etched in the universe
For all to see

Ray Joyce, Grade 11
Arundel Sr High School, MD

Looking Up

The light at the end of a tunnel.
The finish line.
When you finish what you start.
Build a house,
run a mile,
meet someone new,
getting the courage to skydive,
standing up for yourself.
A sign of accomplishment.
People are screaming your name.
Feeling invincible.

Maria Murawski, Grade 10
VA

Out of Habit

They tell us the neighborhood is safe,
and we should believe them.
They are my cousins.
Much older than me,
with names I only remember
when I see them.
Melba pours water
into plastic cups,
offers us bread out of habit,
and I want to love her.
She is my cousin
but I do not know this woman
who asks us for favors,
to lend her money for a new room.
We take the bread,
it is dry in my throat,
and she is left without bricks.

Erika Jaimes, Grade 10
Appomattox Regional Governor's School for Arts and Technology, VA

The Protective Mask

I wear the mask that shows glimpses of the true me
Everything represented is really what I strive to be
Sometimes things don't shine through as the are intended
We all have negative traits and others become offended

I value honesty and trustworthiness in relationships;
However, hypocrisy often springs from my lips
The more I attempt to show the inside of the mask I wear,
My true character becomes less clear

On occasion, the true Nicholas Browning will shine through
Lending a helping hand out, maybe even to you
In a group of our friends we all empower our masks a little more
Hiding behind our fake identities, we belittle others for —
Nothing more than to empower ourselves behind our protective barrier
That is the mask I wear.

Nicholas Browning, Grade 11
Ocean Lakes High School, VA

Cold Steel

Cold steel shining in the sun.
They are the replacement of my warm arms
That once ran through my blood peacefully and swiftly.
Another dream —
The dream of alteration of the Machine taking over my body.
The dream of the good doctors experimenting with my body.
Waking up to my cold arms to complete functionality
I am now able to control the cold steel better than I ever did before.
It now listens to me and me only.
I can control both my strength and my weaknesses of my augmented arms
To my advantages in this dystopian city.
We cannot stop the future.
The future will stop us.

Ulises Salcedo, Grade 12
William E Tolman High School, RI

Championship Game

It was the Championship Game and everyone was excited,
we waited for the puck to drop to start the game.
Everyone was in the rink, not one uninvited,
they all watched as DMA claimed their fame.

We were up six to four
when I got in to show my ability.
I really tried to score
but instead I got a penalty.
I hit a kid too hard
even though the crowd went wild
but I was not barred
the refs had not reconciled.

With two minutes left
we were down a man
we succeeded and the opponent was bereft,
we had the best game plan!

The other team needed to go back to their camps
because we were state champs!
Dillon Conway, Grade 10
Delaware Military Academy, DE

What Is Life?

What is life? A question asked many times.
Many men throughout the ages have tried to answer.
Some answered in prose, while others did rhymes.
Every man had what he thought was the right answer.

They are all different, none may be true.
What can make life better? Also many times asked.
Again many men answered, each had their own view.
Once more, the answer seems forever masked.

Many answers were given throughout the years.
The pursuit of dreams, nature, to others give
Other theories have given people fears.
Some have said there is no reason to live.

The answer to life, nature does not give,
Only with company, do people live.
Markus Honig, Grade 11
Ocean Lakes High School, VA

Isolated

Locked in, never to be noticed
Deserted in a dark forest, away from everything and civilization
Somewhere no one will go and you will never be seen
Screaming does no good, no one is around for miles
A place where not even the sunlight reaches
It's just pitch black, reminding you that you are alone
Forever and for life
Emma McDonough Doane, Grade 10
Noble High School, ME

I Am Just That

I cannot pretend
That I know what you're going through
Already I can see
Unfamiliar habits, an alien appearance,
And a brain grown somewhat different than mine.

But I do know this:

That all who have passed by this place,
This big blue ball of love, anguish, and progress
All have lived,
All have suffered,
All have wished,
All have felt regret,
All have hoped for more,
All have wasted precious time,
All have pondered,
Here by the wayside.

But most importantly, all have loved another.

So, my friend, though I am not all-knowing,
And just a human being like yourself,
I am just that —
A human being like yourself.
Molly Tracy, Grade 12
Great Mills High School, MD

Raining Memory

I stirred honey into warm water
and hugged it with my palms
I drew a face on the window
and watched it cry without a sound
the rain kept falling

I remember walking in the rain
and twirling and laughing
I thought it made me special
and he did too, and he smiled
those rains had long gone

one day a raindrop fell in my eyes
blurring my last vision
of him as I turned away
and all the rain in the world
came pouring down

honey smelt of him asking
when would the sky be clear
then I can see you again
but the rain still dripped on
I wish it would stop
Biqiao Yin, Grade 10
Thomas Jefferson High School for Science and Technology, VA

Hiding Behind a Lie

I wear the mask that hides my soul
Protecting me from ice cold words.
On the outside, I'm dull and gray.
But on the inside, I live another way,
My passionate soul lies deep within
Still I wear the mask and pretend.
I'm locked inside without a key,
And only truth can set me free.
I'm reluctant and quiet if you can't tell,
But on the inside I want to yell.
All these emotions I'm holding in.
It'll all burst out in the end.
I have a creative and wild side
But I cover it up and smile wide.
My mask is plain and hides my spirit.
Judgment's cruelty is why I wear it.

Erica Oakley, Grade 11
Ocean Lakes High School, VA

The Night

The child stirs
In the night
Fighting the urge
To turn on the light
He wants to be
Extremely brave
In the cold dark room
That is his cave
The wind howls
He freezes with fear
He tries to block out
All he can hear
He tries to settle
And resume his peace
He takes one deep breath
And his bad thoughts cease

Kailey Baker, Grade 11
Holy Cross Regional School, VA

Sisterhood

Broken glass on the ground
Dishes unwashed
Toys on the floor
Cookie jar open
Missing money
His leg is broken
Where's the dog?
Cracks in the china
Ripped up paper
Torn up textbook
Drawn on checkbook
Crying children
Confused mother
Sister did it!

Faith Logan, Grade 10
St Johns College High School, DC

We Sway, We Sway

Erupting from madness
your muscles were shaped
eroding your bones were carefully taped
exploding from cosmic wind you appeared
and then year after year after year after year
you're born again
and I steal you
for the one last time
erupting, eroding, exploding, your time is precious
emotions erupting eroding exploding
you're born again

Caitlin McCutcheon, Grade 11
Appomattox Regional Governor's School for Arts and Technology, VA

Temptress

Temptress, siren, beacon of my desire,
Bittersweet, always avoiding my hold.
For you, I would trade any sum of gold.
Your eyes are lit by an inner fire,
I get endlessly trapped by their mire.
You were created of the finest mold,
Being in your presence never gets old.
Alas, never being able to acquire.

Whenever possible sneaking a glance,
Admiring from the darkest shadow.
If ever given the unlikely chance,
I swear that I would never let you go.
Your beauty has absolutely no bound,
I'll never forget the day you were found.

Shawn Simmons, Grade 12
Holy Cross Regional School, VA

Child of Mine

Through hard times
You call me
You don't want to turn away
Just think of my LOVE
And I will come and say
I will not leave you
Nor forsake you
Because you're a child of mine
And I will take you
To a place of peace
And joy that's so divine
You'll never want to leave me
Or say a dear good bye
Because I will love you
Unconditionally
Sweet child of mine.

Erin Rahim, Grade 10
Easton High School, MD

Mask

I wear the mask that all must see,
Holding me back from being free,
An exterior, as hard as steel,
But no one knows how I truly feel,
For things aren't always as they seem.

Some say strong, others say tough,
When really those two, aren't enough,
Finding my inner feelings is no easy task,
I wear the mask.

Sensitive and sweet, that's the true me,
Otherwise known as a softie,
Kept hidden, this secret shall be,
Wearing the disguise is the key,
I wear the mask.

Chas Blais, Grade 11
Ocean Lakes High School, VA

Summits Did the Same

Alpine meadows call to me,
Hushed by means of charred debris.
So trapped within pastoral plains
I find my destiny remains.

Unless a wind, to this way comes,
Blowing ash from where it's from,
Smothers all that's left behind
As my ascent leaves basins blind.

But one request has yet to heed
The notice of thought's frame.

I beg you not to call my name
Though summits did the same.

Tessa Crews, Grade 12
Rappahannock County High School, VA

Watching the Stars

We watch the stars.
Dreamily, they float above our heads
In the openness of their world.

We find it hard to see.
We find it hard to listen to anything
Else that comes from the stars
And tries to touch our hearts.

We look, but don't see.
We cannot help but to remain
Removed—distant
From all that we love
And all that we believe.

We do not dare to reach above us.

We cannot do anything,
He says.
The stars are too far for us to reach.

We solemnly stand
Gazing above
Watching, dreaming, yearning
Yet still,
We are still too meek to act.

Katherine Lee, Grade 11
Thomas Jefferson High School for Science and Technology, VA

Respect

what does respect mean?
do you have what it takes?
does it come with a cost?
please help me learn from it.

a seven letter word,
holding a very valuable meaning,
respect is doing what is right,
even if there is no trophies.

open doors for the elderly,
pulling your pants up,
not using a woman,
not abusing your power.

not laughing at the handicapped,
not calling teachers by their first names,
not cursing or judging others,
not telling people what they are supposed to be.

respect is seeing the good in everyone,
appreciating somebody for who they are,
supporting the hopeless through motivation,
sharing everyone's success.

Sandra Okowa, Grade 12
Chesapeake High School, MD

Disappearance

I am walking on the beach
With wild breakers roaring in my ears.

I have no idea where I am or how I got here.
I can't remember anything at all.

All I know is the rough sea grass
Tearing at my feet
And a sky too gray for gulls that now stand huddled,
their heads beneath their wings.

They say when you listen to a seashell
The sound you hear is your own blood
Rushing through your ears.
So is the sound I hear right now only a magnified pulse?
Am I trapped inside my own head?

I trip over a piece of driftwood and fall to my knees,
Leaving watery hand prints in the sand.
An edge of foam washes over them.
They melt away without a sound.

Getting up, the grass still blows,
The sky is gray, the waves still roar —

But I have disappeared.

Jennifer Coleman, Grade 10
Atholton Adventist Academy, MD

Richmond

The two-hour Ride
Feels like such a short time
I can see — there's a familiar Skyline in the distance
I know we're closing in

Down Roads we go through the city
As high as the Buildings' ceilings
Twisting and Turning — through downtown
I know we're closing in

The smell of the River
The Noise of the cars down below
Wind through the trees — the Quivering leaves
I know we're closing in

Down the road with Monuments
Of fallen soldiers and such
Bushes—and beautiful houses lining the Sidewalks
I know we're closing in

Turn into the gardens know as Sauer
The Courtyard is filled with blooming flowers
Brick and Beige — behind a green lawn
I know that I am home

Jessica Sutherland, Grade 11
Norfolk Collegiate Middle/Upper School, VA

Time Well Spent
You never backed down
You never said enough
You never wanted to quit on us
We've grown so much closer
I'll always be your little girl
Playing in the yard and adopting a dog
Stealing home to win the game
All the great times we've had together
Will never be forgotten
Jessica Alexandra Sandifer, Grade 11
Holy Cross Regional School, VA

October
O range
C olored
T rees
O n
B risk
E vening
R ides
A.J. Mahlon, Grade 12
Rivermont School-Tidewater, VA

Hope
Hope makes me want to wake up;
Hope gives me the power to love;
Mother told me not to cry as she left.
Hope keeps me strong,
Believing that she will return one day;
Hope gives me the strength
Something good will happen one day.
Hetson Fortes, Grade 10
William E Tolman High School, RI

Spanish II D Bell
Just Kings and Queens
Not knowing one another
A marriage was formed
Between Beauty and Violence
And so the story goes on
Collin James Poppert, Grade 10
Norfolk Collegiate Middle/Upper School, VA

From East to West
Ocean to ocean,
New York to Los Angeles,
Lakes to beaches,
Rivers to Deserts,
Me to my family
Cabell Thomas, Grade 10
Norfolk Collegiate Middle/Upper School, VA

A Walk Through My Life
I walk through life with so much weight on my shoulders
Always looking ahead thinking of ways to pass these boulders
They'll always be here no matter what
Even as I walk the stairs of life they'll still be a problem but
I'm never turning back or walking back down
Because I have too much going for me to have dumb stuff bring me down
The sky isn't the limit with footprints on the moon
And I'm moving closer to my dream I always tell it I'll be there soon
I always reminisce on all my happiness I let it take me away
As I face hell today
When I step back and I look at the reality it puts fire back under my belt
And causes me to ask God for help
For he is my strength, my Lord, and my Savior
Don't forget him for he is something major
Always there for me when I think I'm alone
Always loves me when I don't get it at home
He gives me the courage, wisdom, and even knowledge
He can do the same for you
Just call him when you have no clue of what to do
'Cause he helps me through what he puts me in
And he'll never put me in a problem that he doesn't think that I can mend
Lynnae McIntosh, Grade 12
Ursuline Academy, DE

Cheekbones
In one moment, his eyes are blue, a color too wild to be tamed by Crayola.
A pale blue as sharp as an icicle, a knife ready to
cut the skin. And in the next, they're green.
A bright green like new spring grass. But they are nothing
compared to his cheekbones.

On set, his hair is a dark mop of curls, sweeping across his face,
adding a certain charm and sense of neglect.
Off set, it's a short cut of ginger, like the red center of a super nova.
But it is nothing compared to his cheekbones.

The cheekbones that start right below his ice or grass eyes
that stick out, ready to peel away the skin that
clings to it for dear life. The cheekbones that send mutant
butterflies to my stomach, make my heart race like horses on the track.
But they are nothing but a small characteristic compared to the man that owns them.
Candria Hicks, Grade 10
Appomattox Regional Governor's School for Arts and Technology, VA

I Feel the Snow Coming
It's a childish thing I suppose.
To jump up and down in the kitchen as it snows,
To turn on the TV as the weathermen pose,
To be on edge as the children watch the man call out the schools that are closed,
To giggle and laugh as their schools are called out,
To race out the back door into the freezing cold realm of winter,
To see them grab their warm coats and wool hats,
To watch as they build snowmen in the pure white landscape,
And to wonder when they would be witnessing such beauty themselves.
Kavya Krishna, Grade 11
Centennial High School, MD

Remembrance*

Life is too hard to say goodbye.
I never thought it would be so hard; and all I can think is, why?
Even though you are gone that doesn't mean I will forget you.
Forgetting you would be like forgetting to breathe.
It just doesn't happen.
My life will never be the same and since you are away I have changed.
Knowing that tomorrow is never promised, I try to live each and every day like my last.
You never know when God will choose you.
He might choose you now, or He might choose you later.
The memories I have are still with me today and I promise somehow, someway, I will be with you.
I have shed a few tears only because it doesn't seem real.
I never really thought of life, until I saw it taken.
I miss you like crazy please believe me.
I know you are up there; way above.
God truly has an "Angel of Love."

Mariah Morton, Grade 10
Morrison School, VA
*In Loving Memory: Robbie Campbell: March 15, 1994-February 18,2012

The Mixed Blood Speaks of Rivers*

I've known rivers:
My ancestors told me of rivers as ancient as our blood, and older than our Nahautl, Swahili, and Spanish tongues.

They told me;. "Nuestras almas had florecido profunda como los rios," "Nafsi zetu likikuwa kama mito."
"Our souls have flourished deep like rivers."

They fished in the Dawa River of Kenya.
They built the step pyramids with rivers running so their world could hear the fierce teponaztli drums.
The huts were built near the Congo so it lulled the children to sleep.
They heard the singing of the Mississippi when Abe went down to New Orleans,
And they've listened to the war near the Rio Grande.

They've known rivers:
Ancient, different rivers.

Our souls have flourished like rivers.

Swandella Spragans, Grade 11
Appomattox Regional Governor's School for Arts and Technology, VA
*Response to "Negro Speaks of Rivers" by Langston Hughes

Unstoppable

Sit and I'll tell you a story
about a girl and how she grew up in this world.
She was born when the sun shined, and young when it faded.
The light leaving her world never left her jaded.
She got older when the clouds came. She started to see the world as it was.

When the rain finally fell it only made her stronger. She never thought "how much longer."

She grabbed life by the horns and never let you forget that not believing in her was the only thing you would regret.
She never liked impossible, she would rather think implausible. But once she put her mind to it she was just UNSTOPPABLE!!
Maybe someday when the sun shines I'll get to meet this hero of mine.

Selena Slaughter, Grade 11
Parkdale High School, MD

Playing Cinderella

We revere our fathers.
No man ever seems so perfect.
So loving and big,
so warm and strong,
so smart and funny.
Their embrace would make our day.
Us, in our little pink tutus,
playing Cinderella,
following our king around.
We would do things for him that we would do for no other man.
We would do things for them, just to be with them.
We go to train museums.
We go to hardware stores.
We'd wash the car with them in our pink tutus,
just to have his smile,
to know that we've done good.
All we wanted was to please him, our king.
To feel accomplished and special,
to be Daddy's little princess.

Jessica Winters, Grade 11
Holy Cross Regional School, VA

Echoes

And she cried.
She had drowned in her tears.
She had drowned in her sadness; in her invisible pain.
It was inevitable, she wrote.
She knew she would fade away.
The pressure on her heart,
the ghosts of her past stomping on her chest...
It was all just too much.
We never thought her heart would slow to a stop
and the world would stop too.
We never thought she'd give up.
Never thought her eyes could be so empty,
or her laugh so absent.
All we can hear now are her cries —
echoing from a distance.

Anna Coulombe, Grade 10
RI

Mask

I wear the mask that fronts happiness
Though inside that is not always the case.
Although I appear perpetually high spirited,
Oftentimes I feel very lonely.
Though I have many friendships,
I sometimes wonder about their sincerity,
For they are all only three years old or less.
I know it may sound petty,
But the thought is always hanging over me.
Of course, it's not necessary that others know this,
And I don't wish to burden them with my personal sorrows,
So I wear the mask.

Jacob Morgan, Grade 11
Ocean Lakes High School, VA

Master of Puppets

Strings taut at the ready
Wooden hearts pound in hollow chests
Motion frozen, suspended
By carefully spun threads of
Hopes, stories, and dreams
Unblinking eyes strain to see
Curtains swing smoothly open, the show has begun
Minuscule clay feet dance to a predetermined song
Unconvinced by the puppets' silent, halfhearted screams
Their bodies continue to spin gaily across the open stage
Each desperately hoping to catch the master's eye
The crowd stares transfixed
Even as the first falls from heaven
A convoluted parody of an angel with shredded wings
Striking the earth with a lifeless thud
Severed strings float down to grace a body cast aside
A single tear drops to the dust
Freedom at last from the hands of a mad puppeteer

Summer Courts, Grade 10
Home School, VA

Our Love Is Slowly Disintegrating

Our love is slowly disintegrating,
Like the red-orange leaves falling from the trees,
We are only held together by string,
Just hanging on until the first real freeze.
Families carry out traditions of old,
Even bears hibernate with their partner,
Instead of leaving them out in the cold,
I'm the only one who lost a lover.
Flowers in the garden are in full bloom,
They remind me of how we started this,
Without any worry or any gloom,
But full of love, blessing, and happiness.
We bring our real loves together thereby,
Sun shines for us with rainbow in the sky.

Na Jeong Kim, Grade 12
Holy Cross Regional School, VA

Dreams

I sit inside my room thinking of all of the stuff that comes to mind,
I put the pencil to the paper to see what I can find,
What's locked up in my brain is referred to by some as lyrics,
Music is my passion and poetry is a form,
Normal life strikes dreams and they fade away into norm.
I stay inside my room thinking of lyrical maneuvers,
Fire comes from my mouth shooting like a colt,
Louder than thunder and faster than a bolt,
Lightning strikes when my pen touches my pad,
The dreams I once dreamt of are the reality I have,
I only need one shot to make it all right,
To get back on the saddle and start a lyrical fight,
So I leave off with this and saying all that means,
If you have them, don't stop chasing your dreams.

Dallas Mata, Grade 10
Holy Cross Regional School, VA

Not of This World

Dancing through the narrow streets
Underneath the deathly heat
It blazes bright that sun above
Filling the earth with all its love
A careless thought and homeless dream
Is stitched up in the world's seams
I may not know as much as they
I care not for the war at bay
My soul it sings an angel's song
The one I have known all along
The soldiers you can hear them now,
Marching through the snow
They come with swords and guns
Destroying all the lively ones
If only we could have been taught
Exactly what war has brought
Then maybe it would have been avoided
This world's final moments,
But as for me, I will dance through these streets
For this world is not my own
Mine is in the heavens above, the place that I call home.

Elizabeth Lee, Grade 11
Glen Allen High School, VA

Sonnet I

The waves of a man's misfortune thunder,
Crash and fall upon the calm shore of thought.
Shifts peace of mind, happiness torn asunder.
Forever trapped, alone, and overwrought.

Swiftly as it came the tide falls away,
For the moon returns bliss and felicity.
You are my orb of the night, my ballet
Dancing into my heart, a symphony.

The moon sets, the sun rises in your eyes,
Restores my sanity, no more flection.
Pure beauty, you are the stars in the skies
Sparkling, blazing, natural perfection.

Like the celestial bodies above,
I must climb to heaven to reach your love.

Brandon M. Davis, Grade 12
Tabb High School, VA

Flying Down a Slippery Slope —

You go flying down a slippery slope —
Speeding past the old folk —
We hit the powder slope — so soft you think you float —
The feeling's unworldly —
Better, than any fake snow —
Ascend — up the chair lift —
Descend — down the mountain —
Skiing is not a hobby, it's a gift —

Joe Godwin, Grade 11
Norfolk Collegiate Middle/Upper School, VA

No Snow This Winter

The cold winds blow,
But, where is the snow?
I go outside without my jacket,
The wind still blows with such a racket.

I checked my hats, gloves and sled,
but they just sat there in the shed.
I ride my bike on the road that is dry,
Where is the snow? I am going to cry.

I check the TV for the weather,
They tell me I just need a sweater.
I wish I could be building my snow fort,
But I am just playing on the basketball court.

Maybe next year we will get a snow storm,
And the weather will be like a winter norm.
This winter, the snow is in low supply,
This weather is weird, maybe a blizzard in July.

Conor Hotchkiss, Grade 10
Delaware Military Academy, DE

Transcendental Cadence

Brown swirling leaves in the wind,
Trees looking dethroned and thin,
Colors fading away
Life aging day by day,
Blank flakes descending from the sky
On the iced ground they lie,
Red noses and smoke puffs,
Chilling air of which the groundhog has had enough,

Shadow is not seen
Leaves return to green,
Colors spring from the ground
Commencing the common buzzing sound,
To the ground leaves are sent,
Back to brown swirling leaves in the wind

Zakiya Sidney, Grade 10
Leonardtown High School, MD

I Wear the Mask

I wear the mask that hides my true self,
People see me as a firework, bursting with energy,
But in reality I am quiet and keep to myself.
I come off as confident and proud,
But I have all the same insecurities as every other girl.
I like to be around my friends,
Because when I am, I light up with joy.
My family doesn't see the quiet side of me,
So they don't really know how I truly feel.
I get very emotional at random times,
But often tuck my sadness away, as if it doesn't even exist.
I wear the mask!

Nicole Agren, Grade 11
Ocean Lakes High School, VA

One Word

The tears. The hurt.
The endless pain.
The one word
That broke the linking chain.

Her viciousness. Her lie.
Her cruel remark.
The one word
That extinguished the everlasting spark.

My heart. My love.
My dear friend.
The one word
That brought about the bitter end.

Our past. Our memories.
Our hours of fun.
The one word
That had one meaning: we are done.
Yona Sadik, Grade 12
Bais Yaakov High School, MD

They Shine: A Tribute

Skies split wide
Howls singing in chorus
In joy
In sorrow

Living today as if
No tomorrow will come
Running
Breathing

Alive but not well
One among them
One among us
We will never see

They do not die
For in us
They shine,
As never before.
Rebecca Green, Grade 12
Forest Park High School, VA

A Trial

Guilt
Nervous, scared
Bullying, shooting, killing
River, truck, bridge, farm
Trying, helping, testifying
Happy, free
Innocent
Maikor Perez, Grade 10
William E Tolman High School, RI

We

We make life too difficult.
We wake up every day worrying.
We hardly wake up with a smile.
We go through the day worrying if the future will be bright.
We worry too much about our image.
We look at others that have it all.
We do anything to have it all.
We get down on ourselves.
We go to others for help.
We sometimes receive help and at other times don't.
We can wake up with a smile on our face though.
We can wake up knowing that we are alive.
We can go through the day knowing that at least one person loves us.
We have friends that have our back.
We have loving parents.
We also have that one special someone.
We can take a deep breath knowing that not everything is bad.
We know that no one's life is perfect.
We all make mistakes.
We shouldn't get down on ourselves.
We make life way too difficult after all.
Kris Grajewski, Grade 11
Holy Cross Regional School, VA

The Land of the Unsaid

Where does it all go?
All that we don't say
What's left untold…
To the land of the Unsaid.
That's where all I don't say goes, all I keep inside,
Everything I want to say, but don't…I keep it all in my mind.
The things that would have been too much and the things that weren't true,
Things that would have made me seem less mature,
All the things I wish I'd told you.
The land of the Unsaid. A rather interesting place—
Clouds of love and lakes of hate,
Mountains of "I love you's".
Jokes untold, remarks silenced,
Truth hidden, feelings hushed.
The land of the Unsaid,
One only knows of its location—it lies in a secret place
Where it will never be found, not earth, nor space.
Within my mind
Is where it all is kept
Bound in chains
All the Unsaid.
Sydney Frank, Grade 11
Tuscarora High School, MD

Lovey-Dovey
The past few days had been particularly rough. I was losing an internal strife.
For the time had come, unexpected for sure, I had lost the love of my life.

As I wallowed in pity, I decided to run. The air would do me some good.
I ran, and I ran till I could run no more, and in front of me, a mysterious wood.

As I walked slowly through the dark dim wood, I saw a most peculiar thing.
An abandoned house with a tree in the front, and attached to it, a little swing.

I approached the house, very cautious at first. The swing started to move.
I glanced over startle, and to what did I find, just two peaceful little doves.

Me, mad at myself, took it out on the fowl. To frighten them is what I sought.
I yelped and I hollered, I even threw stones, but they sat there together, and didn't fly off.

After I calmed down, I started to think, perhaps my feelings were wrong.
I wanted to believe love didn't exist, but it was with me along.

Those birds unknowingly were my saviors, once again I see the light of day.
So I mustered all of replenishing strength. I dialed her phone number, and the phone rang.

"If one advances confidently in the direction of his dreams, and endeavors to live a life which he had imagined, he will meet with a success unexpected in common hours."
— Henry David Thoreau

Jared White, Grade 11
Ocean Lakes High School, VA

I Wish
I wish to over come the fear I have inside me
I wish to prevail on the journey that has been set in front of me
I wish to see beyond my mistakes and learn
I wish to mark and defend my place in this world that we live in
I wish to strive to the greatest of my expectations

I wish to always see my loved ones smiling at me
I wish to never disappoint anyone
I wish to achieve the goals and meet the expectations my family has placed on me
I wish to live my life the way that I want
I wish to take the hard way out, for that's the only way I'll learn to be on my own

I wish that people would love others due to how they are and not the way they look
I wish that the media would stop polluting our minds
I wish that our country would ease our debt instead of increasing it
I wish that poverty in countries will cease to exist
I wish that there were no more crimes, so the fear of our loved ones being taken from us will disappear

I wish to graduate with my fellow companions
I wish to do well in the future in whatever I choose to do
I wish to love freely and to have someone love me as much as I will love them
I wish to live life to the fullest
I wish to see the faces of everyone in my life smiling,
arms open wide to embrace me at the end of this rigorous journey we call life.

Fiona De Guzman, Grade 12
Oscar F. Smith High School, VA

Color

Why am I defined by the color of my skin?
A simple spectacle consists of colors within.
But stating the obvious seems like a sin,
In this society, reality never wins.
Who is to judge when you have no jurisdiction?
We all seem to talk, and only the ears of silence listen.
We pave the way for hate to penetrate.
When the truth is all said and done, it is already too late.
We seek for protection like the coverage is great,
We only end in neglect and suffer our own fate.
We are so far gone, finding love in a hopeless place,
That bitterness aims strong.
It is the poison you taste.
Then you point fingers at the color.
Do not define me by my traits,
Focus on the ambition on my face,
Sit back and listen as I win this race.
Overcoming color is my mission,
I have no time to waste,
I will survive a genocide before a racist takes my place.

Pamela Jones, Grade 10
Luray High School, VA

Seeking Transcendence

"An ounce of action is worth a ton of theory" — Emerson
my static position
harmful to my whole self
seems unnerved when watched
they see the events unfold in my line of vision
silent as time passes again and again
until it is too late
too late for even me to intervene
and stop my mistakes
time that was spent daydreaming
has caused opportunities to slip away
and with tear filled eyes
i watch them fall to the ground
i saw my soul devalue
because of my failure to act

Sara Fernandez, Grade 11
Ocean Lakes High School, VA

Just Because I'm Skinny

Just because I'm skinny
doesn't mean I'm bulimic or anorexic.
Doesn't mean I hate food.
Just because I'm skinny
doesn't mean I'm a model.
Doesn't mean I'm insecure about my body
and doesn't mean I can have any guy I want.
Just because I'm skinny
doesn't mean I think I am better than everyone else.
Just because I am skinny doesn't mean you know me
so please don't act like you do.

Ashley Harpin, Grade 12
Cumberland High School, RI

The Shark

The shark was nimble in the deep blue sea,
    Just as nimble as she was dangerous.
    Stay far away if the beast is hungry;
    Her ruthless hunger will leave you heartless.

    Although her form was truly elegant,
    Soon did emerge her once-hidden dark side.
    I could not see, in time, her temperament,
    But now I know today I would abide.

She saw my weakness; she smelled my red blood,
    She assaulted me while I was still fresh.
    I was then lapsed; hidden by a black hood,
    My heart as fragile as a piece of mesh.

    Perhaps one day such beauty I will find
    And likewise grace makes us forever bind.

Dillon Butler, Grade 12
Woodbridge Sr High School, VA

Flamed Pursuit

The raking of brittle talons,
Delicate like faeries as they balance bone and scale
The whisper of a slithered note
From behind the bars of an ivory jail
The shimmer of a moonlight kiss
That sets Her scarlet armor on fire
The steady pulse of wind through wings
That drags Her ever higher
The haunting gleam of ruby eyes
That have their treasure set.
The chilling rage of enmity
That tints Her boiled breath.
Silence.
Strike.
Kill.
The mighty Dragon's had Her fill.

Brittany Crow, Grade 10
Woodbridge Sr High School, VA

The Lost

It is so cold,
I am freezing,
I do not know where I am,
I wish my mama were here,
It is so late,
I am so tired,
So hungry;
all I can think about as I sit on the bench is
Why my mama is not with me,
I rest my head on the hard cold bench thinking about
what I should do next.
When I hear someone yelling my name, it is my mama.
She was looking for me this whole time.

Torika Hamilton, Grade 10
Salem School, MD

Masked Identity

I wear the mask of quiet indifference,
It hides my angst and smothers my voice,
This mask a ruse, a false appearance,
Keeps my troubles and anxiety within,
And barricades my opinions from the world.

Why let the world pierce my somber veil,
And reveal my fear and sentiments?
No, rather I will only let them see me as —
I wear the mask

I speak, yet, unfortunately, none hear
My words sound hollow and return to silence.
I move, yet none notice it, my actions become spectral.
Apathy becomes my norm, silence my companion,
I leave the world unknowing of my inner self,
I wear the mask!

Wihan du Plessis, Grade 11
Ocean Lakes High School, VA

Just Because

Just because I'm a guy
It doesn't mean I'm a slob
It doesn't mean I don't care how I look
It doesn't mean I'm gay because I do.
Just because I'm a guy
It doesn't mean I'm macho
I shouldn't have to be muscular to be masculine
Gyms suck, I'm happy being skinny
Just because I'm a guy
I have feelings too
I care about how other people feel
I'm allowed to cry too
Just because I'm a guy — don't judge me. I didn't get a choice

Wesley Hayden, Grade 11
Forest Park High School, VA

Just Because

Just Because
just because I'm impulsive
it doesn't mean I'm uncontrollable
it doesn't mean I need help
it doesn't mean you should judge
just because I'm impulsive
it doesn't mean I can't have fun
it doesn't mean to run
it just means I have troubles
just because I'm impulsive
it doesn't mean to hate me
it doesn't mean I'm indifferent
just because I'm impulsive-please still love me

Taylor Scholvin, Grade 11
Forest Park High School, VA

All That Matters

The need to escape this city
Leave it all behind
Just sit on the beach
Take in the ocean —
The sunset and steady rhythm of the waves
Nothing to worry about
No problems in the world
Those steady waves lulling you to sleep
Your arm around my shoulders
Holding me tight
It doesn't matter if we talk
All that matters is being here in this moment
You and me
The ocean
And the whole world
Be my escape
I need you here
Take me to a place
Where all that matters
Is you
And me

Nicole Sites, Grade 12
Holy Cross Regional School, VA

Underneath the Mask

I wear the mask that shows my flaws.
It shows the anger on my face.
It reveals the tears that long to fall.
It displays my joy for all to see.
It portrays the love inside of me.
I wear the mask!
Many people pass me by
Seeing nothing, but big innocent eyes.
So evil won't come to bother me,
I wear the mask.
Inside me glows the light within;
That no hurt soul could ever dim.
It explodes in excitement: pure and true.
How could it ever tarnish blue?
The mask and I are crab and shell.
Without it my trueness would never sell.
The me inside is unique forever.
With great passion for family, friends, whatever!
Though there are many who will never see
The beautiful soul inside of me
Because I wear the mask!

Kiara Oquendo, Grade 11
Ocean Lakes High School, VA

Dedication

The rough, wild ocean
Swaying sometimes maybe rough
The wind blows hard on the sea
A wave rolls right by

Noah Roistacher, Grade 10
Norfolk Collegiate Middle/Upper School, VA

Is It Still a Mask?

I wear the mask,
That erases my pain.
It shields my heart,
While my mind goes insane.

I wear it at school.
I wear it at home.
Sometimes I wear it,
Even if I'm alone.

I'm sad, I'm scared,
I'm insecure.
I have a sickness,
That lacks a cure.

But my mask is happy,
And my mask is sweet,
Because my mask is everything,
Everything but me.

Ashley Dalenberg, Grade 11
Frank W. Cox High School, VA

Speculation

Darkness.
Total and complete darkness.
Voices.
There are none.

Silence.
An eternal abyss.
Never ending.
Unmistakable.

Hatred.
Irreplaceable.
Reverberating, multiplying.
Consuming me.

Darkness.
Total and complete darkness.
Never ending.
Because it never really began.

Saleha Malik, Grade 10
Woodbridge Sr High School, VA

Musing

She walks through the violet meadow,
The wild flowers tickling her feet.
She reaches down for a closer look,
Plucking the stem with her fingertips
Before bringing it to her face.
She breathes in the sweet scent
As her eyes flutter closed,
Her thoughts consumed by him.

Kennedy Hall, Grade 11
Glen Allen High School, VA

Ode to My Soul Mate

As if my love could be sealed with just one kiss,
As if life could be replayed within seconds of death,
As if your smile could send my stomach into a flutter of butterflies.
I tell you that this, right here, is the closest I've ever been to happy.
Happy; not to be confused with content,
To be content is to be at ease, but to be truly happy,
That can only be found in the true acceptance of life.
The beauty of a whisper in the night when sleep has blessed its gift,
The fire of a friendship turned into love,
The bare touch of skin, so contrast in likeness, but when together, so blissfully alike;
You ask what you mean to me and my answer is subtle.
Everything, I reply, as if one little word could encompass my whole answer.
You smile, you're content with the answer, yet a sorrow lingers within your eyes,
I know what it is you want but to answer it would take years.
A lifetime, perhaps, until I've finished describing that which is indescribable.
By then I would have wasted your love away, as time stops for none.
My answer is so subtle in context, but so immense in meaning.
Let the words and actions of my love be the answer you wish to find.
For in time, if you allow, the answer will be clear
As the wrinkles around your mouth will explain our life story.
Happiness, you see, is what you have given me, and what I, in return, must make you see.

Mikayla Adams, Grade 10
Woodbridge Sr High School, VA

The Story Teller

He skinned the trees for their precious bark,
the backdrop to his stories.
Blackened shards held by his callused hands
draw the characters, etching them into the bark and his mind,
the mind of the story teller.

Words mused from the stars open a new portal
to the men of the sky
who watch the bold and spirited.
How the heroes quest, and the tyrants fall,
And mighty scaled beasts with the eyes of owls
exhale scalding breath,
and cover the sun with their bodies alone.

The story teller points to the stars and says, there is Giselle,
the girl who became a swan.
Over there is Orien, the mightiest hunter.
He tells us of a sorcerer who lives in the mountain,
and sends fire from the sky,
His magic comes from himself, the story teller says
But my magic comes from the past.

Kaitlyn Britt, Grade 10
Appomattox Regional Governor's School for Arts and Technology, VA

Crystallized Realities

The skies mirror dreams
We dwell upon it's crystals
We live by it's creed

Khristian Ortiz, Grade 11
Forest Park High School, VA

Wandering

I wandered down the road,
Not knowing exactly where I'd go,
But I had hope.

Natalie Kanter, Grade 10
Norfolk Collegiate Middle/Upper School, VA

The Shout of Victory

Wading through monotony
I heard the shout of victory
The challenge was now overcome
The day was done
The battle won
A triumphant cry rang through the sky
I heard the shout of victory
All the people gathered 'round
Drawn by the hope
Of the new day
All their hearts were filled with glee
I heard the shout of victory
Their feet were light as feathers could be
They danced until the sun had gone
And among the stars as one
I watched enraptured, now could see
I heard the shout of victory
And thought: why not me?
And out of the mire of life pulled free
I cried the shout of victory

Rebecca Boia, Grade 12
Archbishop Spalding High School, MD

The Boy I Fell For

Tall, dark and handsome
That's how I imagine him
The boy I'll fall for
Athletic, smart
And witty he is
The boy I'll fall for
Caring, sensitive
And loving
That's the boy I'll fall for
Then there's you
With your crooked smile
And braced teeth
You can't sing
And you're a little too tall
You
With your caring ways
And adorable laugh
That makes my heart go crazy
You
The boy I fell for.

Amber Lowery, Grade 10
Woodbridge Sr High School, VA

Spring Time

As warm weather shows
Our spirits begin to grow
The sky gets brighter
Flowers grow large with color
The sun shines brighter than ever

Brianna Mitchell, Grade 10
Norfolk Collegiate Upper School, VA

Guardian Angel

Once trapped in-between the dark wings of my soul
I've finally become something that can be released from sin
For the protection of my love is the reason I've flown
These wings of mine finally blooming because of what is heaven sent
Now I have been given an eternal goal
Protect the one I love as if her heart were my own
Keep her from vanishing into the darkness whole
She is truly someone precious that much has now shown
A task that is so heavy a burden
Unto my divine soul I shall not protest
I give her my loyalty to never give in
To bind our hearts sincerely together without a regret
Once the day has come to which the angel who had fallen
Arises to reclaim his wings those that were once dimmed
The evil will have claimed my luminous heart once again
But the love I kept for her will not diminish
I rendered these words to my love until that day comes
I will continue to love and protect you eternally
Though I'm fallen you can still hold me as your guardian angel
I will continue to love you eternally thru my days of strife
Even as the raven's feathers reclaim my wings to life

Da'jon Mason, Grade 11
Croom Vocational High School, MD

Spring

When spring comes the air becomes cool in the morning and moderate at night
Spring is time for a renewal of gorgeous flowers like tulips, daffodils
Leaves begin to form and prepare to change colors during the fall
It's a time where animals are born like bunnies and baby chicks
Spring peepers are small frogs that come out at night and peep

At night the temperature is perfect for having picnics and gatherings at night
Couples can stay outside till the sun sets or light a candle
In the afternoon men and women work on the lawn to make it pretty and inviting
Women plant more plants to spruce up their gardens
Bees start buzzing and getting nectar from the beautiful flowers

Spring is shiny, warm, inviting and appealing to the eye
It's also a time when the Easter Bunny gives candy to children
Parents hide Easter eggs and let the eager children hunt to find them
Thrilled by what they found
Crack the egg and eat all of the candy
That's what spring is all about

Aidan Swienton, Grade 10
Holy Cross Regional School, VA

Trapped

She is trapped in light and warmth.
She is surrounded by her friends, she can admit it to herself too.
She has been touched and loved, she feels the warmth of another's touch, she
Has been told she matters. She sits on the edge of rainbows, only kept safe
By the chains of joy. The love for everything else, she buries in her
Happiness.

Jake Black, Grade 12
Appomattox Regional Governor's School for Arts and Technology, VA

The Blue Dress

In the middle of the night she waited patiently,
Under garlands that hung from the old, white gazebo.
The silk flowed behind her like a peaceful stream,
And the graceful ripples hugged her delicate body.
The blue dress sparked a fire,
And he smiled back gently.

From a distance she seemed timid,
But the light in his eyes softened her face.
The faint music strolled through the air,
When the brilliance of her dress brought him to his feet.
Her scarlet-blushing cheeks were hot and her eyes unsure,
But his inviting hand still waited in the chilled air for hers to take.
She gazed into his deep green eyes,
And touched the smooth blue silk on her hip.
She hesitated approaching him slowly,
And took his warm, comforting hand in hers.
She was finally ready to join him,
Under the cradling branches and the midnight stars.

Rhianna Ross, Grade 11
Glen Allen High School, VA

The Mask That Hides

I wear the mask that hides my fears,
It hides my weaknesses and dries my tears.
The broken road that lies behind me,
Is paved over with yellow bricks,
Smooth and unwinding.

My pretense is plastered with laughter and grins,
Each day I repaint those over and over again.
The heartbreak and betrayal are pushed to the bottom,
They may be concealed but they are never forgotten.

My love may be genuine and my friendship sincere,
But being broken leaves a certain level of fear.
The fear of being dragged again down the road that's behind me,
Is tucked safe away behind the mask where no one can see.

Megan Phelps, Grade 11
Ocean Lakes High School, VA

Bullet

I watched the light flash before my eyes,
I saw my life right before me,
I saw all the wrong and the right,
I saw the stupidity I went through
I saw you hit me like a bullet,
I saw me slowly fall for you every second I was with you,
I saw me slowly drift from my world to yours,
I saw my heart beat for you,
I saw my jealously with you,
I saw the way I drifted away with you,
I saw how you brightened my day,
And I saw the day I fell in love with you.

Anna Spradlin, Grade 12
Independence Secondary School, VA

Years

Years…
They come and go
Every 365 days
And then we start all over again
Days, Weeks, Months
All make up a year
Years…
Contain one of everything
Birthday, Christmas, Easter, Graduation and so much more
You celebrate all the good times and bad
That together made up the year
Years…
Rely on the one day of the year
New Year's Day
We make resolutions
For a better year
This time around
We want to make it right
Because we only have
365 days before another passes us by

Katelyn "Katie" Lott, Grade 12
Woodbridge Sr High School, VA

Timeline

Yesterday I was gone
Today I am strong
Once I was a victim
I seem to be carefree
You think I am who you want me to be
But really I am the king of my world

At the beginning I was dependent
Three years later I was wild
When I was 10 I experienced death
By 15 I was wavering in who I was
Today I stand confident and strong
In 7 years I'll be who I wanted to be
In the future I'll be wise and respected
Passing down what I know like my ancestors before me
But today I am happy

Joshua Cain Castanon, Grade 12
New Directions Alternative Education Center, VA

Imprisoned

Like a prisoner in the south, I feel trapped
Here no one is genuine
The fast life has been stolen from me

Mama raised me without any worries
I'm orphaned from freedom and my old self
I want to be back to my natural habitat

I feel I am imprisoned
I feel I am imprisoned

James Garrett Jr., Grade 10
New Directions Alternative Education Center, VA

I Make My Life

I have a life held in my hands
nobody else can make it good or bad.
It's my choices and my feelings
and experiences that make me.
Though I am not always accepted
it is up to me to be the better person.
I stand for what is right
and I stand for what I believe.
Though others don't like it,
their feelings don't make me.
I have to be the judge of myself,
and I have to choose the path of life,
that I will take,
so that I can be what I want.
If you stand in my way,
that is unwise,
for I will be a dominate figure,
making my world what it ought to be.
I want nothing but goodness,
so that is why I strive,
to be goodness in every possible way.
Lara Ballintyn, Grade 10
Padua Academy, DE

The Mountain Path

Choices stand before the mountain
Two different paths, or three, or four
Each way leading to no way certain.
Now comes the decision of the hour,
Which life should we decide upon?
This path we walk afraid to fall
But, criminal stands this life in cons.
Everyone shall eventually hear the call
Down one path alone we may tread
The decision to remain solo dread
This fear that may always sift ahead.
We all will stumble apart in time
To learn our own path within this line.
Always sifting through these rhymes,
And walk away from the murky brine.
The Mountain still stands, daunting
Beckoning in the newest paths.
A silhouette against the sky, haunting.
Bringing out the darker wrath,
That send us running from truer paths.
Amy Verburg, Grade 12
East Rockingham High School, VA

The Boomerang Child

The baby is born
Clings onto his mother's hand
He quickly grows up
Becoming distant from her
Yet eventually comes back
Emily Cole, Grade 10
Norfolk Collegiate Middle/Upper School, VA

Not Earth

If war and violence ceased,
If nature was at its finest,
If everyone got along,
It would not be Earth.

If people were kind to all,
If people were responsible,
If people were trustworthy,
It would not be Earth.

If all this would come to pass,
This wonderful, serene state,
It would not be Earth.
It would be Heaven.
Lili Nizankiewicz, Grade 10
Homeschool Plus, VA

Friends

Days grow long
Nights go long
Years can pass
But friends will stay

Adventures grow slowly
Journeys go fast
Experiences can fade
But friends will stay

Time grows thin
Lights go dark
Life can end
But friends will stay
Jacob Laurent, Grade 10
Holy Cross Regional School, VA

Throw Me Back

But I guess it's too late,
And I wish I'd never taken the bait,
Now I'm floppin' on the ground,
Not makin' much sound,
Prayin', prayin', prayin',
That Poseidon will come to save me.

How I got here,
I don't know, but you sure did have to row,
Now I hope you're a
VEGAN,
Or at least s'il vous plait,
Have chicken tonight,
Instead of fish filet.
Marshall Moreau, Grade 12
Tunstall High School, VA

The Sound of Snow

Silence:
the sound of snow;
falling gently,
without noise.

Simply falling.

Touching the ground softly,
without a murmur,
it sticks,
or melts seamlessly
into the ground.

The world around
stands still
as it compiles,
growing ever taller.

In silence it rises,
burying the ground.

Silence:
the sound of snow;
falling gently.
Silence.

Silence.
Sam Winters, Grade 10
Holy Cross Regional School, VA

Alone: A Plea to a Friend

Why is the world so cruel?
Why can't you care for me as I care for you?

So unfair the hand that's dealt,
Anger is the only emotion to be felt.

But, out of great hate can come great love,
Like some kind of twisted joke from above.

I beg and I plea,
But you ignore me

And I'm left…
Wishing
Hoping
Waiting

In vain

I am…
Alone

Just me and my pain.
Shea Ankers, Grade 11
Kettle Run High School, VA

Three L's

Head throbbing, ears ringing
from the gunshots outside my window
3 people shot
helpless, hopeless and now lifeless.
It's like I can feel him breathe his last breath.
Blood violently drips from his chest
I silently sit,
listening to Lupe, The Roots and A Tribe Called Quest.
All the words to those '90s songs are coming true
as if nothing has changed since then.
Helicopters, unmarked cars and drugs flood my 'hood.
Pretty soon there'll be flowers and teddy bears
on the corner where the lives were taken,
but who took these lives?
Nothing will be said
Lives gone too soon for us
but right on God's time.
All I can do is shake my head.
I want my roses while I'm here, not when I'm dead.
A lesson to those who choose to waste their life away,
3 lives taken in 3 seconds you chose to waste.
Danielle Rouse, Grade 11
Woodstream Christian Academy, DC

Happiness Is Not Hard to Come By

They laugh at me because I find joy in the
Little things.

When it seems
Everything
Has been snatched from you or
Everyone
Has abandoned you —
Like having a rug pulled out from under you —
And you are alone with your cuts and bruises,
You cannot help but
To bask in the greatness
Of life's simple pleasures.

Because if you cannot find happiness in that,
Where
Will
You
Find
It
?
Julia Su, Grade 12
Thomas A. Edison High School, VA

Shredded Peaces

When there is war, peace cannot be found
The bombs and the bullets shred it with their sound.
When there is peace, war is done and gone
Until someone creates another war that simply can't be won.
Amanda Esmacher, Grade 12
Forest Park High School, VA

Haunted

Time is running out, and there
is no way to pinpoint the exact
time that life became a primal struggle
to not die — and there are millions of
haunted faces just like his, fading fast,
in this camp nicknamed Death, and the
year is 1944, amusement lingering in
the cold eyes of uniformed men, and once
he'd heard a rumor that the Americans
were coming (too late for that, he thinks,
but doesn't dare say it out loud) — but, oh,
what a relief it would be to die, free from
cold and ash and stone walls, and as if
his body has heard this, his vision blurs,
his mind spins, the echoes of dead men ringing —
lost heroes, fallen angels, you haven't done
anything worth remembering, stop this,
he thinks, but it's too late, and the light
goes out of his eyes in the year 1944
in the camp Auschwitz, nicknamed Death
Smrithi Srikanthan, Grade 10
Chantilly High School, VA

Enigma

I wear the mask that has two parts.
First is the front that is divided in two.
One side is bright, which is friendly to others.
While the other is dark, and can sometimes be cruel.
And yet both of these personas act as a wall.
Because showing my true self, is something that is hard.
Like a tiny ray of light, in a thick cloud of fog,
The true me is there, but not all can see it
And while many think they know me,
Only some have a clue.
But sometimes a few, a very select few,
Manage to break through my wall, and can see through the haze.
Maybe one day, I will take off my mask.
And show to the world, my true face at last.
But until that day comes, I shall remain a mystery
That only so many can recognize, and even fewer can solve.
Marcus Holman, Grade 11
Ocean Lakes High School, VA

Basketball

Basketball is more than a game
One must play with passion
To be the best
One must have high motivation
Basketball is a game
One must seize the moment
But the moment must come to the players first
Basketball is a game
Basketball is competitive
Win or go home
Hoolima Simbo, Grade 11
William E Tolman High School, RI

Rebuilding Panther

The smell of sulfur permeates the air
Shattered glass litters the floor
Graffiti covers the walls
I turn and see a baby doll
Lynched
Covered in blood
Who would do this?
Why?
Is it their home life?
Are they angry at the world?
This was an elementary school once
How could it have come to this?
I must help these people
They need me
And I need them.
The storm clouds have lingered too long
It is time for the sun to shine again
The flood waters are finally receding
It is time
Time to rebuild a broken land
Amy Defnet, Grade 12
Poolesville High School, MD

They Lie

I hate fairy tales, they lie,
There is no such thing as a happy ending.
No handsome prince is going to
Sweep me off my feet and whisk me away
To his magic, fantasy life.

I hate love stories, they lie,
They give us false hope of undying love.
No one is suddenly going to
Realize they love me no matter the odds
Stacked sky high against us.

I hate life, it lies,
Gives us dreams of magic, of love,
Of happily ever after.

But sometimes life isn't about the
Happily ever after,
Sometimes it's just about the living.
Alexandra Quinn, Grade 10
Holy Cross Regional School, VA

That One Girl

A flower may die,
The sun may set,
But a girl like you I'll never forget.
Your name is precious,
It will never grow old,
It's engraved in my heart,
Like letters of gold.
Kyle Hall, Grade 10
Woodbridge Sr High School, VA

Mask Identity

I wear the mask that hides my fears
It smiles and laughs, inside there are tears.

Thousands of pieces delicately placed, make up my mind, my soul, my foolish pride.
The mask is fearless, I can do it all.
The pieces inside, about to fall.

This cruel society says many things,
"You're not pretty enough."
"You're not smart enough."
"You're not good for anything."
These words don't scar my disguise.
It's the pieces hidden behind my eyes.

They started to drop, one by one.
Now only a few remain to hold me up.
My confidence has shattered, my pride is gone, it appears to me the battle is done.

I wear the mask that hides my fears.
It plays with my mind, it covers my tears.
Outside I show I can't be broken,
But inside, I'm afraid, the damage has spoken.
Kate Vanderpool, Grade 11
Ocean Lakes High School, VA

Lift Off

I'm getting ready to take off,
I'm almost ready to lift off,
All I need is the countdown,
Mamma please don't hold me down, I know its going to be hard,
But you're gonna have to let me spread my wings really far,
I know some will let me down, but I know you never will,
Mamma show me how to fly out of this tree we call home,
Show me how to get the worm, show me how to sing to my family from far away,
Mamma can you please show me the way?
I'm getting ready to take off,
I'm almost ready to lift off,
All I need is the count down,
Daddy am I strong enough to go on?
Daddy don't hold back the tears, hold your little girl real tight,
You can still kiss her goodnight,
Some people say I'm more like you when it comes to working, is that true?
Daddy do I have the strength like you do?
Daddy can you help me fly like you?
I'm getting ready to take off,
5, 4, 3, 2, 1
Lift off.
Adriana Freiling, Grade 11
Lackey High School, MD

Spring Time Is Here

The flowers are blooming,
Birds are chirping,
It is the first day of spring.
Alex Railean, Grade 10
Norfolk Collegiate Middle/Upper School, VA

The Leaves Fall

Wind blows through the trees
Leaves softly fall to the ground
Autumn has arrived
Caroline Asam, Grade 10
Norfolk Collegiate Middle/Upper School, VA

The Fall
They were introduced one day
And became the best of friends.

They solved the puzzles and fell in love
They let come what may.

But insanity tore them apart

And the first watched the other fall.

So they both lived without the other

Till the end of it all.

Eleanor Cesafsky, Grade 11
Holy Cross Regional School, VA

Colors of My Heart
Reds of passion
Exploding from my heart,
Orange of pure flames
Burning in my eyes,
Blues of sadness
Engulfing my very soul,
Pinks of sweet poetry
Flowing through my veins,
Greens of happiness
Come in bright rare flashes,
Blacks of the unknown
Floating around my mind,
These are the colors of my heart.

Krystal Harrell, Grade 10
Homeschool Plus, VA

In the Night
I hear a cricket in the back of my mind
I see a small light down the hall fade away
I feel a bit of comfort
I need to fall into my dream world
Where I can finally have peace

in the night
I am the luminous moon holding on.

In the night I am not normal,
I am unpredictable,
Every day.

Autumn Price, Grade 10
Tunstall High School, VA

King of the Jungle
Deep under a tree the lion lies,
Cleaning his paws,
King of the jungle

Marlena Sacks, Grade 10
Norfolk Collegiate Middle/Upper School, VA

Serafina Pekkala, After Reading "His Dark Materials"
This witch is wise
and her old age can only be seen
if you look into her eyes.
She is old but she doesn't need anything.
Her back arches off the dry earth
and her wrinkle-less skin shines
palely against the dirt's dusty brown.
Sprinkles of earth spill from her navel.
Serafina doesn't need to breathe.
Her lungs, filled with grainy sand,
are of no use to her. Her life comes
from her verdant, closed, eyes and her thin, black roots.
The ends of her hair have buried themselves
into the soil and life blossoms
like a halo around her head.
All she needs is herself and the rejuvenating feel
of the moonlight on her breast
that her willful existence craves.
Her youth is eternal. No food, warmth or lover
can sustain her. She could lie here sleeping
for fifteen thousand years and rise the next day the queen of Nigeria.

Mina Williams, Grade 11
Appomattox Regional Governor's School for Arts and Technology, VA

True Friends
Every day we share together
Our thoughts, and plans…how God brought us together
We've been best friends for quite a while
Thinking about it brings a joyful smile

We've cherished many memories, more than we can count
And that is proof He has blessed us with a huge amount
Those memories of cooking, cleaning, talking, and playing
Our times of joking, laughing, being serious, and praying

For every piece of joy and laughter that we have discovered
I know why He has given us each other
We always make each other smile
And then go walking and talking for a mile

He knew we were perfect for each other, that's why He put us together!
"For everything there is a season, a time for every matter under heaven"
And every day we share together
I thank God we have each other!

Mikhaela Whitley, Grade 10
Family Learning Academy, DE

Grow Up
they tell me to grow up and be "mature," when i say that you're too "cool."
"cool" to you means getting high and partying everyday.
"cool" to me is getting good grades and making that winning goal or making friends.
being "mature" to you is drinking.
being "mature" to me is being above the influence.
you can keep telling me to be "cool" and "mature," while I'll just tell you to grow up.

Anthony Testa, Grade 10
Delaware Military Academy, DE

Heart-shaped Boxes and Candy Roses
Diminutive circles
illuminate the cracked sidewalk.
A decrepit bench perches in the deep
shadows.
An African American man
sits blanketed in darkness.
Crisp
new suit and tie.
Polished shoes
shiny enough to be mistaken for
stars in the promising night sky.
Perfecting
his luminous red tie
he rises.
Rounding the corner
leaving the stemmy rose
with velvety smooth petals
and a heart-shaped box
on the bench
in the darkness.
Morgan Scearce, Grade 10
Tunstall High School, VA

Confused
Torn from this world
to my own,
seeing the life
that's never shown
Finding truth
in the lies,
living what's left
before it dies
The life untrue
unsure, not found
is it under?
or above ground
Confused like a moth
flying in day,
unsure where to go
or the right way
My journey will end
before confusion sets,
stuck in this life
trapped by its nets.
John Branch, Grade 12
Dinwiddie High School, VA

A Warm Day
The wind blows softly
The little birds sing out loud
The butterflies fly
The sun in shining so bright
Today is like the heavens
Marnie Abraham, Grade 10
Norfolk Collegiate Middle/Upper School, VA

Dulce et Decorum Est Cadere in Amore
When I held his hand, I felt
only cool skin and stones in my stomach.
I kept waiting for the knots in my nerves,
waiting for warmth like being buried
under the covers in December when
the snow, the street lamps, and the shadows
on the trees made everything look noir.
But I only had the laughter like the chatter of pretty birds.

You had told me to start with a crush, not an effort.
Sly flirting, arms touching, fingers brushing
hair away from upturned, pink stained lips.
You said dulce et decorum est cadere in amore.
It is sweet and proper to fall in love.
You must not remember that I tried that already.
You didn't find it as sweet as I did.
Hannah Rae Bracey, Grade 11
Appomattox Regional Governor's School for Arts and Technology, VA

Tonight I'll Sleep Tight
"Sleep tight, don't let the bed bugs bite."
Every night he was there as we knelt and recited the Lord's prayer.
Praying for just one more day. "Don't leave yet, Please just stay."
A bear hug and kisses, traditions a teenager secretly misses.

Days have passed by, and in the blink of an eye,
I'll tuck myself into bed tonight; Forgetting every worry and fright,
Although still, always on my mind, I attempt to forget Dad's no longer part of mankind.
Drops fall like rain from my forlorn face, thinking of the goodbye I've embraced.

I lay in bed feeling all alone, though I know he's watched as I've grown.
An angel tucks me into bed, giving kisses atop my head.
Reminding me of the time when every day, side by side was sublime.
Then when morning reaches, I rise and shine and know Dad's walking only one step behind.
Katie Cyr, Grade 12
Hampden Academy, ME

Death
Honestly, I am scared of death.
I'm scared of how, why, where, and when,
I do believe in God, Jesus, and angels in Heaven.
But death to me represents pain and darkness,
Then again, life is like a baby bird's life in a nest.
When you are first born, you're fed and protected from the predators or prickly pine cones,
But as you get older, it becomes a necessity to do things on your own.
Death scares me from end to end,
We can't live forever, so why do anything that will cause our lifeline to bend?
Life is hard and feels like diamonds,
But is it really worth cutting it short and dying?
Jordan Sollenberger, Grade 10
Tunstall High School, VA

Okay

A piece of me is empty. I've become a hollowed out cave, dank and dark.
The furniture echoes out hints of the past, calling me to go back to the good old days.
Every movement a memory, every memory pain.

It's a choice I made to stop the destruction of my heart, which was sure to burst.
To purge myself of all the unnecessary longings that were slowly consuming me.
But now the fire inside me is raging more then ever, the need for happiness greater then my need for sanity.

I would give everything to return, take back all the words I've shouted,
Make it all right again and forget the future and what it holds.
I just want to be okay again.

Amanda Johnson, Grade 10
Woodbridge Sr High School, VA

Carolers

An array of people are walking down the street; singing and celebrating the night before Christ's birth. They stop at each house singing songs of joy, peace, and love, on the most tranquil night on Earth.

Their voices blend together in perfect harmony; and echo all through the town. Their strong sounds break through the brisk winds, which makes them shiver, but never causes them to frown.

The townspeople enjoy the Yuletide music, while their children are asleep in bed; dreaming of the toys that St. Nick will leave during the night. They dream of dolls and wagons that are red.

The snow is falling and the wind is howling on this cold eve, but the carolers stay warm, dressed in their best attire. The know that once the night is over, they'll return home to plum pudding and hot apple cider.

Now the night has come to an end, and all the carols have been put away for another year. However, the Christmas spirit has entered their hearts, where it will remain forever dear.

Philip Davis, Grade 10
Delaware Military Academy, DE

Her Broken Eyes

She
is fragile, they say. A wisp of a feather that might blow away
and never come back.

She
sees the world fragmented
in amorphous pieces of fragile weight
through crystalline eyes veiled by a fringe of Indian-carpet eyelashes
that curl like a child's fist
She knows the world and its misanthropic burdens. She knows
lines and curves and bleeding fingertips.

But she does not know the gold dye of a sunbeam or the blue
embrace in her piece of sky.

Tonight is dark, an ebony envelope.
She
will lay outside alone
And gaze on spectral angels and brush
their gossamer wings. And I watch and I know that
one day she may gain a pair of wings herself and fly away forever.

At the raw age of eleven, she
lost a war and lived — but she has
broken eyes.

Alice-Yanhong Lu, Grade 11
Thomas S Wootton High School, MD

9/11

On 9/11 2001
New York experienced something that wasn't fun
Osama bin Laden came up with a plan
And he did this because he was a nasty man

To kill America he did try
By not allowing four planes to fly

There was a ball of fire after the first plane hit
They had to bring in a big emergency kit
People were jumping from high and low
So to their aid many did go

There were many heroes on that day
They tried to help out in every way
The people who risked their lives the most
Were printed in the New York post

They were courageous and very strong
But with their help the clean up still took long

10 years later from that day
It's still a shock what can we say
People today are still afraid
And hopefully al-Qaeda will be repaid

Shaina Sitrin, Grade 12
Bais Yaakov High School, MD

I Want You

Launching me to indescribable states wisely
Getting me through routines with advice daily
Sharing our untold history, embracing it tightly
Ingesting truth, accepting reality, all memorably

Presenting less than willing to, I see otherwise
By simply glancing into your mesmerizing eyes.
I see hope, I see forever, I vividly see our lives
Trust tears with lies, hearts crack with goodbyes.

Your words have blossomed into reality,
Capturing my fragile organ, beating lightly.
Reaching, feeling, grasping it all momentarily,
Uneasily unfolding ourselves, uniting slowly.

Wild dives, trenches deeper, our love never dies
Coming as one as darkness cradles us to sunrise
Intertwining through fights, through kisses, through cries
You are my angel, you are perfect, you are my princess.

Kathy Torres, Grade 12
Woodbridge Sr High School, VA

Shattered Passion

Time seems to have stopped in this world of mine.
The moment I saw his lips touch your cheek, I knew I was lost.
Forever trapped in a never-ending maze of heartbreak,
I find myself swimming in an ocean of tears every day.
Try as I may, I cannot escape this sorrow.
You've chosen his heart over mine.
A fact I cannot seem to comprehend.
But the world holds a great future for me.
I know I must move on, and forget your lovely smile.
After the mark you've left, I'm not sure if it's possible.
Without you the roses seem to have died.
The sky shines a different kind of blue.
And the light from the sun passes over me without care.
He brings joy to your eyes, and tears to mine.
I love you so much, words cannot explain.
As he holds your hand, I realize what I must do.
Let life unfold itself and be happy for the love he's given you.
I may not be the one to warm your heart,
But I'll always be the one to hold it close to mine.

Drew Dickerson, Grade 11
Holy Cross Regional Catholic School, VA

Bullfighting

Run, jump, dodge
Jump, dodge, dive
Dodge, dive, spin
Dive, spin, lasso
Spin, lasso, taunt
Lasso, taunt, crash
Taunt, crash, punctured
Crash, punctured, dead

Greg McKnight, Grade 10
Forest Park High School, VA

Desire

Have you ever wanted something so badly
You could taste it on your tongue?
Could you feel it pumping through your veins?
Did it consume you ?
Were you swallowed whole by your desire?

It's an unquenchable thirst
A fire that can't be doused
It burns brighter and stronger with each passing day
It's a wildfire burning out of control
Swirling in a cloud of emotion
Pushing you closer to the edge.

It shadows you, haunting you dreams
Eventually it swallows you, taking control
Powerless and weak, giving in and letting go
The fire smolders
Leaving nothing but ash.

Mary David, Grade 10
Holy Cross Regional School, VA

Love a Friend

It's never too hard to be a friend,
Don't bend the truth to make the right friends.
Don't be a fake!
Lend a helping hand!
Take a helping hand!
Learn!
Don't turn the wrong way.
Don't push people away.
Don't walk away from a true friend;
'Cause they're as real as a friend can be.
It will pay off once you let people in that care.
They will stay with you through the roller coaster ride of life.
Don't let pride hold you back from doing what is right.
If you do,
You will lack sight in doing good things and
everything will seem like a fight.
Think, speak and seek positive and
You'll be a positive person.

Katelin Moorehead, Grade 11
Salem School, MD

The Art of War

Swords clashing, like lightning flashing,
Hammers smacking, like thunder cracking.
Colors of red everywhere,
Dirty smells fill the clean air.
One falls, another stands
Surrenderers raise their hands
Shouting out, "Mercy!"
Sounds falling on deaf ears,
"Make peace with your deity
And face your fears."

Brandon Simmons, Grade 10
Hampton Christian High School, VA

Burden to the Constant Tick of Time

She's an angel with black, tainted wings
Time slows as she breaks through the sky
Her tears cascade, fabric swaying in the breeze
She falls; Burden to the constant tick of time

Tick, tock; plaguing and echoing through her mind
Set for disaster, her mind shattered, eyes blocked
But still she falls, losing her grip on the whip
That cracks as fast as the tick from a clock

Bursting adrenaline through tainted veins
As she looks down; tears pluck at her viper eyes
Licking her salt-encrusted lips, she stares
Her wings are failing to beat, to rise.

So, failing like the constant beep of a machine
Heart stops; time stands utterly still
Looking through a hospital at crying families
That reeked of death washed out and unwritten wills.

Samantha Solomon, Grade 11
Woodbridge Sr High School, VA

Lost Eyes

Every time she gets around me I fall weak, trip
on my words, suddenly can't speak
The way she licks her lips soft and wet, my
palms get sweaty, my heart jets
She inspired me to be everything that I can it's
crazy how I feel this way
She calls my name
Like the lyrics to a love song
Carried to me from the angels above
Nothing can go wrong
When I look at her, same personality as me
I get infatuated and close the gap between us
She makes me smile again
And the feelings we have will never become
Dull

Ricky Hughes, Grade 11
Rivermont School-Tidewater, VA

Listen

Listen to the sound a heart makes
Listen to the sound a heart makes when it breaks
Tears roll down cheeks
Filling the ocean and its streams
As darkness turns today
The pain and hurt are here to stay
Bright blue sky turns dark and mean
Smiles fades away never to be seen
I throw my worries in the depth of the ocean blue
Trying once again to forget the day I met you
Listen to the sound a heart makes
When it mends back together again.

Deolinda Fortes, Grade 11
Charles E. Shea High School, RI

A Heavenly Friend

Pocketing the expectations of others around,
there's not enough room to put a foot down.

Incredulous, though it may seem,
this is something in which I believe.

Talents are many, where attentive is one,
a prologue to life, mine has just begun.

A support system on which I lean on,
shattered between a crack, a guilt, weighing a ton.

Can you hear me mend the hole,
and set off the scale to balance, to equally hold?

My heart cries for company, which it never gets,
You come knocking on its door, a sound I'll never forget.

You came and filled that void,
with an impartial choice.

Be my guide and I will never hide,
or stand on shaken ground disregarding to Your very sound.

I choose to stay sane,
and choose to travel by on Your soul-searching plane.

Keeping me safe is what You said You'll do,
in return I'll give all the love I have within to you.

Ruth Petit-Homme, Grade 12
Parkdale High School, MD

True Beauty

How can you dare,
To even compare,
Anything with Nature?
It need not try
To be but what it is.
We put so much effort into appearances,
Yet Mother does not.
She smoothly captivates with unending mysteries.
Father God is Love,
Mother Nature is Beauty,
Yet does not Father excel beyond all, in everything?
Father created Nature, and still we ignore its beauty.
Feeling the need to advance,
To improve, but what are we improving?
Maybe, the only improvements necessary,
Are within ourselves.
We try to see,
But how far are we looking?
There is a whole other view
From a mountain than
From a couch.

Nicholas Magill, Grade 12
Paul M Hodgson Vocational Technical Center, DE

The Hands of a Prayer

As he gets on his knees
And begins to pray
As he close his eyes
He begins to cry.
He prays that
God
Forgives him for his sins.
"Lord" he cries
"I surrender my all to you.
I lift my hands to you
For peace and joy.
Lord there is no one like you
I am on my knees
Begging you, please
God, wash away all my sins
So my journey can come to an end."
The hands of a prayer.

Zaneta Ingram, Grade 12
Central State Hospital Education Program, VA

Before My Love Remembered Me (Portuguese Amor)

Before my love remembered me —
I told him to forget —
The endless love we had that day —
I know we won't regret

Though every day — we did not waste
The time we had to spend
We'd lie down in Madeira sun
And wish it would not end —

And when the day came to an end
We knew it would go on
For Portuguese Amor is sweet —
And brighter than the moon

Alexis White, Grade 11
Norfolk Collegiate Middle/Upper School, VA

The Marriage

Their ignominious relationship sadly shattered
For a while now
They had been at two different ends of the
World
As others came along
Their love, an onerous weight on their shoulders
Persisted

They drifted together
In hopes to secure their faithful fate
But
Soon, he found his way back to her
Though, slower this time
So, she called upon Him

Devon Winsor, Grade 11
The Potomac School, VA

Breaking Point

Can't lie like this.
Faking a smile just to get through the day,
stress builds quickly, where does it end?
So fragile, being thrown away doesn't help.
Haven't I reached the breaking point?

Can't that change? Can't it be different?
Layer upon layer, students grow large in size.
Changing from a beautiful fall, to an ugly winter,
outside is cold, bare, and unpleasant.
Where is my breaking point?

Fogs roll in and out,
as if it was a mood ring upon everyone's finger.
Dreading what comes next, who goes next.
When does all this stop?
When can I reach my breaking point and start new?

Rosa Yohe, Grade 11
Glen Allen High School, VA

A Rare Treasure

With sunset comes the end of an old day,
Refreshing warmth in the bright, rosy glow.
It sets over the sea, steady and slow,
Oh, over peaceful, sun-drenched beach and bay.
Beside the waters, by the shore they lay,
They gaze at the sun setting far and low.
They never forget times from long ago,
Shared memories that never go away.
But laughter and joy do not always last.
The misery and troubles we all share,
The sorrow even when the storm has passed.
And sometimes life itself is never fair.
The sadness in life is immense and vast.
Happiness is a treasure that is rare.

Onvara Arthornsombat, Grade 11
Holy Cross Regional School, VA

The Death of the Strength Found in Beginning

Waves crashing against the shoreline,
Like birds throwing themselves into clouds.
Without receding to where they came
And without knowing of where they go,
Reaching past the boundaries
That others seem set to define.
The hues of blue against the orange
Pass onwards, onwards in the world,
Stretching the extensions, running too thin:
The ocean overtakes what it cannot command,
A calm rage against that which never took arms.
Spreading its life and lesson towards the sky
As only in force does it begin to waver,
As only in strength does it finally weaken.

Rebecca Henenlotter, Grade 12
Oakton High School, VA

Stress

You change my day
from great to horrible.
You make me feel like
the world is on my shoulders,
as if I was Atlas. I walk around
knowing that you follow me
wherever I go.
I am worried, aggravated, and paranoid
because of you.
You are my ally.
I call you stress.

Carrington Atkins, Grade 10
Tunstall High School, VA

Thanksgiving Hymn

A time for love
To share what you are thankful for
A time to share with others
To say what you adore about people
Tell God that you are grateful for his grace
To remind others that God loves them
To remember that you are very fortunate
To pray for those in need
Praise God for all the miracles
Thanksgiving is not a day to discard
It's a day to cherish

Regan Standlick, Grade 11
The New Community School, VA

Alone...

Days get colder
Time starts to slow down
I wander around thinking
Thinking what if...
What if...I have you!
What if...we start over!
What if...anything...
To get you back
Yet, here I am,
Alone, alone, alone.

Kelcy Fortes, Grade 10
Charles Shea Sr High School, RI

From Greatness

Whenever you fall down,
You have two choices:
Stay down, is your first, and
getting back up is your second.
But can you do it?
When you fall from greatness,
your body tells you, 'You are nothing!'
Be something, and stand up.
Fight your body and protect your spirit.
Be something after you fall.

Sean Davidson, Grade 10
Tunstall High School, VA

For My Mother

I dreamt you told me I was
Losing the Holy Ghost.
My past, a rainbow of hymns
broke itself, like crisp leaves
falling onto the pavement with
a gust of Salem wind.

Translucency reflected my
hallelujahs and doubt covered
me with a grace.

Was it you?

I awoke and found him
sprinting to me with open arms.
I spun into of knowledge
of fear and love. You
call it good and evil.

I released Him to save another
not doing what you instructed.

I guess this is what limbo feels like,
longing to be washed in the blood
but not to slay the lamb.

William Miles, Grade 12
Appomattox Regional Governor's School for Arts and Technology, VA

A Woman's Place

Throughout my study of history
I have come to see a major discrepancy
The "powers that be" often sight
That women's minds are very light

Therefore men vowed when time began, that we would never get voting rights
Moreover, that thinking women would put the world through many plights
That it was not a woman's job to be politically correct
We were supposed to be the obedience models, erect

In later years they stated that if we didn't want to be a societal woman and marry
Then men said in order to conform to the norm we should just go and join the abbey
Few women dared to challenge men or the traditions
Fearing they would be deemed as reckless heathens

In today's times some men still believe it is blarney
To let a woman go off and join the Army
They say these women are harmful and brazen
They'd rather have an inanimate raisin

Women in the past were always pushed around
Just because they didn't want to be housebound
We have fallen silent in this era, it's time we voice our opinions
Before we recidivate to America's kitchens

Maddie Crimmins, Grade 12
Sussex Technical High School, DE

All I Want Is

All I want is someone to love me.
Someone to love me for me.

All I want is someone to love me.
Someone to show me the way,
Someone to pick me up when I'm down.

All I want is someone to love me.
Someone to lean on,
Someone to cry with,
Someone to laugh with.

All I want is someone to love me.
Someone to know me,
Someone to call my own,
Someone to be there, when I'm all alone,
Someone to love me

All I want is someone to love me for me.
Joseph Hamilton, Grade 12
Independence Secondary School, VA

Peace by the Sea

My eyes are tightly closed,
and a hint of salt assails my tiny nose.
A more beautiful day could not possibly be,
for here I stand, facing the sea.

With graduation coming precariously near,
the thought of my future beckons a tear.
To forget my worries for even just a day
is worth everything I can pay.

Now that my eyes are open wide,
from the dolphins to the tide,
the elegance I plainly see
is serving to remind me.

His love will always be mine
and His plan for me existed before time.
I am rid of my fears
by knowing my Father is always near.
Brittany Whitley, Grade 12
Family Learning Academy, DE

Crooked Blinds

They try to hide the explosion
of cream-colored flower buds
and outstretched skeleton branches
that sway in the late winter wind
and stem from a burly trunk,
where the murky-green moss clings.

But I see through the uneven slits.
Alex Beale, Grade 11
St Christopher's School, VA

A Walk Through the Woods

It's warm
And there is a gentle breeze
I am slowly walking in a pine forest
There is a soft crunch as I step on the needles
There are sudden flashes of sunlight as I continue to walk
I begin to hear the chatter of birds as I continue deeper into the forest
There's a silent
Roar that
Grows ever
Louder and
Ever closer
The roots are
Beginning to
Become gnarled
As if they are
Stretching for
Something far off,
Then out of nowhere
Appears a gently winding stream
The stream flows on endlessly and lazily, going on forever and ever
Eventually finding its way into a peaceful lake where it can rest
Thomas Schubert, Grade 10
Holy Cross Regional School, VA

No Light

I used to sing.
This little light of mine
That was in the days when Mama
used to go to church. White laced
socks, black petty leather shoes,
bright yellow dress with flowers.
Pink ribbon wrapped around the thickness
of my ponytails. A half empty purse filled with hard candy tucked under my left arm.
Big brown Bible folded in the crease of my other arm.
I'm ready for church. I'm gonna let it shine, let it shine
let it shine, let it shine
sitting in the pews of the church God has me.
The word of John Mark and all the disciples ring through the yard.
Jesus loves me this I know for the Bible tells me so.
In my older years I walk alone. Past the bootleg spot
on the corner, past the graveyard and the drug house.
Everywhere I go I'm gonna let it shine
I just keep singing and singing
Jesus loves me this I know for the Bible tells me so.
I used to sing. There is no light for me to shine.
Yet Jesus loves me this I know.
Sheryl Harper, Grade 12
Appomattox Regional Governor's School for Arts and Technology, VA

Under the Stars

Bright speckles in the sky
Around me so quiet
Fresh air feels so good
Virginia Harding Marshall, Grade 10
Norfolk Collegiate Middle/Upper School, VA

A Young Maiden's Desire for Freedom

She longs to fly among the birds
to the forest
where she will be set free.
Sammi Rappaport, Grade 10
Norfolk Collegiate Middle/Upper School, VA

The Beach

The beach is beautiful,
With the sand all white and warm.
The waves go back and forth,
Never beginning never ending.
The dunes are blown away,
And the long grass whistles in the wind.
Children are playing in the water,
Their parents are reading,
While watching carefully.
Tall sandcastles are built,
And sunscreen is layered on.
It is loud yet quiet,
Hectic yet peaceful.
The beach is beautiful.

Annie David, Grade 10
Holy Cross Regional School, VA

Key to My Heart

The celebration of you
While the days turn to night
Are of the moment I saw you
When wrong became right

A love of a lifetime
Rare but true indeed
Forever with no lust
Is my guileless creed

A lock on my heart
As you hold the key
With the knowledge of love
We'll forever be.

Tiffany Smith, Grade 12
Thomas Dale High School, VA

Lost in Wonderland

I look around this strange new place,
dizzying sights that begin to expand
I've been here before in my fantasies
it seems I am lost in wonderland

here, I thought, wishes would come true
surrounded by creatures who care
here, I know now, all sanity is lost
a dream has become a nightmare

I run till I find the beckoning door
on the other side, I hope to prevail
now I know that dreams are misleading
they are no coveted fairy tale

Elizabeth Main, Grade 11
Holy Cross Regional School, VA

Partial Confession

Forgive me if I don't display
The way you make me feel.
But I have never felt this way
So I'm not sure this is real.

I'm sorry if I hide my eyes
I don't want to show my gaze.
Because when I look at you
I'm lost in bewitching haze.

I try my best to show my love
But often I'm left stuck.
I find myself at a loss for words
To express my immense luck.

I'm lucky that I found you
I'm lucky, this is true.
I guess what I am trying to say
Is I think I love you.

I'm just too afraid to show it
Because I'm not sure it's true.
I'm relatively sure it is.
But when I know...
I'll tell you.

Jeremiah Watts, Grade 11
Leonardtown High School, MD

That Summer

Oh Father Time, please turn your clocks
Back a couple years.
Take me to the good ol' days —
The summer of no fears.

I miss our backyard barbecues
And picnics in the grass.
Just you and me, and me and you,
We made the moments last.

With lips stained blue from popsicles
And tangled, sun-bleached hair,
We babbled on for hours and
We laughed without a care.

With kicked-off sandals cast aside
And suntanned legs so bare,
We'd sink our toes in cool wet mud
And breathe the summer air.

If only things had never changed
Why did they have to end?
Those precious, breezy summer nights
I spent with my best friend.

Brianna Bagalkotkar, Grade 12
Tabb High School, VA

In My Hand, in My Heart

I held a Moment of Time in my hands,
Briefly.
Then the Grains of Sand
Slipped through my fingers.

I held a Ray of Sunshine in my hands,
Lightly.
Then Night fell and I
Had to let it go.

I held a Rainbow in my hands,
Softly.
Then Clouds blocked the light and
It disappeared.

I held the Wind in my hands,
Strongly.
Then it whispered and howled and
Blew away again.

I held Love in my hands,
Gently.
Then it moved into my Heart and
Has never left me.

Jessica Gauldin, Grade 11
Chatham High School, VA

My Surroundings

The clouds so fluffy and white
I sit here looking to the sky
Today the sun is so bright
I think as I lie

Everything here in my surroundings
So pretty and colorful
I think of what is around
There is grass, flowers, and other things

The grass is so tall
So skinny like a pin
Some grows against the wall
So green and thin

Flowers so beautiful
The bees gather their pollen
The petals are so colorful
Bees make sweet honey

I get very frightened
As the sky starts to darken
The porch light starts to brighten
My mother tells me to come in

Anna Filiaggi, Grade 11
Holy Cross Regional School, VA

Dry Desires

Sometimes I sing to the cactus
and stroke her until my blisters burst
I dream of the distant mirage
and drown in its mirrors I once cursed
Sometimes I tease the scorpion
and harvest the beetle's wings
In ultimate prayers for rain
I'll beg the water to heal the sting
Sometimes I slither afar horizons
to curse the silent skulls
And at the sand I'll scream and thrash,
laugh at its wrath and sunken holes
Sometimes I don't hide my cruel glares
and run against the wind's fierce blows
I cruise the wasteland's deep hell pits
to wait for the sky's answer to show
Sometimes I scorch beneath the sun
and I'll try to let myself fly,
but sometimes I'll just let my blood boil
beneath the curdling sky.

Lindsey Barszcz, Grade 10
Woodbridge Sr High School, VA

Straight Hangers Are Useless

We were created
in the confounds
of a French style sun room.
On top of censored out
magazine clippings.
With the ear buds
still clinging to the vibration
of our drums.
But we just gazed
through the mirrored glass
at the roof men working
with the chain strung to their ankles
and a weight at the end.
And we mocked the antiques
as they mimicked their balding owners
and cracked their frames
just to spite us.
So we cursed aloud
and covered our feet in wet cement
and tried to sit up.

Thomas Payne, Grade 12
Tunstall High School, VA

A Beaver's Fear

There once was a beaver,
Who looked at Justin Bieber.
He shrieked and he ran,
For he was not a big fan,
And then decided to leave here.

Breanna McGreevy, Grade 10
Stearns High School, ME

Summerfine

When I imagine feeling free,
I think of relaxation.
Of smiling in perpetual comfort.

A feeling of refreshment
pervades my soul,
and I feel as though I'm laying on
the soft summer grass,
looking up at the sky
and telling someone a joke
they'll think is funny.

Soft cotton shirts,
a cool, gentle breeze.
Soft-soled
sneakers, ankle socks,
and freshly-dried jeans.

Long car rides, me sitting
in the back seat, her head
on my shoulder.
We're going to Disneyland...
Her head's still on my shoulder.
We're still laughing.

James Rives, Grade 12
Appomattox Regional Governor's School for Arts and Technology, VA

Softball to Me

It's 5 a.m. and were already out the door,
We got up a little after quarter to four.
We get in the car to get something to eat,
We pull up to Dunkin Donuts that's where we all usually meet.

We get in the car for that long two-hour boring ride
And when we get to the field it's really cold outside
Our team starts to warm up to get ourselves prepared,
We look so precise and sharp the other team looks scared.

The team starts to come together like we're going to war
Next thing you know we hit, we run, we steal, and we score score score.
In a blink of an eye we're in the fourth game of the day
It's hot and were tired
And we're still ready to play.

The practices, the running,
All the preparations we've done,
Finally pay off 'cause now we're number one.
Where can you go to get all this done?
This is why I love softball,
It's so much fun.

Courtney Allin, Grade 10
Delaware Military Academy, DE

I Wear the Mask

I wear the mask that hides frustrations
And protects the heart from harmful penetrations
The wall that stands portrays a smile
That hides the tears just for a while
As my face hides in humiliation.

I wear the mask that exhibits confidence
As it shades the feelings of incompetence
Full of joy and rejoice
It feels as if no one hears my voice
Begging for them to see the real me.

I wear the mask that with zeal laughs
For I have experienced true sadness
And even though I seem so strong
It is because I know and hide my weaknesses
Many may judge me wrong
Because they know I don't belong.

I wear the mask...
Natasha Diaz Carrasquillo, Grade 11
Ocean Lakes High School, VA

Little Bird

Look past your iron bars; leave your steel cage behind
Reach for those sunny skies; soar among the dreams of hope:
Fly, little bird, fly
go on, spread your wings
and show the world
that hope will never die

Look past the withered silence; leave the shadowed night behind
Reach for the silver stars; revel in the sweet music:
Sing, little bird, sing
go on, smile and chirp
and show the world
that peace will always ring

Look past the fallen ashes; leave the leaden mist behind;
Reach for the vibrant threads; live rather than survive life:
Dance, little bird, dance
go on, just spin and twirl
and show the world
that love still has a chance.

Sarena Tien, Grade 12
Mills E. Godwin High School, VA

My Labyrinth of Darkness

Clouds,
Stars,
Mazes
Of the night,
Have me feeling lost
Yet this is my sole comfort zone.
Thao Huynh, Grade 12
Woodbridge Senior High School, VA

The Celebrity

There was a celebrity who walked with finesse
She held her nose way up high and wore a tight dress
She did her best to look gorgeous, it was easy to see
She carried a purse, and in it, a canine named Fifi
She really looked striking, sitting in her chair
Caking on more makeup that she just had to wear
It was all part of her image she set
Fake breasts, fake nails, and a fake nose, I'll bet
When she wants a quick drink, she will look at a man
And he will whip out his wallet, quick as he can
She will smile and flirt and laugh at his jokes
But at the end of the night she'll leave him, like all other blokes
I won't explain all that I think
Only that if air was heavy, her head would sink
Now onto the good, for not all is bad
This girl was trendy; she knew what was the fad
Also, she has more money than I
Wherever I walk to, she could easily fly
I do envy her, a little at least
I would drive golden cars, and everyday there'd be a feast
Ethan Caldwell, Grade 10
Sussex Technical High School, DE

A Twist in Fate

I was born dead in a merciless place
I walked through the Valley and stared death in the face
"Tick, tock" says the clock as the cuckoo bird pops
Try to hold on; the last grain of sand drops
Our upside-down minds, misplaced in the stars
Our brothers and sisters watch us from afar
I went to the future to return to the past
I won the race first, but I came in last
The back of the bus is the front of the line
An age-old end to a beginning so fine
Material hogwash humanity consumes
But I saw the dark in the lightest of rooms
The deaf man listens to the mute's tall tale
As the blind man watches the whole ordeal
Standing alone in a crowd full of people
A heathen sits down and prays at the steeple
Our lives slowly pass by
In the blink of an eye
The moon and the sun are eternally friends
Everything starts, but what starts must end
Alexander Campbell, Grade 12
Freeport High School, ME

Don't Leave

I watch you walk away,
Leaving my sight and never,
Returning again.
My body begins to ache,
Since you have just walked away
Emily Bashara, Grade 10
Norfolk Collegiate Middle/Upper School, VA

Why Not Be Yourself?

Most girls do the same things.
Wear the same clothes and cake on all of
that makeup.
But why?
Every girl should be CONFIDENT.
They should not put on all that makeup,
and should wear what they want.
No girl should be a clone.
Everyone is their own person.
Every person should express themselves
in their OWN way.
When every girl is the same,
what's so great about that?
NOTHING
Be your OWN person
LOVE yourself
Be HAPPY with who you are
YOU are UNIQUE
Don't let anyone tell you differently.

Christine Wolanski, Grade 10
Delaware Military Academy, DE

Colorful Memories

I remember the lazy days,
The sun out bright as the light stretched
Out amongst the cascade of blue that
Laid parallel of my own lounging form.
I can still feel the ticklish sensations as
Blades of grass brush against my cheeks,
As if soothing me to sleep.
I felt safe, content, unbeatable,
Unstoppable.
What I loved most was the
Distinct smell of gingerbread that
Would never come out of my clothes.

It's like that every time I close my eyes,
But when I wake up, I can still feel myself
Longing for those days, and my heart aches
For the smell of gingerbread again.

Morgan Richardson, Grade 11
Woodbridge Sr High School, VA

Frantic

Hands shaking,
Legs falter,
Breathing's uneven,
I look up,
Eyes wide,
Lips parted,
I announce my name.
Addressing my audience,
My voice escapes,
Runs through my teeth.

Mona Osmer, Grade 11
Forest Park High School, VA

Untitled

I lie.
I lie about what I'm doing, where I'm going, and what I just ate.

I steal.
I steal food when I can't starve myself any longer, the scale that I'm prohibited to use,
and my mom's trust, which she thinks is so strong.

I hide.
I hide my discoloring nails, my dirty deeds, and my shrinking body.

I believe.
I believe that I'm ugly, that I'm not skinny enough, and that everyone hates me.

I regret.
I regret that I've betrayed the ones who love me the most,
that I've harmed my body in ways unimaginable,
and that I've stopped caring about the most important things in life.

I'm trying.
I'm trying to get better, to resist temptation, and to learn to love myself.

Jasmine Pickering, Grade 12
Appomattox Regional Governor's School for Arts and Technology, VA

The Logic of Life

Meek Mills, dream chaser
Martin Luther King, dreamer
Rodney Young, procrastinator
Americans, wasters
High school teens, bulliers
Homeless people, beggars
If Martin Luther King Jr. was alive right now, he would be mad
The only thing we changed was all the laws that we had
Now we have those girls who are dissing other races online
So now I can watch videos of bullies on Youtube about how I can be defined
But I forget, I should not complain
Since I live in a house with a lovely door frame
One of my dreams is to create a homeless shelter
I will keep trying to do so till I'm an elder
You see, I don't feel like wasting anything for no reason
So I'm going to keep my dream, even if I get arrested for treason
While I'm in my cell, I will talk to the talking wall
The wall will listen and hopefully never call
My conscience because my mind is crazy
So it calls my mind, it will finally figure out I'm lazy

Rodney Young, Grade 11
Delaware Military Academy, DE

Endless

Down by the ocean
I look to the horizon
I see endless waves
Time seems to last forever
Will I ever be endless?

Zach Miller, Grade 10
Norfolk Collegiate Middle/Upper School, VA

Time

Time passes faster
Even faster than we think
If you sleep too long
One day here, the next day there
Wake up and wonder what was

Anyssa Reddix, Grade 10
Norfolk Collegiate Middle/Upper School, VA

My Car

My car, my sweet car,
It goes from 1 to 60 in 4.5 seconds;
My car, my sweet car.
Not really a car for the ladies,
But, it does the job for me!
My car, my sweet car,
My way to show my mood.
My car, my sweet car,
Freedom!

Dylan Rojas, Grade 12
William E Tolman High School, RI

Suspicion

Suspicion lifts her head above the bushes,
Peering into the unknown.
Her long lashes obscure her vision,
Clouding her mind with lies.
She steps forward with caution,
Nerves locking up her hooves.
A blaring horn, a sudden rush,
Doe eyes shine in the light
As her fears are confirmed.

Mariel Frey, Grade 11
Glen Allen High School, VA

The Wall

I built them tough
And I built them tall
I built them to protect
What's inside —
But thanks to me it
Will never see the light of day
It's in a safe but dark place
But it doesn't have to worry
About its wounds reopening

Taylor Mills, Grade 10
Tunstall High School, VA

Drifting

When awake
I daydream of
Sleep
Wrapping his cozy fabricated
Arms around me
In a warm embrace
Sending me adrift
Though never letting go
Until I wash ashore

Amber Cluesman, Grade 10
Cape Henlopen High School, DE

My Role Model

The burning sensation has you running back for more
It opens up a whole new world of possibilities to explore
You become tolerant to the pain of others
And a woman I wish I didn't have for a mother
You try to kill away all the memories and make yourself believe
But when you wake, you remember everything and realize the hurt will never leave
You're stuck in this apathetic moment, while I'm still growing up
You don't remember my jokes or my secrets
You only fill me with disgust
You never came to see my play, when I got the lead role
Or even a single soccer game at my school
The pain inside is anchored and incredibly bare
I can no longer spread my wings in your polluted air
The fumes from your failures are suffocating
I must break free from your chains and learn to fly
There is no more waiting
In leaving I must let go of my past and give my wounds time to heal
It has stolen every part of you I could have had
And now there is nothing left to steal
But everything you are, is everything I will never be
It has shaped a Role Model, don't you see?

Caitlin Blades, Grade 11
Woodbridge Sr High School, DE

Where Our Destination Lies

Lend me your hand and I'll show you a world sublime,
We'll soar like gulls — sailing on the breeze —
Laughing at the wind and tasting sweet sunshine.
My, what a sight we'll be.
Lend me your heart and I'll show you care like you've never known it;
Tell me your despairs and I'll put them to ease,
Show me your fears and I'll dispel the beasts,
I can't fight fate, but I can give you all that I have
And I can hope that it's enough.
So come along and smile like you always do,
It very much becomes you.
We'll turn this world upside-down in our pursuit;
In tumbles and somersaults we'll search with all our might.
And even though we don't know what we're looking for —
Or what we may find —
Gladly I will chase dreams with you
If that's where our destination lies.

Amber Grawl, Grade 12
Courtland High School, VA

Tea Time with Nonnie

Nonnie's finger has touched her lips so
Now we bow our heads, and close our eyes, and hush…
Now before you begin wondering what it means or don't we count God's sheep to sleep
We wait for all the eyelids to open so we can
Lift the rose chanel off Nonnie's cheek, sift it with sunshine dandruff
And pour the petals-powder-and-particle parfum
All over the tea set.
This is Nonnie's secret to polished silver and earl grey.

Addie Eliades, Grade 11
Appomattox Regional Governor's School for the Arts and Technology, VA

Trust No More

Trust is the name we all wanted to have
Lying is the shame we've all been given
Terror of the heart spoken before deaf ears
Never wanting to listen so we live in fear
Of what will be said and what might be spoken
Will I be mended or will my heart be broken
We always give up before we're allowed to fail
So our souls become cold and stale
Washed in The Blood renewed and freed
But still feeling like I'm tied to a tree
Lost and searching for the true missing love
Saying bye-bye like a free white dove
Screaming at the moon to get your point across
But my life is just a meaningless lost cause
I give up!!!
I'm through!!!
Sad to say I'm done
Don't worry about me…
I'm the deceiving son

Romello Sincere Raycrow, Grade 11
North County High School, MD

When Traveling

A chill in my bones from the feel of the glass,
and a longing I hope will come to pass.
The meadows and fields a vivid gold and green,
sway gently towards something unseen.
The brilliant crimson and tangerine trees,
caught in an embrace by the mountains beneath.
They twist and quiver as we roll by,
I do my best to suppress a sigh.
Faintly, they seem to be whispering,
or perhaps it is a song they sing.
It's stirring a feeling that I can't bear,
a restlessness that I can't compare.
I search the cobalt and white patched sky,
to find what's missing,
but I'm not sure why.

Carinne Boord, Grade 12
Woodbridge Sr High School, VA

The Best of Us

No one can be the judge of us
Because they'll never understand.
The way our words flow together, a babbling brook
The simple way life controls our friendship.
We learn to accept all things of each other
Including the flaws, the imperfections.
I sit and remember,
The echoes of fading laughter,
The memories together
That lie fragmented, scattered throughout time
Because though it may have been in pieces,
I gave you the best of me.

Kadie Bennis, Grade 11
Woodbridge Sr High School, VA

Admiration

Diamond
A little white diamond in front of a background of black sky
A tiny droplet of rain amongst a world that gets madder
Black, black, well is that all they see?
They offer their tricks and their kicks
Getting back nothing if only vain
How I wish it would rain
Comfort is the color
Oh I long for it to pour out here
In the city of waste

Ruby
The red beam
Seeps through a gray patch in the sky
Thin as paper, but never giving in
Always guiding and giving us hope
The only time that seems bright enough
Is the crack of light
When hope is abandoned
And all is but forgotten
It never seems to forget its place

Ashley Gray, Grade 10
Woodbridge Sr High School, VA

My Friend, My Hero, My Mother

Someone who showed me true love, giving me life.
A person that I will always count on.
Someone without fame, but special to me.
You never stopped to wonder.
And you prayed I could learn.
That is who you are.
A star that showed me the way when I could not see.
A person that I can teach and learn from.
You are the ideal and vital to me.
You make me see life with other eyes.
You gave me solutions when I was lost.
I would never change you for anyone else.
All I need I get from you
You do so much for me, creating a huge debt.
A debt that I can not repay.
I pray God to help me
Make you as proud of me as I am about you.

Karine Barreto, Grade 12
Charles Shea Sr High School, RI

Always Alone

Starlight, so very bright, shining down to the surface of Earth,
Pure white, on a dark night,
Beautiful, and of boundless worth.
I wander outside, and I can't help but sigh,
While everyone else stays locked in their homes.
I stand amongst loveliness, looking up at the sky,
Longing, waiting, alone.

Eric Howell, Grade 11
Amherst County High School, VA

Girls With Makeup
Makeup is a girly thing
There's bronzer to look
Brown
There's mascara to look
Longer
Eyeshadow to
Pop them
Eyeliner to make them look
Bigger
And lipstick to look
Bolder
No girl NEEDS makeup
Too much is ugly
You gotta have
Confidence
Orange isn't a skin tone
Natural is the way to go
Brittany Harvey, Grade 10
Delaware Military Academy, DE

Shadows
Laying back and smiling
what a beautiful world is this
the birds whisper in my ear
death rising up above heaven
wiping the final tear
open your eyes once more
seeing you were there the whole time
but the whole time with her
ripping the scarred hole in my heart
lies come flowing through
seeing that the past
never really was true
and even if I stay
you'll still cry till the breaking of dawn
curled up in the corners of life
tucking you in at night is my way
my way of saying goodbye
Katie Dryer, Grade 10
Delaware Military Academy, DE

Time
Time.
It eludes you still.
You stand erect,
on the train platform,
absent minded,
just
waiting.
Your eyes blink,
only a moment.
And then you see
the swirl of smoke that has long been gone.
You've missed your train.
Maria Kellam, Grade 11
Lake Braddock Secondary School, VA

Blue
Is that feeling in the bottom of your gut;
Resonating and lingering, never seeming to fade.
It's lies and never knowing what is true and what is false,
It's mistakes and always looking for what is right in a sea of pandemonium,
It's a ship sailing in the midst of an ocean with no direction.

It's the tear crawling out from one's eye and rushing down the cheek,
A skydiver without a parachute.

The list of regrets camps out permanently.
This, oh this, is not a symbol of anything.

It's the feeling of not being good enough, even though you have given it your all,
and it seems as if no one in the world is on your side.

When a man's best friend is put down for good,
All happiness is shattered.

Blue can only be erased if it is pushed to the side and forgotten,
If not, one is only left with despair.
Cole Hyman, Grade 11
Glen Allen High School, VA

Sweet Mother
I love you sweet mother; I will never forget you;
I will never forget how much you suffered for me.
All the things you went through to make me happy;
All the love and caring and respect and advice that you gave me;
When I'm hurt, you're hurt; when I cry, you cry; we share secrets together.
You have been in my life since birth;
You're not only my mother, but also my best friend;
Your arms are always open for me;
I run to you whenever there is a problem.
You keep me standing up high;
You're the reason I'm alive today;
You made me the person I am.
I miss you so much, Mother
I miss all the fun times we had together
And all the things you taught me.
Every day I dream about having you close to me;
I try not to worry too much, but I can't help it.
I wish I had you by myself at all times, Mother.
You're the best mother of all; I love you more and more.
Susan Kanga, Grade 10
William E Tolman High School, RI

Birds
They chirp so early in the morning
While they sit in their trees
They fly above the clouds
And make you lose sleep
They swoop in front of cars
Making you slam the brakes
They eat the food that goes to waste
Katie Renesis, Grade 10
Norfolk Collegiate Middle/Upper School, VA

Anxiety
A llow me time to grow
N othing is set in stone
X -hale
I nhale
E xpect change
T alk things out
Y ou are in charge of your emotions
Zuriely Quiles, Grade 12
William E Tolman High School, RI

The Still of Morning, Otherwise Silence

I live in a world where music doesn't exist
Where the only sound is the pounding of my heart and the biting breeze on my lips
My world has only the rough textures of the guitar strings, their subtle vibrations being nothing
but a ringing, a ringing in my fingers
The birds open their mouths, and I see no music
The band leader speaks only poetry
The radio is naught but a hunk of metal and plastic
The man with his back turned
It's all nothing but subtitles in the world where I live
The fog of the morning muffles the chance
that a falling leaf could touch the ground and break its heavenly, monastic silence
A man on a bench with nowhere to go, just another alley cat's day
He says nothing, and hears nothing in the fog of waking
His eardrums are broken, but there should be sound, he knows
The park is quiet, and the air is broken
He's broken, and he is of the fog, the mist
Ephemeral like a ripple in the air or the fleeting, final chords of a song
There is no music but me and the world
None but the touch of my fingers and skin
against the world and perhaps
The reverberations of a beat throughout my ribcage

Brian Loftus, Grade 11
Holy Cross Regional School, VA

Double Identity (Bravery vs Fearfulness)

My surface may be smooth, but my surface is my mask.
My mask makes me suffer with anxiety.
It is glued, stapled, and compressed to my body.
My mask controls every move, every gesture, every groove.

Ever varying and ever-concealing
My true identity has escaped from me,
Now, I run and hide but prison walls are everywhere
My voice and hands tremble,
Others see me as weak, timid, and cowardly. You think less of me,
And the sardonic laughs are killing me.

I truly possess the bravery of a war hero, who has the aptitude of victory.
The warrior has been tormented, and the strength tested numerously.
After each feat the faith and strength become unimaginably stronger
It cannot win one battle however: it lashes at the nervousness with the strength of a thousand gravities
It screeches and has prepared for this battle for a century
But the fearfulness that others see is too heavy, and sadly cannot be extinguished
So you see, I have a double personality.
I wear the mask.

Andrea West, Grade 11
Ocean Lakes High School, VA

Voices

Voices are ringing, listen, listen,
As they tell us a story,
One of glory or of defeat,
Sadness and laughter, listen, listen.
The voices are strong, some are weak,
Some loud, some soft and quiet.
Cold voices that give you chills,
Or the musical voices that warm
Your heart when it is ill; listen, listen.
The old cracked wispy voices worn from decades of use,
Or the young voices, fresh and ready for use,

The voices of hearts all around.
The voices of the world, the voices of nature,
The voices of the broken, of the abused,
Of the fearful, of the hungry, of the crying
They tell us a story; listen, listen…

Armand Wine, Grade 11
Homeschool Plus, VA

Raging Clue

Why must my girl always do this to me?
I love her to death and can't be without
But she is running around town with he
Love for me I am beginning to doubt

I may seem to act like I do not know
Countless times I have seen your face flush red
I never thought you would stoop so low
You honestly thought you had me misled?

So continue the lying and cheating
I will pick up what's left of the pieces
Answer the door with a happy greeting
Just looking at you, my life decreases

Listen to her with a frown and doubt
"Don't let the door hit you on the way out"

Zach Keaton, Grade 12
Holy Cross Regional School, VA

Afraid of Change

Afraid of Change
That's like being afraid of life
It makes you envious of the Earth
So fearless, and unafraid of any change
From blue skies to gray nights
From winters breath to summers shine
From falling stars to dusty rocks
From a moon that comes, and goes
That sometimes never shows
Afraid of change that's all right
Courage and love will give you strength
For life.

Kaitlin Bampton, Grade 11
Forest Park High School, VA

The Orange River

The river is orange.
It has always been.

From the extrema of time
to the extremum of our time
flows the mighty veined river.

And in the delta
is all the centuries— millennia
of man's coarse red blood.

And over top is the yellow spheroid,
the palette orb, the indifferent paint drop
of a somnambulant pseudo-artist.

There, it is. The celestial zenith,
centerpiece of our cosmic scherzo,
refracting in our watered-down depths.

And the medium reflects orange—
passively and grotesquely orange.

So many rivers converge in an orange sea.
So many suns radiate of apathetic aridity.

And so, each day sanguinely adds
the sanguine blood of neutrality.

Into the orange river. Evaporating.

Elvis Fix, Grade 10
Gaithersburg High School, MD

The Possible Impossible

There are some
people in this world
who would tell you
that no matter
how much you try
you will fail
to do whatever
you set
out to do
then there are those
who will encourage you
to no limits
no matter
what the situation
that the
impossible is possible
those people
are like to
diamonds in
the rough
Mr. Zane

Dylan McLean, Grade 10
Temple Academy, ME

The Night Terrors
Awoken at night
Shuddering in my bed sheets
Sweating through clothing
My deepest fears haunting me
The night terrors had begun

Ryan Russell, Grade 10
Norfolk Collegiate Middle/Upper School, VA

Heart Breaker
See they call me the heart breaker
The one who hurts for a living
The cold-hearted girl
The one who could never love

Maybe the heart breaker just wants to be loved...
Maybe I break hearts because I'm scared someone will break mine.
Maybe I don't want to break hearts.
Maybe I'm just scared I'll fall...

In love
With someone
Someone good.
Someone loving.
or...
Someone who's no good.
Someone that'll hurt me.

Maybe I don't deserve to love...
Maybe I have to be patient...

Only time will tell
One day
Un dia

Alexis Carey, Grade 10
Bladensburg High School, MD

Grades 7-8-9
Top Ten Winners

List of Top Ten Winners for Grades 7-9; listed alphabetically

Keelan Apthorpe, Grade 8
St Anne Catholic School, TX

Kelly Brown, Grade 8
Fairbanks Middle School, OH

Natalie Ciepiela, Grade 7
Landisville Middle School, PA

Golda Dopp, Grade 9
Davis High School, UT

Madeline Elliott, Grade 7
Holly Middle School, MI

Lydia Heydlauff, Grade 8
Gilbert Middle School, IA

Mariella Jorge, Grade 8
Madrona Middle School, CA

Kaitlin Kilby, Grade 8
North Kirkwood Middle School, MO

Maryann Mathai, Grade 8
Windy Ridge School, FL

Jacob Nelson, Grade 8
Leesville Road Middle School, NC

All Top Ten Poems can be read at www.poeticpower.com

Note: The Top Ten poems were finalized through an online voting system. Creative Communication's judges first picked out the top poems. These poems were then posted online. The final step involved thousands of students and teachers who registered as the online judges and voted for the Top Ten poems. We hope you enjoy these selections.

What I've Learned

I've learned that what you think is right, isn't always right.

I've learned that people may not be your friends forever, but the ones that are, are true friends.

I've learned that everyone is different and following your own style is okay.

I've learned that it isn't appropriate to talk out of hand while attending Mass.

I've learned that a good sense of humor can help break the ice.

I've learned that you can do almost anything if you set your mind to it.

I've learned that breaking free and not being as shy as a sheep can benefit, especially when it comes to making friends.

I've learned that going for the bigger wave can be worth it, even if you don't make it till the end of the risky ride.

I've learned that trying something new and what seems boring can be exhilarating and the best thing you have ever done.

I've learned that looking back to the past does you no good,
    but looking toward the future can help you prepare for things to come.

I've learned that if you study hard and put forth much effort, exams and other big tests can be much more stress-free.

I've learned that being obsessed with something (Redskins) can be very upsetting near the end of the season.

I've learned that you can't waste life worrying about simple things that usually don't even happen.

I've learned that St. Patrick's Day is totally awesome, mostly when you have a red beard that matches your hair.

I've learned that famous people will never be my true role models or heroes.

I've learned that having a close and loving family can help shape who you are.

I've learned to always trust the little voice inside of you because it is always right.

I've learned that basketball is one of the most fun and intense things I have ever tried.

I've learned that spiritually I wouldn't be as religious and happy as I am without God
    because he has taught me so much valuable information.

Nick Curtis, Grade 8
Most Blessed Sacrament Catholic School, MD

Items for Soccer

To play soccer you need a jersey, custom for you;
    your number on the back is your new identity on the field.

To play soccer you need your own comfortable cleats;
    some are pronounced and vibrant, some are subtle and dull.

To play soccer you need undying strength;
    the stamina to run the whole entire game even in the blazing, late summer heat.

To play soccer you need the ability to learn from your mistakes;
    being able to take every flaw from each game and improve the next time.

To play soccer you need the courage to step up and play at the level of your opponent;
    the game will be rough and intense.

To play soccer you need intricate footwork; every movement, every fake out must be definite and defined.

To play soccer you need teamwork; no one can be blamed for a loss, you go in as a team, you come out as a team.

To play soccer you need a field, whether it is lush, crisp, green grass or coarse, unpleasant dirt;
    the more diverse the terrain, the greater the challenge.

To play soccer you need a ball, the center of the whole game; many are masked with hexagonal pieces,
    but some have special, unique patterns.

To play soccer you need the dignity to walk off the field with your head high,
    chin up, even after a devastating, crushing loss.

To play soccer you need the desire. You have to want to win. Nothing is given. Never.
    You have to step on the field and give 110%.

Every single time.

Emma Engel, Grade 8
Most Blessed Sacrament Catholic School, MD

The Smell of Summertime

As the wind softly sweeps through my hair, like socked feet sliding on the floor, I prance over to the river.

I dip my hand in the water and feel the cold current rushing towards my Nannie's log cabin.

My heart skips a beat, as I watch the sun fall down into nonexistent bliss, and say bye to the warmth.

And I can't help but wonder what tomorrows day will bring, and how marvelous it may turn out to be.

Skye Green, Grade 8
Princeton Elementary School, ME

Making Friends

The little kid is lonely,
he needs another friend.
So he pulls out some fatty foods,
and gains an extra ten.

Before you even have the time,
to see the kid is chubby.
He gains yet another ten,
and puts it on his tummy.

By now the kid's a social god,
his friend-making will never cease!
But before you even notice,
he's morbidly obese.

But there's no need to worry,
he has more friends than you've ever seen.
There's Cap'n Crunch, Ronald McDonald,
and his girlfriend, Dairy Queen.

David Caravas, Grade 8
Norfolk Christian Middle School, VA

Love

Love—
dancing hearts,
glancing eyes,
holding hands,
touching fingers,
caring forever;
always heard "haha,"
ending never,
yet, always changing.
—reflect—
changing always, yet
never-ending,
"haha" always heard;
forever caring
fingers touching,
hands holding,
eyes glancing,
hearts dancing
love.

Rosie Soucier, Grade 8
Princeton Elementary School, ME

One Small Wish

Only to fly
To hope and dream
To see the sky
And in between the sands of time.
Watching the silver lining form
Like wax on candles, slowly
Growing by giving up quantity,
But gaining love.

Sophia Sar, Grade 7
Friends Community School, MD

The Old Book

the cracked edges and
worn pages that creak
as I turn them
unfold a romantic tragedy
or thrilling adventure.

as the story unravels
this book becomes my friend
or foe as its
heavy scent fills my mind

the last page turns
and with it

the back cover of the
old book closes

Only to be opened again.

Hannah Shearer, Grade 9
Homeschool Plus, VA

Spring

Thump.
Drops of water pound
The thirsty Earth.
Silence.
Worms wiggle out,
From their little dirt homes,
Smiling in the sun.
Spring.
Grasshoppers dance,
Jumping from blade to blade.
Bees buzz from flower to flower,
Making sure they receive
Every drop of nectar.
Birds fly high in the sky,
Singing their joyful song,
Peering over everything
To watch.
Spring.

Michael Charlton, Grade 8
Holy Cross Regional School, VA

My Mom

She is a bodyguard, strong and protective
She is a lollypop, always sweet
She is a diamond, sparkling and beautiful
She is a wolf, always protecting her young
She is a puppy, fun and playful
She is a wise man, overflowing with wisdom
She is a textbook, giving me knowledge
She is a cheetah, fast and agile
She is a child, always fun to play with
She is my mom

Sam Kohler, Grade 8
Stevensville Middle School, MD

Rebirth

Spring has come,
it's finally here.
The change is amazing.
The plants are growing,
and the grass is greener.
The lyrical sounds of birds chirping,
you know life is in the air.
When the weather gets warmer,
and the days get longer,
I know that spring is here.
I work out every day,
and feel much stronger.
I look ahead with anticipation,
to the lazy, dog days of summer.
Going to the beach,
basking in the sun, relaxing
and lounging by my pool,
Oh the joy that spring can bring
I know life is born again.

Tim Picard, Grade 7
St Rocco School, RI

The Meet

Adrenaline
I can't feel my arms
Legs motionless
Thoughts clear

Eyes fixed on the only thing that matters,
The finish line
People fade away
Voices muffled

The gun, the boom
Feet pound
Breath fast
Legs numb

Worries gone
Almost there
Teams cheer
I finish

Sarida Pisarnpong, Grade 8
Blacksburg Middle School, VA

Africa

Brown sand
Spotty lions and cheetahs
Rainy days
Hot days
Sunny days
Crystal blue skies
White fluffy clouds
That's why Africa is so fine.

Fassil Fa-Yusuf, Grade 9
Bladensburg High School, MD

Holly

You ask what I love and I tell you this:
What I say is I love my dog, Holly.
When I leave she is the first thing I miss.
What I love most is she is part collie.

When I get home she always makes me smile.
Holly does not look like a normal dog.
With her by my side I could run a mile.
She looks like a wolf even in the fog.

When I look at her I am never gray.
She loves to lie in the warm, yellow sun.
Her coat looks really beautiful in May.
When she sees a squirrel she starts to run.

Together I want us always to be.
Just my little puppy, Holly and me.

Hailey Fisher, Grade 7
Trinity Lutheran School, MD

Slurpee

The benefits of Slurpees are varied,
So many flavors it's too hard to choose.
They always taste so great it's just scary.
The tang of them will relight ev'ry fuse.

Some people might say that they like icees
Some people think that they make such a mess.
Some folks hate drinks that are thirty degrees.
But I think Slurpees are a big success.

Slurpees have very high distribution
But icees are just so boring and bland.
And Slurpees are a good substitution,
For the other bad posers and name brands.

Slurpees are so much better than the rest
They don't know the meaning of second best.

Malcolm Ferguson, Grade 7
Trinity Lutheran School, MD

Nothing Beyond Never

to be true to you is like nothing beyond
to be true and fine is nothing but a lie
to be true and be told, why hold
why care why cry it was only just a try, just a lie.
no looking back, no fears, no regrets
Never look back, remember
Just a lie.
You thought forever, and he thought Never
Just a lie.
No more tears, no more lies.
now you got the perfect guy.
That will think forever, no lies, no cries.

Candis Madore, Grade 9
Fort Fairfield Middle-High School, ME

Watery Grave

Like fog on the horizon
And wind through your hair
A cat creeps slowly, without a care
All wizened
With age
And hunger
Crosses the path of a younger
Tom in a cage
They acknowledge each other
In the way that cats do
Then our cat goes away with less than a mew
On he goes, without an ail
Our cat now has reached
The place he was going
So he drops the load he was toting
Now at the beach
Our cat says farewell
And he jumps in the water
With just a slight totter
There is no more to tell

Morgan Sciacca, Grade 8
Brunswick Jr High School, ME

Ode to a Fish

Swish goes the fish
In his vast undersea world,
Swimming in schools,
No books or rules.
Freedom to live in the moment like a child
Eyes wide open, never closing.
Scales glisten, like salty sweat.
He is an acrobat,
Performing in an ocean circus
Hungry shark appears, like a bully in a deserted alley.
Time stands still, trapped against his will.
He is the target, there's no way out.
Adrenaline rush earns a split-second chance
He is a bullet on fire, swimming for his life.
Darting in and out,
Through a cold maze of ghostly coral reefs,
Until blinded by the sun, like a flashlight in the dark.
All is calm and bright.
The coast is clear, danger no longer near.
Swish goes the fish.

Blake Boddiford, Grade 7
The School of the Cathedral of Mary Our Queen, MD

The Warmth of Heaven

The rivers are blue
with so many things to do.
On a bright and sunny day
the warmth in the air brings so much cheer.
As the sky dims down
I think to myself God has blessed us here!

Carlo Merola, Grade 7
St Rocco School, RI

My Baby Sister

My baby sister is a mess.
But she isn't a buzzing pest.
Her name is Khloe Rayne.
Also she's sweet as a candy cane.

She goes to a mall…
to play with a ball.

I'm glad she was born…
On that JANUARY morn.

Curtis Howard Jr., Grade 7
Rockbridge Middle School, VA

Ode to Jesus

Thank you Jesus
For all you do

You paid the price
For all my sins
Even though I don't deserve it

You give me eternal life
Thank you Jesus
I give you my praise

Blake Cash, Grade 7
Rockbridge Middle School, VA

Basketball

B all
A ll Star
S hooting
K illing
E lite
T all
B e
A ll
L ike
L ebron James

Chris Smith, Grade 7
Rockbridge Middle School, VA

A Summer Night

Sitting in front of the fire
Listening to it crackle
Watching the flames dance
On this warm summer night

Sitting so quietly
Listening so carefully
To hear all the noises
From the trees I hear them
That's the summer night for me.

Marissa Chapkounian, Grade 8
St Rocco School, RI

If I Were in Charge of the World

If I were in charge of the world
I'd put all the bad guys in jail when they did a crime
If I were in charge of the world
I'd fix the economy because I hate hearing people go on and on about gas prices
If I were in charge of the world
I'd end long lines because I hate waiting for football autographs
If I were in charge of the world
I'd make no high prices
In school there would be no class but gym
There would be no waking up until 1:00 PM
If I were in charge of the world
You wouldn't have to go to work
If I were in charge of the world
Students would teach teachers.

Christian Bushey, Grade 7
Corkran Middle School, MD

Family

Family over everything
We love and hate
But at the end
We cry together

You see your mom cook
You see your dad smile
You see your brother's eyes light up when he plays video games

You can hear the most beautiful words "I love you" come out of your mom's mouth
You can hear your baby sister laugh and it just makes you smile
You see your mom cry and it makes you wonder why?

Family over everything

Ashley Alfaro, Grade 8
Corkran Middle School, MD

Listen Closely

Listen a voice once told me,
Listen to the stars,
Listen to the moon,
Listen to yourself,
Listen closely.
Hear how they softly whisper to you, to your soul,
Listen.
Believe in yourself, believe in others, believe what they say.
For what they say is nothing but the truth.
Listen closely to what they warn you for, for I might be the only thing you can trust.
Listen closely to the stars,
To the moon,
To yourself,
Listen closely.

Mattie Stull, Grade 7
Western Heights Middle School, MD

Kony 2012

Kony 2012,
Their childhood gone,
Taken away at a young age,
Parents left in rage,
Children forced to fight,
They hold their weapons tight,
Children worry about who will get kidnapped next,
An organization came up with a plan
Stop Kony 2012,
There is a video made just for Kony,
Some people think it is phony,
Joseph Kony you should worry,
We will find you in a hurry,
We found Bin Laden,
We will find you too,
It's all over the news,
Yes, texts, tweets, and emails,
Traveled all across the world,
Just to find him,
It is giving some people the blues,
Because it impacted the whole world too.

Bailey Holmes Spencer, Grade 8
Norfolk Collegiate Middle/Upper School, VA

Message 2 Society

I try to enjoy life's blissful atmosphere
While evading the ignorance of society

The beauty of the world is swallowed by hate
And destruction seems like the only outcome

But destruction itself can be substituted for another answer
The answer is inside the mind,
Instead of inside the chambers of a weapon

The strength of a thought overpowers the strength of a fist
The brain's outstanding intellect zooms past a bullet

Live through the inevitable battle of life
And then tell the story
Life is war — then you make peace

Dermaine J. Chambers-Walker, Grade 9
Charles Herbert Flowers High School, MD

Opening Night

Whispers of nervousness come out of every mouth
We're about to go on!
The thrill of joy and excitement that stirs behind the curtain
The crowd falls silent
The stage goes dark
Now it's the crowd's turn to whisper so eagerly
Light steps travel across the stage
Curtains open, lights flash, and the crowd erupts in a roar
And the nervousness melts away

Hayden Zavareei, Grade 8
McLean School of Maryland, MD

Monochrome Transition

The air was crisp and the skies were dark
Against the silver moon, a contrast so stark
Its dim light shining gently upon the trees
A blackened wonderland of autumn ease

The leaves were red and turning brown
As they fluttered softly to the ground
Scattered through the air by a breeze so light
Carried away into the autumn night

The air was chilled and thus came frost
All signs of summer peacefully lost
The glimmering white lying upon the grass
The pulchritude of winter had come so fast

The snow arrived one darkened night in November
This was indeed a lovely sight to remember
A world of monochrome, pure white and black
Beauty the scene certainly did not lack

Keariel Peasley, Grade 8
Riley School, ME

The Woman With a Blank Face

Her face is blank, who will love her?
She is happy, but who will love her?
Her face is blank, but her heart is loving.
She is not loved, because she has no eyes.

Who would kiss her? Without lips?
She has beautiful hair, but a blank face is she.
She cares for the poor, helps those in need.
Soft skin, warm hearted, but a blank face is she.

Who will love her?
She wants to show how pure she is to you.
They say what matters the most is on the inside.
So, would you love her, would you?

SaraJane McDonald, Grade 7
Rockbridge Middle School, VA

Horse Crazy

One breezy evening, in the late summer
My family and I went out to a rodeo to watch my brother ride bulls.
We went back in the shoots to wish him a good luck.

Meanwhile, we were just wandering around
Neighs and mad outraged deep bull grunts
It was like music to my ears
Hay and shaving were trapped in my nostrils

"For Sale"
A cruddy sign hung above a stall
And unsurprisingly we walked out with a two year old Quarter Horse
Now I'm horse crazy.

Charity Smith, Grade 7
Rockbridge Middle School, VA

Sometimes

Sometimes beautiful things are hidden
Beneath the surface of our skin
Sometimes miracles are blooming
Somewhere deep within

Sometimes words are flowing
From the lips of the betrayed
Sometimes hope will blossom
Someplace we never thought we'd stay

Sometimes love is fragile
In our hands it feels like it will break
Sometimes it will shatter
Leaving us broken in its wake

Sometimes the dark will rule us
Until we let the sun lead us to the light
Sometimes anger will be our last resolve
Until our true hearts lead us to the victory of our fight

Leah Berry-Sandelin, Grade 8
Mahoney Middle School, ME

The Forest

Deep in the forest,
The trees wave their long, spindly arms,
Taking in all of the warm air and sunlight of spring.
The frogs serenade the forest with their croaking,
And the birds flash their colors in the treetops.
Ferns rustle when a fawn dashes through the woods.

Emitting woodland fragrances into the air,
The pine trees and daffodils soak up water
From the stream that trickles between the massive boulders.
Raspberries and blackberries become perfectly ripe,
So that they shine like jewels,
Easily let go of their handholds on their bushes,
And spray sweet juice when bitten.

Emil Welton, Grade 8
Trinity School, MD

The Artifact, the Portal, and the Living Receiver

It's hard to believe
How life flashes through time
An artifact of "the travel."

Can we just travel
Back to when you believed
Come with me, we don't have much time.

Have you seen the portal of time?
The living use the portal to travel.
The portal that makes you believe.

Do you believe in time travel?

Carla Leanzo, Grade 8
Norfolk Collegiate Middle/Upper School, VA

Only on the Horizon: An Ode to Coronado, California

Your palm trees sway in the salty ocean breeze
I adore the sand that remains ubiquitous
as a quiet reminder of the close-by beach

Your sunsets are more than amazing
because the sun dips so softly behind the mountain range
filing the earth with a radiant orange glow
that softens into a deep blue
and lingers like the last note of music

Your bright blue sky contrasts
with your deep blue ocean and bright white sands
like colors picked by an artist's expert hand

Tall skyscrapers along the horizon
reminding everyone from tourists
seeking a pleasant getaway
to residents who have never left the island
that a large, bustling city is only minutes away
but yet is far enough away that one doesn't think of it
Just like one's trouble and sadness
Far enough away that it only appears along the horizon

Megan Morford, Grade 8
Norfolk Collegiate Middle/Upper School, VA

A Child's Wonderland

Children live in their own dreams,
to escape a place that is not what it seems.
So jump into their world of the night,
where there are moments of delight.
It is not what they seek,
it is just a peek,
into an imaginary place,
where everyone will know your face.
It is not all peaches and cream,
there will also be screams.
When the night closes in,
you are about to begin.
The journey takes you here and takes you there,
with rarely a scare.
When morning comes around,
I realized what I have lost and what I have found.

Arielle Truax, Grade 7
All Saints Catholic School, DE

Inside, Outside

Inside, I feel pain, I'm broken down
Outside, I'm well put together, but no longer now
Inside my mind, I make sense
Outside, I don't
Inside, my heart is nothing but pain
Outside, you see only stitches
Inside my mind, I see things clearly
Outside, I can't make it come true

Josseline Rojas, Grade 9
Bladensburg High School, MD

I Am Ty'quan Cunningham

I am a basketball and football player
I wonder if my grandfather is coming
I hear stuff that's not happening
I see things that are not there
I want to go to Paris
I am a basketball and football player
I pretend I'm a ninja
I feel like someone's touching me on my shoulder
I touch a wall and think it's a car
I worry about my brother
I cry never
I am a basketball and football player
I understand RELA class
I say I believe in God
I dream about being a real football player
I try to play UFC
I hope to be famous
I am a basketball and football player

Ty'quan Cunningham, Grade 7
Wicomico Middle School, MD

Who Are You?

I don't know who you are anymore.
Did I even know you at all?
Where is your head these days?
Sometimes I feel like you're a stranger.
Other times I feel like we're closer than ever.
You change to fit the crowd.
You act different to seem "cool" I guess.
You insult your closest friends.
You criticize every little thing I do.
Do I know you? Or the better question.
Did I ever know you in the first place?
All I want to know is.
Who are you?
Or do you even know?

Hailee Horling, Grade 8
Mill Creek Middle School, MD

What Love Is

When you love someone you will have patience.
When you love someone you will be so kind.
You two will flow together in cadence.
You two will come together as a bind.
When you love someone envy is a not.
When you love someone you don't get so mad.
You two should be combined together as a tight knot.
You two should always be very, very, glad.
When you love someone you give protection.
When you are in love there is always trust.
Love does not always reach its perfection.
You think you're in love make sure it's not lust.
When you love someone there is always hope.
Both of you will always be there to cope.

Evile-Currat Kabongo, Grade 9
Bladensburg High School, MD

Prejudice

It's hard not to stare at someone,
Who is a different color
Or who has a disability.
People may look different,
But, really, they are the same in God's eyes.
When I think of prejudice,
I think of a flower bed.
A flower bed needs different kinds of flowers,
To make it beautiful
Just as the world needs all different kinds of people,
To make it beautiful.
In a flower bed all the different types of flowers join together.
This is how we should think of our world today,
Everyone is different,
But, together we form one beautiful human race.
Everyone should look at people in the same way,
With respect, compassion, and an appreciation for the beauty
That each individual brings to the world.

Meredith Fish, Grade 7
All Saints Catholic School, DE

Sailing on Friend-Ship

Years ago I boarded a ship
To sail across the ocean with you.
With a journey unknown,
We sailed the calm seas with sails held high
And tales to be told.

We sailed the rough seas with nothing to be said
And only each other's trembling hands to hold.
Through the wildest storms and calmest seas,
We used each other's shoulders to laugh and weep.

Years have passed,
With hearts held high and heads held low,
But never once did hands let go.

Throughout the years we have sailed the seas
On what we now call Friend-Ship.

Shaira Khan, Grade 9
Norfolk Collegiate Middle/Upper School, VA

Greed

If greed was a color
It would be black
As cold and dark as being outside in the night.
If greed was a taste
It would be just like raw meat.
If greed was a feeling
It would be as hot as a wildfire.
If greed was a smell
It would be as sour as a carton of milk gone bad.
If greed was a sound
It would be annoying as a swarm of bees.

Jessica Morelle, Grade 8
Mount St Charles Academy, RI

Ice Skating

My friend and I go ice skating then hear the still ice cracking beneath our skates.
We look frightened as we run off the lake into a pile of white fluffy snow.
As we walk over to the house we see smoke coming out of the chimney.
We are welcomed inside by the smell of firewood burning in the fireplace and steaming hot chocolate.
We sit down by the warm fireplace while the hot chocolate burns our throats.
After our long entertaining day we go upstairs into the warm bed and fall asleep right away.

Michelle Deshaies, Grade 7
Biddeford Middle School, ME

Ode to My Gun

Oh how your lovely shade of walnut brown matches the deer in which I'm about to shoot.
How you shoot so swiftly like the wind, you make me want to shoot you again and again.
The smell of the gun powder blasting out of the barrel "bang" is the sound that you make.
To see the deer run and then drop right before my very eyes, lets me know that I have done a job well done.
At the end of the day it's not hard to say that you're the best gun that I've ever had.

Keaton Hall, Grade 7
Rockbridge Middle School, VA

I Wish I Had

It started on a Monday morning, like it usually does —
the girls walk in on a typical day.

Their glossy hair and shiny faces in
a grimace ready to pounce.

They are not talking to each other again.
Only yesterday, they were best friends.

But it's okay because tomorrow they will find new friends
to laugh and share memories with.

Twenty years from now they will see
the stupidity of popularity

They will see each other and say "hey,"
and they will smile with faces of guilt.

They're done with popularity. If only they noticed so many years ago
how much they loved each other so.

For in the end, nothing will matter
'cause the glory days are over.

In the end, they wish they never did
spend their time rising to the top.

But in the end, they are at the bottom,
for they have forgotten how to bury the hatchet.

Cate Woodward, Grade 7
Cape Henry Collegiate School, VA

Heaven or Hell

Heaven —
peacefully quiet and relaxing, the hum of energy is the only sound
with the soft colors of blue hues and white blankets for miles
golden skies with a shiny sun
the soft breeze on your pale skin is a comfortable warmth

drifting through the meadows and by the rivers
gliding through the vibrant flowers and grasses
the feel of the cool water is soothing

traveling anywhere and everywhere
from the ocean to the desert, trees to the plains
anywhere you want
because this is your happy place

Hell —
loud, ear piercing noise, the hum of music and people everywhere
with dark colors of reds and blacks, gray skies and no sun
smoke and dirt covering everything

drifting through the empty highways and clubs
hands tucked, closing by your sides
the feel of dirt and slime is gross and makes you sick

stuck here, crying and shaking
having no one
hearing the screams of many victims
you just might be next

Morgan Knowles, Grade 8
Glenburn Elementary School, ME

Prideful Memories
Best day ever
When I was five
I learned about basketball
Went to the basketball court
My brother taught me how to play
Taught me the fundamentals

Few years later
I was better and started to play
I was good enough I played for a league
We had won
The championship

For some reason I don't play in leagues now
When I rise to a higher level
I will become better
I will play
I will be a pro

Gabriel Matthews, Grade 7
West Frederick Middle School, MD

Angel
I was once
a girl who was adrift
in the stark cold sea
and I would cry out
"Nal guhaejwo, nan neomu eolyeo balabnida"
"Save me, I am too young to die!"
I drifted along
waiting for an answer
to my hopes for salvation
finally you came
on gossamer wings and lifted me
so high
I could have touched the stars
"Dalcomhan cheonsa"
"Sweet angel,"
My heart swells with the breeze
and we drift away…

Kaitlyn Theberge, Grade 8
Mount St Charles Academy, RI

Peace
Peace is like a flower blooming
Peace is like the wind blowing through the trees
Peace is like the sun setting
Peace is here
Peace is there
Peace is everywhere
We are the symbol
We are the source
We are the reason
Can't you see
What we need to be?

Colin Schraudner, Grade 7
St Clement Mary Hofbauer School, MD

Ode to a Pancake
The pancake
Moves with a sizzling flipping.
He passes fruits and vegetables
Just carrying on in their day.
Like an aerialist,
The pancake spins a 360
Before its flop.
The beige pancake lies still
In fragrant bliss.
A camouflaged moth whose wings won't beat
On the pine floor.
Our hero coils his crispy edges
Of syrup soaked stickiness and gathers his courage with a war cry,
As the sniffing hunter closes in, like a locomotive.
Rendering his gluttony goodness
To a wad of flour and surrender,
He sticks to the roof
Of a Labrador's mouth.
Even after our aerialist falls, SPLAT
He is a delicious triumph.

Luke Scaletta, Grade 7
The School of the Cathedral of Mary Our Queen, MD

Silly Peers
Whispers, whispers in the air,
What a terrible sound to hear.
Secrets, secrets over there,
Something not for me to hear.
Gossip, gossip always near,
One thing we all fear.

Liar, liar let me hear,
What is going from ear to ear.
Smiles, smiles everywhere,
All so fake and filled with fear.
Silence, silence a quiet tear,
Something not for the world to hear.

Wondering, wondering if happiness will reappear.
Grinning, grinning from ear to ear,
Those who make their terror clear.
Silly, silly are my peers,
Many trying to bring sadness near.

Rebecca Nicholson, Grade 8
Linkhorne Middle School, VA

Never Ending
I have no friends.
I make people miserable to the death.
Nothing can yet defeat me.
I travel like a thief everyday, but in thousands.
What am I?

Cancer

Jose Crosby, Grade 8
Stevensville Middle School, MD

Grace of Passing

Mice of mute,
Wind of whispers,
Talk is silent,
Speech is denied,
Not a thing to be heard,
No breath,
No movement of the body,
Still of silent,
Quiet of the grass,
Dark and soundless as fog
Undetectable, unusable,
Aim is off,
Not a path to be seen,
The roads are twisted and turned,
Roads of truth and wonder,
Roads of false and despair,
But a light guides me,
I follow this light,
And I received death welcomingly and not dreadfully.

Samantha Starstrom, Grade 7
New Windsor Middle School, MD

A Rock Unopened

Hard as a rock
A rock unopened,
Unopened because of the firm outer shell,
The outer shell protecting the insides,
The insides that are so precious,
Precious and untouched,
Untouched from everywhere else,
Everywhere else still knocking on the secrets,
But the secrets stay the same,
Same as they have been forever,
Forever inside until one day cracked,
Cracked and exposed,
Exposed for everyone to see,
To see what lies beneath.

Victor Layne, Grade 8
Norfolk Collegiate Middle School, VA

We Are All in the Same —

I am standing on a boat,
watching the horizon underneath the sun.
With me I can see other people.

I don't know who they are, these people.
I don't know how to escape this boat.
It moves forward somehow below the burning sun.

We are heading West, following the sun.
I am joining these people
on their journey, because there is no way off this boat.

I am with a lot of people on a small boat going West with the sun.

Shay Maney, Grade 8
Norfolk Collegiate Middle/Upper School, VA

The Sun and the Wind

I am the sun and the wind
I am the draw of breath
The hesitation between life and death
I am the foe and friend
Both the beginning and end
I am war and peace
The suffering and the release
I am the good and the wrong
The small step between weak and strong
I am the darkness and the light
The difference between day and night
I am a nightmare and a dream
The mind tricks and things that aren't as they seem
I am the truth and the falsities
Both calm and calamities
I am the balance
I am not one for you to challenge
For I am the sun and the wind.

Renee Brittigan, Grade 9
Woodbridge Sr High School, VA

My Kingdom

My feet make footprints on the soft, white shore
The calm rhythmic waves echo all around
This is my kingdom without any doors
I go here when I don't want to be found
Seagulls sing and call out above my head
The foamy water brushes against me
This is a place where nothing need be said
A calm place called the Serenity Sea
Dolphins jump and splash in the breaking waves
Fish glide alongside, as quick as lightning
Then they disappear into submerged caves
Swimming down so far it is truly frightening
I take one more look trying not to cry
Promising to come back before I die

Emily Calhoun, Grade 7
Kilmer Middle School, VA

Second Chance

It's just I can't let you go
Without you I wouldn't know
How to smile with no reason to
For every reason was because of you
I can't go out knowing we were once there
I wanted to tell you how much I missed you, but you wouldn't care
I tried my best to be someone I'm not
I ended up telling lies and now I got caught
I'm scared to tell you how I feel
I'm hurt and I'm waiting to get healed
I know we made mistakes before
But I promise you there will be no more
I love you so please don't go
I just want you to know.

Karen Marineros, Grade 9
Woodbridge Senior High School, VA

Opening Day at Fenway
The grass is green.
The clay is raked.
The gates are open.

The roster is complete.
The lineup is ready.
The anthem is sung.

The umpire screams, "Play ball."
The first pitch is thrown.
A new year has begun.

A title could be won.
Timothy Wade, Grade 8
St Rocco School, RI

One Cold Snowy Day
This ice cream is like a cold snowy day;
There is the cold wet surface,
Topped with chocolate, as gooey as mud.
Then it is topped with whipped cream,
As white as snow.

As soon as it all hits your mouth, it melts;
As if sitting right under the sun.
Then all that's left is chocolaty cream;
As if it is a liquid muddy substance.

When a new ice cream is made,
It is like a new snowy day.
Kiley Sellers, Grade 8
Norfolk Christian Middle School, VA

Soccer
You kick the ball,
You run and might fall,
You make the goal and get cheered on.
One point more,
Do you hear the screaming fans?
The ball goes out,
You toss it back in,
Keep running, shoot, and aim,
This is how you win.
I bet you want to know what sport this is.
Can you guess?
It's better than the rest.
It's soccer.
Giana Ferreira, Grade 7
St Rocco School, RI

Fly Tying
A small tiny lure
A skill of knowing their food
The fun of the catch
Justin Santerre, Grade 9
Stearns High School, ME

Bullying
Why can't you see all the bullies these days?
From short ones to tall ones to round ones and skinny ones
They are all around us.

It could start as just a joke or a text
Or an email nonetheless
But what most people don't know is that they are harming another.
You may think it's funny at first
Saying something like "She waddles just like a duck"
Or "He's as dumb as an acorn"
But truthfully, acorns are pretty smart considering they don't bully anyone
And ducks actually waddle really cool and don't bother you.

The truth is the world is full of many different shapes and sizes
From tall to short to fat to skinny
Maybe you just have to look at yourself for a change
And figure out what's wrong with you.
Matt Jennings, Grade 7
Rachel Carson Middle School, VA

If I Were in Charge of the World
If I were in charge of the world,
I'd make every skate park mine.
I'd get every single ps3 game.
I would be the best baseball player ever.

If I were in charge of the world
There'd be one month of school which is recess,
Every holiday would be about me.
Everything for my family would be free.

If I were in charge of the world.
You wouldn't have to do chores.
You wouldn't have to take out the stinky gross trash.
You wouldn't have any boring rules like doing homework before playing games.
Or no more listening to adults.

IF I WERE IN CHARGE OF THE WORLD!
Logan Scott, Grade 7
Corkran Middle School, MD

Takedown
It is a final death situation. Two more points, and we win the match.
I have to wrestle someone a weight class above me, I get on the mat to wrestle my opponent.
He is big like a mini truck. In my head I was scared to death,
So I closed my eyes. I said to myself, "You can win."
Teammates cheering my name, "Cameron, Cameron, Cameron," I can do this,
I opened my eyes with confidence. I was ready to win this.
"Shake hands please," said the referee. He blew the whistle, and the match began.
I am looking and waiting for a takedown. He puts his hands on my shoulder;
I push his hands off my shoulder. I did a blast double into his chest,
He fell instantly, I was amazed. I could really do something like that.
I had to get wrist control quick, For the last point of the match.
Then a loud weeee sound flew over me, It was the whistle; I had won the match.
Cameron Buck, Grade 8
Linkhorne Middle School, VA

The Dance of Life
Life is like a dance
Filled with slips and falls
Twists and turns at every door
We shine beneath the light of which we dance

Darkness, quietness, is all that's heard before we have awakened from that dream
The music is the symphony of nature, of life
Every step taken, every staggered breath taken could be that one last breath, and that one last step
To make the jump or break the fall
Every leap is a new height
A new reason to carry on

The stares, the glances, and the applause
Just gives us one more reason, to live
To dance.

Patience Northedge, Grade 8
Stevensville Middle School, MD

Ode to a Marker
The Markers: the clashing clique; Dumped onto the blank paper, the Wild, Wild West, untamed and uncut.
The jealous, sneaky Green was in a cranky state. He snapped at the Red, spiking him like a cactus. The ill-tempered, fuming Red
was crankier than the rest, leading to an explosion like a volcano.
The Violet busied itself, trying to make peace and positivity,
but couldn't stand a chance at the Red and Green's battle.
It bravely attempted to, but got swirled into the commotion like an ingredient in a chef's mixing bowl. Across the Wild West, the
vain, self-centered Indigo was creating nature's mirror, admirable. As she admired her striking, mysterious beauty, the Red, Green,
and peacemaker Violet came storming over, whistling like a windstorm on a desert. Red shoved Green into Indigo's swirling
mirror, and Green splashed into the deep, thick pond like a cannonball, panicking. Polite, passionate Orange tore in, its hat close
to blowing away. Parading behind him were the caffeine loving Yellow, the Blue, looking for some water, and the self-pitying,
depressed Gray, waiting for the storm clouds over its head to give up. When they reached the rainbow-looking windstorm, they froze
like boiling water in Antarctica. The Blue, who was hoping to find something with water, cannon-balled into shrieking Indigo's
masterpiece. Before anyone could react, the markers heard excited voices…Children's voices…Art class!!!

Haley Halvorsen, Grade 7
The School of the Cathedral of Mary Our Queen, MD

Hope
Hope gives us strength to appreciate another tomorrow. Hope gives us that push when it seems you can't go on. Hope gives us power
to keep pressing on. Hope helps us to keep believing keep expecting. That in the night when it is cold and dark. And it seems like no
one is there. To just keep going. Because in the morning the sun will rise and light your trail so you can see. And it won't be dark
but light. And it won't be cold but warm. And you will feel the warm rays of sun coming down upon your face. And you won't feel
alone anymore for the sun and all its beauty and radiance is right there shining, smiling down on you. And hope is what guided
us through it all. It's what gave us the gift to go on. Hope was that tiny voice inside of you the entire time advising you. Pushing
you. Encouraging you. Forcing you to go on. Not letting you quit until you made it through. A light at the end of the tunnel. Relief
from the weight of the world. An encouraging smile. Hope is a spark. Hope is a house in another country. Hope is a child waiting
for mommy or daddy to come back. Hope is the dream of one day being okay. Hope is only for 2 years. Hope is the rainbow after the
storm. Hope is the tears in my eyes. And the smoke in the air.

Imani Green, Grade 9
Princess Anne High School, VA

Pencil
I am a pencil not too big not too tall.
I am a unique pencil I can erase all my mistakes and the smaller I get the more memories I make.
Yes I'm a special wooden stick I get used everyday and when my beginning touches the end that's it for me.
Yes I am a pencil.

Allison Barrera, Grade 9
Bladensburg High School, MD

Ode to a Lacrosse Stick

It waits in my room,
lying in its case.
The dirt smudged along its head
after a long day of practice.
It waits for game day.
The shaft so great in my hands, as I slowly trace the confusing
patterns it makes.
When I'm out in the field, I stand in the center for the face-off.
The two sticks pressed hard against the ball
waiting for the official to blow the whistle.
As I snap my wrist and lift my arm to flick the ball in the air,
it lands in the head of my stick, pressed against the laces,
like a spider web, frozen in my pocket.
I dodge, I spin, and I fake a pass,
as I sprint down the field, cradling,
and passing the defender.
I get close to the crease and make a bounce shot to the left corner.
As I make it, everyone cheers
and my teammates hit shafts with me.
I jog back to the center, head held high,
my stick in my hand, and ready to do it all over again.

Caroline Kosco, Grade 7
The School of the Cathedral of Mary Our Queen, MD

Companion

A tear, small and round, slowly slipping down a cheek of a girl
The small tear, slick and shiny, lands on the ground
Where her beloved dog lay
Sweet and kind, with those warm chocolate brown eyes
Staring up at her
She knew it was coming to an end
The dog's heartbeat was very faint
And her eyes were losing their sparkle
The breaths slowed down
Slowly drifting down, down
She knows her life is ending
She lifted her head one last time
Looking at the person who took care of her
Who loved her
Then slowly her big eyes closed
She took a breath one last time

Katy Riechers, Grade 8
McLean School of Maryland, MD

The Letter Y

I'm in the middle of every eye,
I'm at the beginning of a yawn,
I come after every why.
And it's nice to have me.
Without me you can't begin every year.
I may be a vowel, or sometimes I'm not.
And without me, it wouldn't be yours, it would be ours.
What am I?
(The letter Y)

Gabby McNeill, Grade 8
Stevensville Middle School, MD

Ode to My iPod

I see you there, on my desk
Your screen cracked
From when I dropped you
You cut my finger
Your headphones tangled, one ear bud broken

I can do anything with you
From music to movies
Temple Run to *Angry Birds*

I keep you locked and safe
With a code only I know

I can't record video
Or even take pictures
But you have many other features

I can go on YouTube
Or browse Safari
You may not be the newest
But you've also helped me, so much

You do what I ask
You certainly aren't perfect
But hey, you're mine

Jack Francis, Grade 8
Norfolk Collegiate Middle/Upper School, VA

As We Add Years

Some say as we add years,
We lose part of what we once owned,
And it forever disappears;
But as something we've condoned,
There must be something different.
As we age, our senses deplete,
Our eyes unable to encompass an event,
Our ears in need of a repeat.

Some say as we add years,
The Earth becomes a better home.
A worldwide utopia nears,
As if protected under a safe dome:
No more heartache and sickness,
Reassured safety delivered on a screen.

Some say as we add years,
The planet's fate lies with the young,
That elders no longer test the future frontier,
But the young learn from their tongue.

Some say as we add years
Our minds lose their activity,

But I say it is only years that make our minds active.

Michael Ortiz, Grade 9
Norfolk Collegiate Middle/Upper School, VA

Every Single Night

Your eyes shine like stars
In the middle of the night
They give an illumination
A never-ending light
You remind me of the sun
Your personality burns bright
But you don't know I dream of you
Every single night

Your voice, so smooth and sweet, like honey, with every bite
It chills me to the bone
And gives me such a fright
I like it when you smile
It makes everything seem right
I don't know if you think so
But I think you're worth the fight

I love you like no other
You're always on my mind
But I just don't know if it's me
You dream of every single night.

Reagan Adams, Grade 7
Hardin Reynolds Memorial School, VA

This Is Life

I feel there should be peace;
With peace there should be happiness;
When there's happiness, there needs to be responsibility;
Responsibility comes with being ready.

Being ready is just a part of growing up;
Growing up means you take on more challenges;
Taking on more challenges just makes you stronger;
Being stronger isn't everything. You also need skill…
Skill, just another word for being smart.

Being smart takes time;
Time is all we need to live.
Take the time to live smartly;
Being smart helps to become successful;
Being successful is how we live.

Yalaina Dupre, Grade 9
Norfolk Collegiate Middle/Upper School, VA

Just Stop!

I'm little, but I will grow tall.
I'm breakable, but I will not fall.
They think they can push and nudge me,
Thinking it's just a game.
But while they're pushing and nudging, I'm going insane!
I could say no; I could say, "Stop!"
Do they hear me? Do they listen?
Do they respect me for who I am? —
Then why can't I just say, "Stop?!"

Raleigh Thomas, Grade 7
Homeschool Plus, VA

Life Principles

Don't let the rain get you down
Never play with people's hearts
Keep everything close and people even closer
Pop the misery and wickedness away
Remember anything and everything
Breathe in life
Breathe out pain
Rumors aren't a part of you, just next to you
Make a wish on a star
And be who you are
Cut it short or let it go
Be a kid, and never pretend to live
Color outside the lines
Fly instead of falling
Get frizzy not dizzy
Be curious
Smile at your enemies
Protect yourself
Don't harm yourself
Drink in the freedom you were given
And forgive the forgiven

Tabitha Arms, Grade 8
Blacksburg Middle School, VA

Leaves

Autumn trees toss their leaves away,
Waving goodbye to summer,
Behaving like acrobats — twisting, flipping, twirling,
But looking like fireflies with flashes of the brightest yellow,
Or like the burning orange of fire,
As if shooting sparks were raining down from the sun,
Contradicting the clear blue of the sky.

But as they finish their routine,
Making a final dismount onto the Earth,
Becoming splotches of paint against the dull dirt
Until the artist runs out,
Their fiery colors now contradict a rich brown canvas
Until they fade into the image,
And match what is now left of their artist.

Lonnie Garrett, Grade 8
Trinity School, MD

I Remember

I remember when my brother came home with big news
I remember he said he passed the test for the Army National Guard
I remember my Mom started to cry
and I was confused not knowing what the National Guard was
I remember my brother saying the military
I remember my Mom saying you will be alright
I remember my sister coming into the room
even she started to cry
I remember my brother saying this is what I want to do
But my favorite memory is yet to come

Shannon McDonald, Grade 8
Mount St Charles Academy, RI

Safety
Quietly, I approach
My paws slowly splash their way into the Everglades swamp
My dinner lurks just minutes ahead
I hear gunshots
I am now the victim

Our species has been endangered for many years
Florida's environmentalists die for us
We are Florida panthers
Our home, the Florida Everglades

I hear more shots
I run for my life but the bullets grab me
My eyesight deteriorates and I fall into a deep sleep
When I wake up, what I see is something I have never seen before

When I wake up, I don't know where I am
But I must be safe
Zachary Levine, Grade 8
McLean School of Maryland, MD

Sparkling Waters
A soft breeze of fresh air
Creates calm, continuous ripples on the water.
The sun peeks through the morning clouds
And shines down upon the lake.
Its rays reach the lake's surface,
Creating a radiant, rippled reflection of light
As if the water is decorated
With dazzling ornaments of silver
And covered in garland strands.
A flock of geese glides onto the sparkling waters,
Perches upon the peaceful nest of soothing waves,
And floats across the lighted lake.
Ian McCann, Grade 8
Trinity School, MD

Cloud
"I love flying among the birds." — Maximum Ride
Soaring high along the clouds.
Seeing only what birds see.
The dream people have of flying,
Is everything it's cracked up to be.
It's too bad I can't fly forever.
It's so peaceful up here.
It starts to crackle, boom, and rumble.
I have to find shelter and fast.
Boom. Thunder.
I flew down into a cave and
I waited out the storm.

Molly Barkley, Grade 9
Woodbridge Sr High School, VA

Neighborhood Fun
My old neighborhood
Big court where everyone hung out
Played basketball, fought, and rode bikes
Big neighborhood, so there was a lot of people
BB gun wars and running through other neighborhoods
We ran through creeks and had nerf gun wars
When we were younger
And there was nothing else to do
Unless we went to the creek,
And walked around and just hung out
That's all we did
We were boy and girls just hanging out
Adrian Turner, Grade 7
West Frederick Middle School, MD

Drifting in Our Past
Sometimes we look too deep,
Into what we call life,
So we slowly drift away from each other.

We become part of the other
Group, that fell too deep,
Who drifted away from the reality that's supposed to be found in life.

What is life?
It's another
Question too deep.
We end up drifting, wondering too deeply about this life we live in.
Jordan Sibley, Grade 8
Norfolk Collegiate Middle/Upper School, VA

Nothing
A mere little nothing.
Nothing knows not the horrors of the world,
and nothing is asleep at the same time it's awake.
Nothing sees everything
that you and I do.
Because it's constantly there,
with a watchful eye.
And you can't harm nothing,
no matter how hard you try.
If you learn to love nothing,
nothing will be something.

Gregory Mumma, Grade 8
Mount St Charles Academy, RI

Autumn to Winter
Autumn
Blustery, cool
Raking, biking, harvesting
Thanksgiving, wind, Christmas, snow
Snowing, glistening, shoveling
Freezing, icy
Winter
Michaela Seay, Grade 7
St Clement Mary Hofbauer School, MD

The Wind
it didn't mean to
but it did
it smashed the house
the house that was bound
bound to be good bound to be nice
bound to help others

it sucked up the barn
the barn that held animals
many animals
but still it took it

this weird wind was strong
it was mean
the wind was ferocious
it brought rain
it brought thunder
it brought lighting
strong and mighty
IT WAS A TORNADO
Hayley Blankenship, Grade 7
Rockbridge Middle School, VA

When You Left
When you left
You took my heart with you.
But if you break it, you buy it.
So I guess you know it's not for sale.

When you left
I cried a lot more than I should have.
You weren't worth it anyway.
Every minute was a waste.

When you left
You left a scar.
You tattooed your name on my heart.
It causes me pain when I look within.

When you left
You left graffiti on my soul.
You tainted me.
And you tainted my heart.
I hope you're happy. </3
Diana Klemm, Grade 8
Corkran Middle School, MD

Smiles
Smiles are good for people.
Smiles can make people happy.
And smiles can make people feel good.
Smiles can make
a person have a good day.
Katie Mencer, Grade 8
Salem School, MD

A Season Is Lost
Grass replaces snow
As nature defrosts.
The wind stops to blow;
A season is lost.

The rain starts to come,
Drenching the ground,
Unpleasant to some,
But something new is around.

AS the rain begins to stop,
The world's color beings to show.
The flowers start to open up
As everything begins to grow.

The world is now bright,
AS pretty as a butterfly.
The birds all take flight;
Winter has said goodbye.
Rachel Brodsky, Grade 9
Norfolk Collegiate Middle/Upper School, VA

A Busy Street
Childhood innocence,
I stop and remember,
Not having a care in the world,
Not worrying about being judged.

Being told to look both ways
Before crossing a busy street,
Thinking one day,
I would be all grown up.

If I only knew the obstacles to come,
The challenges I would face,
The heart that would be broken,
And the friendships that would end!

Childhood innocence…
It flies by,
And I have come to the realization
I was just a small kid, living in a big world.
Rachel Klavan, Grade 9
Norfolk Collegiate Middle/Upper School, VA

Field Hockey
Pass, run, dribble
Run, dribble, drive
Dribble, drive, run
Drive, run, receive
Run, receive, drag dribble
Receive, drag dribble, run
Drag dribble, run, drive
Run, drive, score.
Nicole Knowlton, Grade 9
Stearns High School, ME

I'm Not…
I'm not athletic,
but I can play.
I'm not poetic,
but I can write.
I'm not a teacher,
but I can help.
I'm not a speaker,
but I can talk.
I'm not popular,
but I'm not an outcast.
I'm not a phenomena,
but I've done phenomenal things.
I'm not fat,
but I'm not thin.
I'm not a brunette,
but I'm not a blonde.
I'm not a genius,
but I'm not an idiot,
and my small traits don't define me,
I define me.
Jennifer Dempsey, Grade 9
Delaware Military Academy, DE

From Darkness to Light
The darkness is coming,
Yes indeed,
The darkness is coming,
And we are in need.

In need of help,
Hiding from the beast,
The anxiety makes you want to yelp.
The day will be here soon at least.

The sun brightens your day;
It makes you brave.
It makes you feel better in every way,
And that is what most people crave.

So when the shadows arrive,
Take the bravery from the light.
It will help you thrive
And even win a fight.
Peyton Fancher, Grade 9
Norfolk Collegiate Middle/Upper School, VA

Friends and Family
Friends
Companions, partners
Talking, playing, laughing
Funny, cool, special, home
Loving, caring, sharing
Blood-related, forever
Family
Caitlin Mays, Grade 7
St Clement Mary Hofbauer School, MD

Daddy's Little Girl

He can never take back all that he's missed
Winter, spring, summer and fall she waited
Another birthday past, she checked the list
Still no. Daddy's work is overrated.

She found "him." The one. There were no doubts. None.
Still no dad. No disapproving father
The fighting continued, it just begun.
That piece of her heart gone, what a bother.

That night she cried, and cried. He'd cheated.
Forever he promised. What a liar.
Her heart's in his pocket he retreated.
Daddy's out there somewhere always higher.

That day she believed would never come. Did.
Dad is home. In one piece. She's still that kid.

Maddy Logan, Grade 8
Massabesic Middle School, ME

Dancing Leaves

Leaves dancing, falling, spinning in the air
Twisting in the breeze, dipping and swirling.
Being blown by the wind, landing with care,
Like a dancing ballerina, twirling.

A display of fireworks, they burst and blaze
A show of colors, brown, red, yellow, gold.
At colorful blankets of leaves I gaze,
and the trees that nurtured them growing old.

The quiet swish of the dying leaves,
Now colorless, without a single hue.
Leaves crackle underfoot, under the eaves,
From the porch you get a wonderful view.

Leaves dancing, swaying in the wind, tumbling,
Fall leaves drop to the ground. Bumbling, stumbling.

Kira Lee, Grade 7
Kilmer Middle School, VA

Swimming With You

There in the shallow pool water I saw it
The creature
So gentle and beautiful
I wish I was as beautiful
As that sea creature
That laid there it…
Was magnificent…The creature
Was surreal and more beautiful
Than anything else, I did not approach it
I was excited but overcome with fear
The creature was just so beautiful under the moonlight
It made me shiver with joy.

Zoey Vooss, Grade 8
Norfolk Collegiate Middle/Upper School, VA

The Last Leaf

Hanging on,
determined not to fall.

Cool breeze swings you back and forth.
Still hanging on.

Small, delicate, leaf of a thousand colors.
Why must it be the last one on the big oak tree?

Heart pounding, the anticipation of dying.
And then getting stepped on.

Little leaf, hang on.
It'll be okay.

Just a little longer.
Just a little bit —

Swoosh.
Crunch.

Madison Decrispino, Grade 9
Chapelgate Christian Academy, MD

The Woman Called Love

Walking with intimate grace, she whispered into my ear
She said nothing, yet I concentrated on her story
I got sensations uncanny, indescribable
I was unaware it was burning fear
I did not know she would be the thing I would miss most
That's how it was always perceived
But I was not a believer in such things, until she crossed my purview
She took from me, she is surely a thief
She is the child in everyone, she is innocent
Yet she deceived me
From the outside she was beautiful, the inside even more,
And painfully so
She sneered at me, she laughed a wet laugh,
She waved goodbye
I went looking for her, but she was everywhere
And out of reach
She knew I would tip the vase on the shelf,
Everywhere I went I knew who had met her
They had so very clearly met her
They had met the woman called love

Caroline Creed, Grade 9
Woodbridge Sr High School, VA

Broken Friendship

I thought that we would be best friends forever.
Now it is just best friend for-never.
You act like I'm never here
I've cried out every tear
I guess there's nothing left to say
I'll try to act okay.

Victoria Haskell, Grade 7
William S Cohen Middle School, ME

Inspiration

I need inspiration
I need it bad
But how can I get it?
I've lost the mind that I had

I can't get my inspiration
I'll get lost in my brain
I promise you one day
I'll go insane

My memory is going.
I've broken my camera and recorder
One day you'll find me
With a sign marked:

"Out of Order!"

Toni Lester, Grade 7
Hurley Elementary/Middle School, VA

I Am a Flower

I am a flower.
I wonder if people see me sitting there.
I want people to sniff me.
I am a flower.
I pretend people aren't stepping on me.
I feel lonely sometimes.
I touch people's hearts.
I worry someday I'll be crushed.
I cry when I am ignored.
I am a flower.
I understand people's feelings about me.
I say one day I won't be forgotten
I dream to look beautiful.
I try to make good smells.
I hope I won't die soon.
I am a flower.

Dena Solieman, Grade 7
Western Heights Middle School, MD

Little Mary May

Little Mary May
Went outside to play
She saw a pole
By a hole
She was not too bright
Or afraid of frost bite
So she licked away
And to her dismay
It was just her luck
Her tongue was stuck
She pulled away
But her tongue would stay
So if you turn right on Conway
Say "Hi!" to little Mary May

Sarah Hawk, Grade 8
Mountain Christian School, MD

Rainforest*

The canopy of the Rain Forest
Is where the birds fly with glee
But down on the ground
Is where there is a little mystery

The darkness shrouds creatures
That swerve through the brush
Chasing their prey
Making them leave in such a rush

The boisterous birds
Of the canopy
Sing their sweet melodies
Chiming in to make jubilant whoopee

As guardians of the Rain Forest
We must strive to do what is right
We all need plans to protect it
From those who cause its blight

Stop those cruel people
Before they extinguish its light
The Rain Forest is important to us
Without it our world wouldn't be as bright

John Maddox, Grade 8
Holy Cross Regional School, VA
*Dedicated to John and Iris Martin

El Burrito

Staring,
Eyes blue and red.
Teary eyed,
Red nosed.

He bears shame
He has disgraced his family
The throne

Reaching…
With a clammy hand
Gripping the handle.
Head low, eyes closed.

Pulling
The cool air flows
Around his arm.
Reluctantly, he lifts the taco
And lets it go,
Into the cold abyss.

With a final kick
BAM!
The door shuts
With a familiar noise.

Ideen Ashraf, Grade 8
Blacksburg Middle School, VA

Jasmine

Jasmine was the best dog in the world
Her hair was always curled
She had a big wet nose
And always sniffed my toes
She was going blind
But we always had a good time
Even though she couldn't hear
She would frolic like a deer
She would lie in the sun
She would always run
Most of the time she was glad
But sometimes she was very bad
She was always at my side
And she always tried
She acted like a puppy
And after a bath she was always very fluffy
She sometimes had a little rash
And she loved to go through the trash

Alexandra Howe, Grade 7
St Rocco School, RI

Spring

The flowers are blooming
The birds are chirping
The rabbits are hopping
The music is popping

Easter is coming quick
Let's hope we don't get sick
Kids getting baskets of candy
Painting Easter eggs feeling dandy

Let's sit together in the green grass
Maybe we can even catch a couple bass
We can even bake a cake
Over Spring Break

Spring is like love
It's delicate as a dove
That was sent from above

Sarah Snyder, Grade 8
Corkran Middle School, MD

Free

City walls,
Containers,
Of the lonely,
The brave,
The strong-willed,
To those who look,
To the moon for their answers,
And those whose hearts,
Dare to be,
Free.

Darden Purrington, Grade 8
Norfolk Collegiate Middle/Upper School, VA

My Friend the Frog
One day I saw a little frog.
I caught him in a smelly bog.
I put him in a big red pail.
But he was eaten by my dog.

I chased my dog across a dale.
I got some help from my friend Gail.
It looked just like the frog was dead.
We both let out a mournful wail.

"But look! He moved! He isn't dead."
My friend surprisingly said!
His eyes are open, he can breathe!
And we have been very misled.

I decided to name him Steve.
Now I can keep him up my sleeve.
I am so glad he did not leave.
I am so glad he did not leave.
Brooke Myrick, Grade 7
Trinity Lutheran School, MD

Sleep
As a boy, it is such a tedious task,
Deciding what night terrors may lurk:
A scary monster? A man in a mask?
He might wonder what is in the dark.

A single dream sets off the imagination.
That dream is like no other.
The boy experiences a terrifying sensation
And shouts for his mother.

As his mother comes to save the boy,
All the monsters disappear.
And as the boy becomes all riled,
His mother whispers in his ear:

"Don't be frightened, my dear,
Whatever you do.
'Tis just your imagination
Playing tricks on you."
Martijn J. Goossens, Grade 9
Norfolk Collegiate Middle/Upper School, VA

What Is a Friend?
What is a friend?
A friend is a person that will listen
even when you're not with them.
A friend is always there for you
even when you're blue.
A friend understands you,
and you understand them to.
That's what a friend is.
Ashley Hickey, Grade 7
William S Cohen Middle School, ME

Words of Writing
Scritch, scratch, scritch, scratch,
Goes a pencil,
Flying across the page,

Click, clack, click, clack,
Go the keys of a keyboard,

Authors type,
Writers write,
All stories untold

New imaginations,
Untold stories,
New minds,
Treasures,
Lying unfound in the mind

Each new generation,
Bringing new ideas,
New lives,
Making new stories

New stories are just around the river bend,
So to speak,
With each of the
Words of writing
Mariah Moon, Grade 9
Woodbridge Sr High School, VA

Ode to an Oak and an Owl
I look up through the leaves,
Into a bright blue sky.
I look down to my feet,
Watch the grasses going gold and dry.

My inside pulses up and down,
The beginning of all life.
I am the center of the forest,
Living off of light.

At night I feel an owl,
Shift beneath my breast,
Her talons dig deep into my skin,
As she flies off to feed her nest.

With my arms I reach to the sky,
Feel the leaves blow by.
I feel the beauty of the forest,
A beauty all mine.

I look up through the leaves,
Into a bright blue sky.
I look down to my feet,
Watch the grasses going gold and dry.
Emilie Hollingsworth, Grade 7
Chincoteague High School, VA

Welcome Home
Days longer since you've been gone,
Nights linger.
Shadows form across the grounds,
Figures are created,
But you are not found.

Though the stars do not wait,
The sun will still shine,
Days still go on,
And the moon still glows,
No one will wait for you to come home.

My heart still beats,
But you are overseas,
Protecting our families,
And soon to be's.
You stand strong,
While I am weak

But when you come home,
There I'll be,
Waiting for you,
By that same tree,
Welcome home soldier.
Jordan Fournier, Grade 9
Stearns High School, ME

Being 14
Being 14 is the next step.
The next step to grow and reach
your desired goals.

Being 14 is the treasure
I was given.
Given to view the world
in a new light;
given to reach adulthood;
given to learn new abilities.

Being 14 shows great responsibility
for everything.
Everything including work,
nature,
and family.

Being 14 enables me to work harder
than last year.
It unlocks new challenges in life,
even at school.

Being 14 unlocks a further part
of our wisdom.
Xavier Pleimling, Grade 8
Blacksburg Middle School, VA

Accident

Eight-mile trail
That is how it started
Riding my bike, with my parents
Everything was fine
Until I looked back
That was when I lost control
I started swerving
Couldn't stop
Next thing I knew, I was flung forward
Over the handle bars
Nothing to stop me, but concrete

I was on the ground
My whole body hurt
I touched my mouth, no braces
My hand was full of blood

I wanted to scream
Instead I cried
I was cut all down my face
I felt pain
More than I had ever felt.
Emma Taylor-Fishwick, Grade 8
Norfolk Collegiate Middle/Upper School, VA

Are You Scared

You see me in your sleep,
Or are you asleep,
Could this be fake,

I'm not sure what to tell you,
Except I'm on your mind,
You might be scared of me,
I'm really not sure,

Please listen close,
And tell me how you feel,
I don't think you like me,
But I don't know because I'm not real...
Catie Williams, Grade 7
Rockbridge Middle School, VA

Basketball

Tip-off, dribble, pass
Dribble, pass, steal
Pass, steal, block
Steal, block, box-out
Block, box-out, rebound
Box-out, rebound, pass
Rebound, pass, dribble
Pass, dribble, shoot
Dribble, shoot, buzzer
Shoot, buzzer, swish.
Game Over
Marc Morneault, Grade 9
Stearns High School, ME

Ice

Cold as ice,
You know it's coming for you.
Cold as ice,
You can feel it,
Panting, rumbling, like a hunter,
Right behind you.
Cold as ice,
The chill
Rises up your spine.
You try to run,
Try to hide,
But it always follows.
The feeling will
Never go away.
It blocks
All the happiness out.
Cold as ice,
You try to escape
From the unknown.
Jonathan Crawley-Fye, Grade 7
McLean School of Maryland, MD

Ode to Dolphins

Beautiful.
Sleek, fast, slick.
They are masters of the sea.
Dolphins.

Chasing a fish through the water.
Almost got it...Gulp!
Yum.
Tasty.

They are happy and playful.
Like a child.
Shooting through the ocean like
A ballistic missile
Leaping into the air
Powering to the surface,

For the joy of being alive.
Dolphins.
Katherine Flynn, Grade 7
St John Neumann Academy, VA

I Exist

I see you in the hallways
do you notice me?
I stare at you from behind all day
do you notice me?
I breathe the same air you do
do you notice me now?
That's when one day you gave me a glance.
That's when I knew, I really do exist.
Goksu Baltaci, Grade 8
Rachel Carson Middle School, VA

Your Someone

You find someone,
Just someone,
It could be anyone,
You say you're in love,
Until something happens,
With that special someone.

That special someone,
That person you trust,
The one you dream about,
The one sitting by you,
Will betray you.

No matter what, you can't stop it,
Or wish to pause it, or even replay it.

That moment,
You wished never happened,
Might happen again,
Maybe not with that someone,
But just someone.

You might find another someone,
Maybe like the someone before,
That will truly be your faithful someone.
Adrianna Brooks, Grade 7
William S Cohen Middle School, ME

Fall for You

In the summer it's hot,
But in the winter it's not.
During spring it will rain,
And in fall colors will change.

Red, yellow, and green are a few,
And all of them will have changed for you.
Because you are the only one in the world
That is pretty enough to be my girl.

Your attitude changes with the seasons
As does mine for many reasons.
One of those reasons is to find
How to be with you all of the time.

We talk to each other night and day
Until we get our phones taken away.
I still have not told you yet
Those words that you want to get,
But please do not get upset.

For I only have this to say,
But it won't be said in an easy way.
I am going to tell you that I love you...
And wait to hear, "I love you, too."
Chris Bianchi, Grade 9
Norfolk Collegiate Middle/Upper School, VA

Ode to a Paintbrush

Oh-so smooth and slender as it coats canvases
one after another; colors after colors.
Its nimble whiskers sway,
as if a fox was searching for its prey.
Back and forth it moved,
at times getting quick and broad;
also, at times becoming slow and simple.
Such precise strokes are taken at times,
to get a perfect outcome;
like a golfer trying to make the ultimate putt.
A paint brush is a curious animal,
always yearning for more,
until satisfaction is given.
Casting wonderful images for
others to see; a paint brush is like
a role model.
But most of all,
a paint brush is a surprise;
it is something to praise,
for a marvelous outcome with joy,
from the fulfillment, of an achievement.

Daniel Tadeo, Grade 7
The School of the Cathedral of Mary Our Queen, MD

Love

Love a strong word
Full of happiness and full of tears.
It also has a lot of cheers.
You see that love brings happiness,
You hear it brings tears,
You see happy lovers with a lot of fears.
"I love you"
The 3 words that make you tingle and smile,
Love is like a roller coaster that goes up and down.
Love is also like a monster
It stomps right
Past.
Love is endless so make it last.
Love…
one simple word but so powerful to say
Love…

Aquela Brown, Grade 8
Corkran Middle School, MD

See

In our lives all we see
is the things only
the naked eye can see
but I see more
I see happiness apart from despair
A lovely future instead of a hopeless past
A world full of adventure then stranded alone
So you see there is more to all the things
the naked eye can see

Leah Ramnarine, Grade 7
Franklin Middle School, MD

White Walls

White walls around me caving in,
desolate of color and glee.
They try to cover up the white walls,
with posters of encouragement you see.
But those walls are still there hiding away,
haunting me, taunting me, I still can't bare to see.

The trash compactor scene in *Star Wars,*
resembles the predicament I'm in.
I look at my test, I still don't know.
Question fourteen, thirty minutes to go
"The white walls have no answers,"
my teacher tells me so.
"So put your eyes back on your test,
or soon you'll have to go."

A flash hits my eye from out the window,
That's where all the color is.
Blue skies, white clouds, lying in the sky.
But not in here, no way in here.
This is where the white walls drip-dry.

Michael Weber, Grade 8
Stone Hill Middle School, VA

Everyone's Dream

Everyone says they dream of world peace,
But when they speak we forget about the deceased
And how they got there.
I can tell it wasn't from all of the "love and the care."

They look at us from their pacific grave,
Asking us dearly to please behave.

Instead we'll just go on a rampage
Like a lion let loose from its solitary cage.

You'd think someone would try and stop all of this madness,
But the people who have the power to, are consumed by the sadness.

Everyone says they dream of world peace.

Samuel Pawlowski, Grade 8
Massabesic Middle School, ME

The Mini Lop

I just lay there right on the floor —
my bushy white tail stuck out behind me —
my strong back straight,
muscled back legs out at a right angle to my body
neatly stacked one on top of the other.
My front legs straight out in front —
my proud head held high, body long and thin —
fur white with black spots —
I am proud —
I am a mini lop.

Matthew Goodwin, Grade 7
Frank H Harrison Middle School, ME

Fragments of a Mirror

Listen close dear, the time is near,
When dreams will become reality,
And you live life in a mirror,
But that's the least of your fears,
For as the hour closes in,
There will be no tears,
Nothing is as it appears,
Leers and jeers hide around every corner,
Reminding you this is never over,
Don't you ever wonder,
Why you live in misery,
You'll never be free,
Unless you break out of this scene.

Michaela Ramandanes, Grade 8
Stonewall Middle School, VA

Frustration

Frustration is a storm.
It sits out,
Becoming stronger all the time.
It builds up as it waits.
It grows and grows,
Until it cannot be contained any more.
It lets loose a fury,
The winds roar about in the storm,
Tornadoes rage through the countryside,
Torrents of rain immerse the streets.
Unable to control itself,
Unforgiving and merciless,
It destroys everything.

Benjamin Lyons, Grade 7
Rachel Carson Middle School, VA

Dance

Dance, dance is what I do,
I love it more than golden hoops,
Every move must be complete,
Look very hard and be on beat,
I point my toes gracefully,
I come to dance three times a week,
Yes, six hours not just three,
That's commitment don't you agree?
When I dance I feel at peace,
Like I can do what I please,
The harder the step,
The better I know I'll be,
My dance studio is where I love to be!

Isabella Colapietro, Grade 7
St Rocco School, RI

March

Spring is in the air,
Flowers bloom while bluebirds sing.
Music everywhere.

Sarah McKay, Grade 7
Hall Dale Middle School, ME

Fixed and Growth Mindsets

No one can change either you or me
If we have to work at it, it wasn't meant to be
I'm not your maid
It's not going to work — you're never going to change
You're annoying me
What do you do for me in return?
I'm fed up with this.
You're ignoring me
Well, what do you want me to do?
We should work on it.
All right, then. Where do we begin?
I'm better than you. You're under me and you can never move
I have my worth to prove
As I rush out of the building, I see them waiting for me
What are they thinking?
Is there something about me they can't help but hate?
No one can change either you or me
If we have to work on it, it wasn't meant to be.
This idea is stupid, can't you see?

Elizabeth Larson, Emily Tellez-Sandoval, Norah Shenefiel, and Kathryn Snyder, Grade 8
Parkside Middle School, VA

The Chain of Night Life

A cool night air rustles the jungle
Making a flock of birds erupt from a towering tree
A salamander slithers along beneath the fallen leaves
Searching for a small insect to eat
A hawk swoops down and snatches him up in its beak

A patch of bioluminescent mushrooms shine like many turquoise suns
Lighting up the soft mist fluttering through the air

Ample supplies of moonlight leak through the canopy
Alighting upon a velvet-winged butterfly floating through the breeze
A squirrel scurries up a tree, escaping the predators below

Shining fireflies hover just above a dark cave
Where a silent snake waits for the unwary traveler

This jungle is a many-faceted machine
It is simply crawling with life

Sam Eger, Grade 8
Norfolk Christian Middle School, VA

The Viper

He is just amazing
Crossing, passing and finishing
No matter who is on him he will strike
Sometimes it's in, sometimes it's not, but in his heart it always goes in
Doing his tricks and doing the moves
If you are defending him you are going to lose
He is known all around, in all of the towns
The beast is rising
Cristiano Ronaldo, The Viper

Justin Rudden, Grade 8
McLean School of Maryland, MD

Ode to a Warm and Fuzzy (Colorful Cotton Ball)
Warm and fuzzy
Sleeps,
Silently in a bag
Colorful like
A rainbow,
Just waiting for a
Person to
Pick him,
Warm and fuzzy
Is like a rabbit
Waiting for a carrot
To sprout,
Warm and fuzzy
Is a cloud floating
Across the sky,
He waits for a person
To be given to,
He goes silently in
Warm and fuzzy!
Is now in a great club called
The Zip-lock
Rachel Burke, Grade 7
The School of the Cathedral of Mary Our Queen, MD

This Cold Autumn Night
I walked by the park in the dead of night
Only to witness the eerie silence
And the scrape of my shoes against the cold hard ground

The moon shone high above the ground
Illuminating the night
Yet there was still silence

Throughout the night there was silence
Even as leaves hit the ground
On this cold autumn night

I walked through the park in the dead of night.
The ground was wet and cold and all I could hear was silence,
On this cold autumn night.
Devon Donis, Grade 8
Norfolk Collegiate Middle/Upper School, VA

Free Boy
Oh, the simplicity of his mind,
no harm has come his way.
He only knows of joy,
not knowing the cruelty of the real world.
He knows not what is to come of his future,
but he doesn't mind.
All he sees is a fresh blanket of snow —
waiting to be treaded on.
It's okay little boy, stay innocent while you can.
Cassandra Donahue, Grade 9
Tunstall High School, VA

Fake
People wear masks,
not masks like on Halloween.
Not masks of goblins and ghouls,
but they're there.

These masks don't hide their faces.
They hide something else,
who they are.

They could take off the mask,
but they don't.
They're afraid.

The true 'them' they chose to leave behind,
for popularity and to be cool,
certain that the taunts that echo in their mind
will never be heard again.
Alexandra Krens, Grade 7
Blue Ridge Middle School, VA

The Beach
Waves crashing against the ocean's shore while
Overhead gulls circle the salty foam.
I could walk this stretch of peace for a mile
Or more, because this feels like my own home.

Warmth from both the sand and sun above me
Heat my core after a refreshing swim
Through the blue green waves of the rolling sea
Whose arms held me as I splashed on through him.

In summertime is when I find my peace.
I'm content spending long days on the beach,
So all year I wait for the sweet release
And hope that sooner, June, the year will reach.

I could never love a city's busy street
Or call it home; the waves are my heart beat.
Jessica NeJame, Grade 9
Chariho Regional High School, RI

Shots in the Past
Basketball court across the street,
Not so perfect to others but it was to me,
A broken net,
Couldn't really see the lines,
The only place that would make me feel better,
The perfect place where I could work on basketball,
Had great friends,
Lucky enough to have friends,
So amazed with all the 3 pointers,
I felt comfortable doing it freestyle
It's a flash drive,
Where all my memories are saved.
Monet Wade, Grade 7
West Frederick Middle School, MD

For Pride

A boy stands on a street corner in the rain
He has been there
Waiting
Waiting for someone to care
Waiting for a spark of hope

He stands and watches the people
A man bumps him and doesn't look back
A mother pushes her stroller out of his reach, as if he is criminal
A teenage girl looks at him in disgust, judging him as she walks
Another boy walks to the street corner looks at the boy,
And waits
Waits with the boy

A spark is ignited
One that is stronger than heat

Still one sits and pulls a hat out of his bag
And sets up a sign leaning against it
He stares into people
Entreating their stop
A boy next to him, knows no better
But walks away
He will not beg

Pranav Gulati, Grade 8
Rachel Carson Middle School, VA

Letting Go

I remember my past…
Born from a cedar tree.
Cut down; harvested.

Crafted into a slender shape.
Given clothes;
Metal shirt and helmet.
Waiting a month after that,
For my master.

Then, living with him.
Each day walking through town.
I felt so special.
People commented on my looks.
I felt so appreciated.
Bids were placed on me,
I wouldn't leave you though.

We were happy…
Now I just lie on the floor,
Collecting dust.
You left me…
Weren't we supposed to stay together forever?

Emma Salecki, Grade 8
Norfolk Collegiate Middle/Upper School, VA

A Day Ago

A day ago
We just had that one last chance
To show everyone what we were made of
A day ago
Was the championship
A heart-beating experience
Either it was now or never
A day ago
Hands were shaking and stomachs were turning
Posters hanging up and fans ready to cheer
A day ago
Could've been our last game together
Close like family we had each other's back
A day ago
We had the confidence and strength
But what we needed was that win
And on that day ago
We became champions
But most important
We became
FAMILY

Sydney DeCesare, Grade 7
St. Rocco School, RI

Goodbye Grandpa!*

i know it hurt you just laying there suffering.
it hurt me too. but now that you're gone,
all i know is that i miss you.

you were fighting the pain off for so long,
my strong old grandpa, sounds like something he would do.
i never thought you would leave. it was a tragic loss,
but now i have learned that it's the journey of life.

the day that you left, january 16, 2012 to be exact,
i remember sitting at home and crying all night.

i know you love me, and i love you too.
so i'm going to be strong just for you!

Autumn Beverly, Grade 7
Rockbridge Middle School, VA
*Thinking of you, Grandpa.

Night/Day

Night
Dark, silent
Quiets the city, people sleeping, nothing to do.
Street lights, stars, clouds, cars driving by.
Muster of voices, always something to do, lights up the sky.
Bright, noisy
Day

Taylor Masse, Grade 8
Mount St Charles Academy, RI

Ode to a Waffle
A sleepy Saturday morning,
Is a soft bird's song,
Way up in the trees,
I stare down at my plate,
A delicious, creamy, soft, crunchy
Waffle.
Thick, sweet maple syrup collects
In sparkly brown pools,
The bubbles like dolphins,
Appearing every once in a while
To have a fresh breath of air.
It sits high upon the waffle's shoulders,
It is a jockey for the horse,
As it gallops up to my mouth.
A sturdy brown surface,
Dough schedules a gathering in the center,
Crumbs drift off like snowflakes
In a blizzard.
The enjoyment of today,
Vanishing in a delicious moment.
Marion Comi-Morog, Grade 7
The School of the Cathedral of Mary Our Queen, MD

Losing a Great Friend (Alyssa Fish)
You will never know how beautiful you are,
It's like trying to hide a stupendous star.
With your bright smiling eyes,
Your short dark brown hair,
And the bronze hue on your skin,
I can't even bear.

Even though you left a time ago,
I just wish that you could've known.
You were the joy to everyone,
Deep inside their crimson heart.
Who would laugh all day and say,
"You know we'll never tear apart!"

You'd never care what anyone said,
And we'd always know you were a footstep ahead.
I just hope that you know,
We all miss you much!
And we all really wish,
You were here my dear Alyssa Fish.
Megan Harford, Grade 8
Dover Air Force Base Middle School, DE

It's Never Been This Cold
This water dripping off my back, it's never been so cold.
Me making a move like that, I've never been this bold.
My heart is the warmest muscle in my body usually,
But right now, this cold just feels like, an, eternity.
And now I'm more sopping wet then you could ever be,
But all I really know is that he'll never be with me.
Michelle Radley, Grade 7
Massabesic Middle School, ME

Sway to the Beat of Me
I am music.
I am flowing and lively,
Playing through the day with ups and downs.
Every day I am a different genre,
Some days I am an explosive rock and roll,
Other days I am a calm classical piece.
When I speak,
People listen with great interest and want to hear more.
I have a tempo and dynamics.
Speaking softly or loudly,
With a certain speed and rhythm.
I have articulation in my emotions,
I can act sweetly or angrily,
Changing from one to the other at any moment.
My life could take a sudden crescendo
When something goes wrong.
Or relax into a decrescendo
When everything is calm.

Music is a part of me and
My life.
Noah Machi, Grade 7
Rachel Carson Middle School, VA

LIFE
Life is like a big world with big things and small wonders
It makes you think why life is so different from everybody else's

You see people smile from millions of faces
You will hear laughs from thousands of people
You see people cry but wonder why

You call life a place where everybody's happy and joyful
But the life we live now is really full of emotions

Life is like a roller coaster that has ups and downs and all around
Life can be hard just never let go
Believe in yourself, be strong and hold on tight !!

LIFE
Kaneshia Afi, Grade 8
Corkran Middle School, MD

My Past Times
I remember when I could see the sunrise from the clouds.
I remember when my aunt went to the park and walked around.
I remember when my brothers played baseball with me
    and when we played video games.
I remember when my mother took me trick-or-treating.
I remember when my grandmother took me to the store.
I remember when I went to the Delaware State Fair.
Even my uncle skateboarded.
I remember when my father played guitar.
But my favorite memory is when I got my first guitar.
Joseph Farmer, Grade 7
Corkran Middle School, MD

Ode to the Sun

The bright yellow Sun
stared down at Earth,
like a small child riding in a plane.
Every morning the sun wakes up
and cartwheels around the dancing Earth.
Who is the sun?
The sun is like a beautiful, little girl,
about four or five years old.
She is expected to live
until she reaches the age of one hundred.
What does the sun do all day?
Well, she floats in the air
and braids her long, golden rays.
The sun is a toddler,
she never sleeps,
and never runs out of energy.
The sun is a tour guide,
Without her we would be lost.
This is an ode thanking the sun.

Cassidy Craig, Grade 7
The School of the Cathedral of Mary Our Queen, MD

The World in Need

Hungry children poor and homeless.
They sing a lonely song of complaints in this life.
We will shine this light. We will shine this light.
Let me reach the world, the world in need.
I know I can't change the world by myself.
Lord, I need your help to reach the world in need.
Single parents most recently divorced,
Looking for love, looking for hope.
We will shine this light. We will shine this light.
Even though there's a dark world, even though death has evil ways,
And all your sin has weighed you down, we will sing this song.
This world is a world that's in need, that is longing to be set free
There once was a man who died for my sins.
He carried the cross for my shame, for my life.
He has done the same. He has done the same.
For this world, this world that's in need.

Adam Cessna, Grade 9
Woodbridge Sr High School, VA

Not Forgotten

Past the loved house full of joy
Among the huge moss-covered trees
Beyond the deadly steep hill littered with trees and shrubs
Below the setting sun the air now cool
Over the decaying fallen tree that never seems to go
Across the forever freezing creak
Atop the deep little secret lake
Made by unskilled hands
Sits the remains of a glorious fort where we defeated the dragon
and sailed around the world and even had a safari.
Never forgotten but a cherished memory to forever hold.

Terese Hull, Grade 7
Rachel Carson Middle School, VA

Ode to a Frozen Lake

On a cold winter's day,
the town's children wake up to find a frozen lake.
The lake is buried treasure to all of the children.
They have been waiting all year for this.
They run to the lake by their houses and skate
like penguins
slipping and sliding on ice.
The children play all day,
until they are called home for dinner.
After the children leave, the lake is alone.
A single cloud in the sky.
The ducks arrive in rows,
soldiers
searching for holes in the ice to look for food.
They march around the ice, row by row,
and yet there are no holes for the ducks to find their food.
They fly away disappointed,
searching for another, less frozen lake.
The lake is growing quiet like a traveling circus leaving town.
Empty, alone, and then gone.
A frozen lake is like time, it comes and goes before you know it.

Katey Kearney, Grade 7
The School of the Cathedral of Mary Our Queen, MD

If I Were in Charge of the World

If I were in charge of the world
I'd make everybody be nice
No hard algebra homework
And hang out with friends and cousins

If I were in charge of the world
There'd be no cold snow
There'd be all spring
And there'd be a big swimming pool

If I were in charge of the world
You wouldn't have jobs
You wouldn't have to have snobby sisters
You wouldn't have any cat litter to clean up
And there would be no prices on clothes that you wanted
If I were in charge of the world

Rebecca Hoff, Grade 7
Corkran Middle School, MD

Stand Strong

What doesn't kill you makes you stronger
Live your life a little longer
If you are a scared bird open up your wings and soar
Push open that door
Don't let people make you small
Lift your chin and stand tall
Because this pain will last only a little while
You are in this not for the sprint but for the miles
After all God just wants to see that smile

Emily Durvin, Grade 8
Mount St Charles Academy, RI

Sleep
The feeling of relief
When my head hits the pillow

I'm done for the day
It's time to rest

Everything is silent
The world is tired too

Shhh say the trees
As they whistle in the night

Pulled up to my chin
The covers keep me warm

My eyes are like a clam
Closing tightly shut

The best time of the day has arrived
It's time to sleep
Tyler Kumes, Grade 8
St. Rocco School, RI

Books
A book is a set of printed pages,
A literary work,
A book is a source of knowledge,
Inside a book, you can always find a perk,
When you read a book,
The words come alive,
A roar becomes a lion,
A buzz becomes a beehive,
As you read,
You lose track of time,
You become lost in the pages,
And before long, it's nighttime,
Fantasy, romance, mystery, myth,
There is a book for everyone,
A book can take you to different places,
An ocean, or a field under the sun,
If you are ever sad,
And you need some cheering up,
Grab a book — find a seat,
Get under a blanket and cuddle up.
Marissa Wharton, Grade 8
St John Neumann Academy, VA

At the Cross
At the cross, Jesus died
Perfect and without transgression.
He shed his blood for you and me.
He freed us from the power of death,
And from the penalty of sin.
Jesus cleansed us of our sin.
Claire Simms, Grade 7
Richmond School, VA

Give
Give me value or give me worth,
Give me life not found on earth,
Give me scorn or give me virtue,
Give me something I can live through.

Take my death or take my life,
Take my longings, troubles, strife,
Take my heart or take my soul,
Take my every single goal.

Break my bonds or break my heart,
Break me up, take me apart,
Break my spirit or my fear,
Break my chains that keep me here.

Fix the wound or fix the hurt,
Fix the world with what you've learnt,
Fix the truth or fix the lies,
Fix the dark, till it subsides.
Cecelia Schmidt, Grade 9
Norfolk Christian High School, VA

iPhone 3G
I hold a lot of information
A lot of apps too
I have the news of the nation
You won't have to rue

You pay my bill every month
Sometimes it's very high
You just go in and pay
And tell the clerk goodbye

Everything's unlimited
Except your call time
Sometimes you're tempted
But you just get on Facetime

You're about to have fun
And purchase Draw Something Free
And maybe even Temple Run
I am the iPhone 3G
Marshai Brown, Grade 8
Norfolk Christian Middle School, VA

Mixture
all this mixture created one bad picture
that I can't erase
all this mixture created one bad picture
that I can't face
if I didn't create this mixture
why can't I face the picture?
all this mixture created one bad picture
that was never meant to be drawn
Simone Dowtin, Grade 9
Bladensburg High School, MD

Love and Hate
Hate is what fuels a war.
It causes blood to fly
and men to die.

Hate is like vinegar.
It's bitter to the taste,
and makes things burn in a haste.

Love is what keeps the peace.
It makes men accept man,
and forgive again and again.

Love is like sugar.
It's so sweet you'll want to savor it,
and it will make your heart flit.
Shaylyn Cyr, Grade 8
Glenburn Elementary School, ME

Winter Day
When it's cold up high near the sky,
the powder is thick and it flies everywhere.

When my board swishes through the snow,
it scatters all over.

The smell of the fresh snow,
smells so great.

I hear the blowing wind,
whistling through my ears.

It feels so good with snowflakes on my face,
I just enjoy snowboarding on a great day.
Cody Provencher, Grade 7
Biddeford Middle School, ME

Summer Moment
I close my eyes
and let the warm, summer sun
shine on my face.
I hear myself as I
breathe in.
Then, I
let it out,
let go,
blow.
Tiny parachutes
drift in the summer breeze,
then land softly
on the green sea,
as if nothing happened.
Katherine Berg, Grade 8
Blacksburg Middle School, VA

Carnival Fun
Take a shower
Comb my hair
Try to wonder what to wear
6:00 we're out the door
Never want to come back anymore
We're like peas in a pod
Going to the carnival
As best friends forever
The food and the rides
The butterflies
You feel in your stomach
When you're going upside down
That's what fun you have at the
CARNIVAL!
Kelsey Clark, Grade 7
Corkran Middle School, MD

Love
Love comes from my mom
When she gives me a hug
And sometimes a kiss

She likes it when I give her a kiss
I spend a lot of time with my mom
Every day I give her a hug

She says that nothing is better than hugs
Care is shown through a kiss
Happiness comes to me from my mom

Every day I get hugs to show love
And kisses to show care from my mom.
Mary Elizabeth Wallace, Grade 8
Norfolk Collegiate Middle/Upper School, VA

The Blind
Of many, some
choose to wall
off, close the blind.

Many are blind,
from the world, some
build a wall.

Through faith — the wall
will break, the blind
will open for some.

Some will be freed by faith —
walls broken, blind no more.
Madison White, Grade 8
Norfolk Collegiate Middle/Upper School, VA

Life of a Teenager
I am 14 years old
I have put school on hold
I don't care about school
because I don't want to look like a fool
I am quiet and shy
I want to be able to fly
I know how to play soccer
I am a good blocker
I am very small
but people still see when I fall
I'm not all "sunny"
but I try to be all "funny"
What's that on my face?
Tears from a big disgrace
That's how my days are
Hoping not to be seen from afar.
I want to be able to fly —
I want to touch the sky
I don't want to be so shy
I feel like I am living a lie
Dylan Danneker, Grade 8
Mount St Charles Academy, RI

The Spring
The flowers bloom,
The trees grow,
The grass gets greener,
The rivers flow,
The sun starts to shine,
The pine falls.
From the trees,
The clouds come out to stay,
The rain goes away
In the spring.
In the spring
The rain goes away,
The clouds come out to stay,
From the trees,
The pine falls,
The sun starts to shine,
The rivers flow,
The grass gets greener,
The trees grow,
The flowers bloom.
Helena Banks, Grade 9
Norfolk Collegiate Middle/Upper School, VA

Untitled
Spring
Flowers, colorful
Sweet, warm, bunnies
Leaves, Thanksgiving, calm
Cool, quiet
Fall
Aimee Twilley, Grade 7
Wicomico Middle School, MD

Sunday Night Football
Tomorrow is her birthday.
It was a cold winter night.

I wanted to give my wife a gift.
I got a call from a boutique.

She loves the scent of roses.
He had taken a red dress.

I did not have anything to give her.
He didn't have anything else on him.

She was diagnosed six months ago.
I was missing Sunday Night Football.

She's not getting better.
One away from quarter finals.

She's in the hospital waiting for me.
I just wanted to go home.

I wanted her to feel beautiful again.
I don't care for thieves.

I'm not a bad person.
All of them are the same.

I need to be with her tomorrow.
He is going to be locked up for three days.
Juhi Sharma, Grade 7
Rachel Carson Middle School, VA

Ode to Volleyball
In hand
It gives so much power
The white ball
The color of snow

It soars through that air
Like a cloud moves through the sky
The ball moves as fast as
The wind blows

The sweet feeling of scoring
A point for the team

Three matches have been played
Only two games to go

Halfway to victory
Energy in the air
Serve, set, sent

SCORE!!!
Haley Jernigan, Grade 7
Cape Henry Collegiate School, VA

Oblivious
Going,
Going too fast,
Too fast to stop,
To stop and see the things around you,
You are oblivious,
Oblivious to everything,
Everyone is,
Everyone is always in a hurry,
A hurry through life,
Life is precious,
Precious time,
Time we are letting hurry by,
By the time we notice it's gone,
It's gone also with our time to live,
Live your life slow,
Slow it down and enjoy all of it,
It could hurry by with a blink of an eye.
Laura Gayle, Grade 8
Norfolk Collegiate Middle/Upper School, VA

The Cycle
Your smile, as bright as the sun's rays.
Your laugh, a thundering blow.
You bring joy to the endless days
And you, are mine to know.

So bright, the sun, that shines on skin,
As pale and bleak as snow,
And when I want to try and get in,
Your kindness starts to show.

But sometimes songs are not so bright,
A scowl smears your face,
And attacks my soul, a relentless blight
Without a letting pace.

So long as my soul shall feel your pain.
The cycle begins again.
James Cooper, Grade 8
Norfolk Collegiate Middle/Upper School, VA

Country
Sun is shining,
wind is blowing.
Beautiful day,
to go out and play!

Singing and dancing,
like flowers prancing.

Them city folks,
don't know what they're missing,
living life in the country
is one beautiful thing!
Taitlen Hundley, Grade 7
Hardin Reynolds Memorial School, VA

Falling
Colors as sharp as glass,
Weight as light as a feather,
Contrast as perfect as a rainbow,
Breeze as calm as the night.

The ground is like a painting,
and the trees are like a sculpture:
Beautiful in every way.
Then things begin to change.

As the dread arrives,
The glass begins to break and shrivel;
The feather becomes nonexistent.
The rainbow fades.

The night gets colder,
The painting disappears,
and the sculptures get bare.
Boring in every way.
Abby Hodges, Grade 9
Norfolk Collegiate Middle/Upper School, VA

Far Too Long
Smoke remains in this ghostly town.
Bodies lay scattered on the ground.
Since the bombs, not a single sound.
This war has gone on far too long.

Once full of life, this town has gone.
It fell victim to the battles.
Explosions caused violent rattles.
This war has gone on far too long.

The war has brought many despair.
Families are sad and weeping,
loved ones are forever sleeping.
Long gone is the town's joyous song.

Many countries are now involved.
The war's not over, so beware.
What's to come may cause quite a scare.
This war has gone on far too long.
Abigail Traver, Grade 7
Rachel Carson Middle School, VA

Think About
Think about who you used to be,
Now look at me.
Think about who you are now,
How'd you get so far down?
Think about who led you to be how you are,
Do they matter any more?
Why do I care you ask…
Because once I was in your past.
Naja Sasa, Grade 7
St Rocco School, RI

Life
A time comes along when you question
your actions
or choices
A time comes along when you lose
faith
or a loved one
A time comes along when you feel
betrayed
or loved
A time comes along when you
realize how lucky you are
and how much you have
These are some of the ups
and downs of life
Life may change but life doesn't
fade
Sydney Welch, Grade 7
Wicomico Middle School, MD

Sisters
Sisters are a pain in the butt.
They are mean.
They are always touching my stuff
Tease me

But…

They are funny and silly.
They like to tell jokes
We do a lot of things together
We go riding
Watch TV
Go shopping
Hang out with friends

I think I'll keep them.
Dallas Terry, Grade 7
Rockbridge Middle School, VA

Innocence
Temptation
is the utter representation
of life's struggle.
But what we do is the trouble,
the choices we make
and the chances we take
to be caught
even though you thought
you still had your innocence.
You have to look back with remembrance
at what was lost
and what it cost
because you are now separate.
Was it worth it?
Hannah Imhoff, Grade 8
Mountain Christian School, MD

Diamonds and Rocks
Diamonds
Elegant, treasured
Dazzling, glowing, adoring
Concealed deep in the forbidding darkness
Watching, hiding, waiting
Undefined, ordinary
Rocks
Kelly Sheehi, Grade 8
Stevensville Middle School, MD

Silver Moon
Silver moon
Lighting up my night
You disappear then
Come back
Oh silver moon
Where do you go
When you disappear for a night
Jason Murray, Grade 7
Massabesic Middle School, ME

Cheerleading
Cheerleading
Tiring, active
Tossing, leaping, yelling
Chanting, screaming, jumping
Caring, supporting, loving
Energetic, cheerful
Fans
Haley Dunlap, Grade 7
Massabesic Middle School, ME

Life and Death
Life
Bright, warm
Awakening, growing, developing
Learning more, becoming wiser, and wiser
Darkening, hardening, hurting
Slow, painful
Death
Thomas Marmo, Grade 8
Stevensville Middle School, MD

Tornabow
Rainbow
Colorful, spectacular
Shining, outstanding, flowing
Nature can be beautiful but threatening
Destroying, spinning, murdering
Infuriated, violent
Tornado
Jackie Sproson, Grade 8
Stevensville Middle School, MD

Difference of Colors
Colors come in many shades,
Like yellows, blues, blacks or grays.

Two that are different in many ways,
are purple, and maybe gray.

Purples can be bright and vibrant,
glow in the air,
They reflect on glass when it gets hit by the sun.

Grays can be dark, gloomy,
and a little depressed,
I can't think of ways that are the best.

Purples can be neon, bright, or dark.
They have many varieties of shades or moods,
It all depends on what you choose.

For grays, there aren't many tones that are very happy,
not very common, it's kind of sappy.
It's really not a fun color.

When you listen just to hear the words,
Even purple sounds more fun, pleasing is a must.

If you could taste a purple, I bet it's like you're eating grapes.
If you ate a darker gray, I'm sure it's like anything bland.

Purples and grays can be also the same, they can be fun or even great.
Jordan Hernandez, Grade 8
Glenburn Elementary School, ME

Baseball in a Nutshell
Baseball is described as boring or easy.
However, baseball is a game of perfection.
With perfection, there also comes failure.
"You learn from your mistakes."
One false move can change the game completely.
A simple out can turn into a base hit if the ball takes a bad bounce.
A stolen base could result from the ball getting past the catcher.
A bad throw could make a base hit into a double or triple.
Baseball is a game of attentiveness.
Situations need to be read before they occur.
Reflexes need to be at their best in case of a bad bounce.
A pitch must be identified as a ball or a strike as soon as it leaves the pitcher's hand.
Baseball is a game of agility.
Bat speed needs to be tampered with, as needed.
A good jump is needed when trying to steal a base.
Endurance is needed to play the outfield.
Baseball is a game of life.
Life has its bad hops and strikeouts.
Bad throws come unexpectedly as well.
Sometimes, people will take your pitch and hit it out of the park.
And even with the balls and strikes life pitches to us, we still play the game.
Casey Cline, Grade 9
Mount Saint Joseph High School, MD

The Story

leaves and rain fall
waves and heat rise
and as the sun breaks dawn
the birds fly north
to begin a new life and
to tell a new story

leaves and rain return to the skies
waves and heat fall underneath
and as the birds return home
the story comes to a close

Isabella Glenn, Grade 7
Hardin Reynolds Memorial School, VA

I Love You

I had a little thought
When I got caught
In your smile.

My stomach flipped
And my heartbeat skipped
When I looked into your eyes.

I felt like I might die
When you said, "Good-bye"
All because I love you.

Alyson Nelson, Grade 7
Hardin Reynolds Memorial School, VA

Dreams

Dreams,
They awake you in the night
Sometimes peaceful
other times full of fright
Dreams,
They often don't come true
because if they did
Life would never surprise you
Dreams,
If you could control them
What would you do?

John Messina, Grade 8
St Rocco School, RI

Falling Leaves

Falling leaves
Colorful, crunchy
Falling, changing, sweeping
Autumn, trees, Winter, cold
Laying, melting, freezing
White, soft
Falling snow

Samantha Stylc, Grade 7
St Clement Mary Hofbauer School, MD

Life as We Know It, Life as We Knew It, Life as We Will Know It

Jumping off swings,
Using your butterfly wings,
Cutting up your knees,
Running from bees
Are all a part of the kids we used to be.

Homework and sports,
Facebook and Twitter,
No time for family,
Only time for friends,
Bad moods and breakdowns
Are all a part of the teens we are right now.

Responsibilities and restrictions,
Jobs and taxes,
Less work but more hours
Are all a part of our lives years from now in the future.

Mary Elizabeth Corliss, Grade 9
Norfolk Collegiate Middle/Upper School, VA

Technology in the Youth's Hands

Ever since the invention of the computer, the world hasn't been the same.
Other inventions, like wireless phones, have also changed the game.
Eventually, laptops soon joined the club,
And even digital cameras began to form their own hub.
Later on, the flip phone introduced the world to texting,
In which the youth discovered new ways of instant messaging.
The flat-screen television was a great innovation,
Because men could now watch Sunday NFL Football in High-Definition.
Most of all, the touch-screen smart phones were probably the best,
Because these little devices gave people the information age at their fingertips.
Devices such as these really changed the earth,
But what really did it were the people who used the devices of this earth.
Some used them for good, and some used them for bad,
But the people who will use these devices are the youth.
No matter what, the youth will always have the future in their hands, and that is the truth.
So what adults need to do now is teach us how to use these technologies for good,
So we can shape the world into a better shape, as we should.

John Erik Taylor, Jr., Grade 8
Norfolk Collegiate Middle/Upper School, VA

Because of You

In my eyes you are the most magnificent thing on the face of the planet,
Because of you I wake up every day,
Because of you I have something to look forward to when I come home,
In my eyes you are better than perfect,
Because of you I climb the mountains of problems and keep trying,
Because of you I never give up on life,
In my eyes you are a magnificent waterfall of beauty,
Because of you I walk with my head high,
Because of you I live, laugh, and love,
In my eyes you are original you dare to be different,
Because of you.

Kaleb Carroll, Grade 7
Columbia Academy, MD

The House I Will Never Forget

My old house was the place where I
spent most of my life.

I made new friends and those friends
turned into best friends.

It was my family's house and no one else's
only ours.

I lived there for 5 years of my life.
The best Years of my life.

Jesse Kauffman, Grade 7
West Frederick Middle School, MD

I Made It!

For all you guys that told me no
I made it. That tried to knock me
down and step on my toe I made it.
That talk behind my back in your
minds thinking please go back I
made it. She's not making it anywhere,
she's black well I made it. So while
I'm here I'm never turning back. God
be with me and keep me on track. I
made it once but this is my twice I made
it from Kramer Middle School.

Annuleesa Thomas, Grade 8
Kramer Middle School, DC

Jungle Aura

A luminous glow
Deep in the jungle of life,
Hues of blue and green.

A bright sun shower,
Tears of rain running down leaves.
Making each leaf shine.

A jungle aura,
Bringing beauty to all life,
Casting a rainbow.

Micheala Small, Grade 7
Harrington Elementary School, ME

Slipped Away

It was just there.
A thought in my mind.
I don't know where it went.
Lost, missing.
Something I will never find.
I was just about to say something.
I don't know what.
It's disappeared.
I forgot.

Noah Golden, Grade 8
Holy Cross Regional School, VA

Invisible Children

How long has it been?
More than 25 long years these children have suffered.
They've been taken away from their parents from their homes.
Suffering, dying, fighting are the things they see and are taught.
Why haven't we helped them?
Children are taken and taught to fight; women are used as sex slaves.
Children are forced to kill…even their own parents.
Nightmares that will never escape their dreams.
Joseph Kony has taken the childhood of many young ones.
Kony is a man; an awful man who needs to be stopped.
The crimes he's committed are inhumane.
All these invisible children are crying for help.
Our childhood is mainly happy.
Playing with our friends outside or kicking a ball around.
Theirs is much different though.
Instead they have nightmares from their childhood.
If they run away, most get executed.
Brothers and sisters see their siblings getting killed or shot.
No one should ever have to witness this.
"Where you live shouldn't determine whether you live."

Annie Gao, Grade 8
Norfolk Collegiate Middle/Upper School, VA

Ode to a Snowboard

Excited on the drive up
The snowboard lies asleep in the trunk
It is eager to get to the cold,
Fluffy snow.
As a small child would be on the way to the circus.
Glimmering black, reflecting the falling snow.
Swifter than an avalanche, gliding through the fresh powder
Leaving a snakelike trail in its wake
Defying gravity as it goes off life-threatening jumps.
Cold does not penetrate its rhinoceros hide
Of high gloss polymers keeping the wet away from its flexible core.
It glides, never failing its trusting rider
Though balance is up to his passenger
It is like a knight's trusty steed
Going where it has to go, no matter what.
Responsive like a well-trained dog
Picking up speed with its smooth underside
Hurtling toward the mountain's bottom
Increasing speed every moment until
It comes grinding to a stop as its sharp edges find a foothold in the snow.

Justin Lopez, Grade 7
The School of the Cathedral of Mary Our Queen, MD

A Wish Your Heart Makes

Whether you're at the carnival or at the beach, there is always a dream you can reach
It doesn't matter if it's big or small, you can make the best of them all
Being a movie star or just being who you are; you know you can always go far
Love, happiness, hurt, or sorrow all of your dreams could happen tomorrow
A simple wish is my command, I'll take you softly by the hand
Make your nightmares pack up and leave, just don't forget how to breathe

Sydney Krazinsky and Lena Underwood, Grade 8
Stevensville Middle School, MD

The Social Life

The social life is something to adore,
Facebook, Twitter, and maybe a few more.
Texting, IM, is in most people's life,
Just by using a cellular device.
But the most social,
Just by using your vocals,
To talk to people who are local.
Laugh, joke, share memories too,
Is how people bring social to you
Although it may not sound,
Like a good rumor to spread round.
Being social could be new,
Even if it means something else to you.

Patrick Walsh, Grade 8
Rachel Carson Middle School, VA

Snow

The crisp January air
Blew on my face.
The powder at my feet
Blew into snowy clouds.
The snowflakes kissed my face,
Lighter than feathers.
They hugged my eyelashes
Until I saw through two white screens.
As my ears and nose turned fire red,
I laughed
Imagining I was the Snow Queen,
My face turned to the sky,
Snowflakes dancing into my open mouth.

Izzy Larsen, Grade 7
Leonard Middle School, ME

Summer

Flowers blooming on the hill side
The snow is melting away
The Chickadees are coming out
The smell of fresh cut grass,
Is a wonderful delight
Laying in a beach chair
looking up at the sun,
but burns are not very fun!
Walking along the beach
with my feet in the sand
And my shades are in my hand
The Sun is now coming out
to say Goodbye winter and hello summer!!

April Allen, Grade 7
Massabesic Middle School, ME

Clouds

Clouds fluffy and soft
White and bright they follow wind
They don't stop floating

Richard Stacy, Grade 7
Hurley Elementary/Middle School, VA

Ode to a Chocolate Chip Cookie

The sun poked out above the horizon.
Along with its neighbors, a cookie was taken out of a fiery
vault and put on a stand with its neighbors.
Its dark colored chips made it
the picture of perfection against more plain creations.
Before the sun had completely awoken,
the gingerbread men buttoned up their coats,
and the sugar cookie decked itself with crystals.
One by one, the cookies were all bought and taken home, except one.
One chocolate chip cookie was alone.
Then a boy came in, shuddering from the winter winds.
The cookie simply oozed with sweetness. It dared the boy to eat it.
The boy was like a hungry dog, yearning for a bone.
He counted his coins and bought the cookie.
The boy chewed the cookie as if it were the last thing he'd ever eat.
It was a ray of sunshine on a cloudy day.
It was as comforting as a lifelong friend who had come for a visit.
The cookie was like pure happiness, the boy couldn't get enough.
The cookie was a counselor. It taught someone that there is more in the world
than hate and greed; there is happiness.

Clare Athaide, Grade 7
The School of the Cathedral of Mary Our Queen, MD

War

War rings forth and brings the thousands,
The millions to their deaths.
War rings forth and brings the hearts,
And puts them on the line.
War rings forth and changes lives,
And puts scars in places we didn't know we had.
War reaches out and grabs us and twists us inside out,
And hold us there.
It makes some think that murder is noble,
And that their death has a cause.
When all it really does is break another's heart.
War turns us into animals,
Animals that don't cry at the sight of hundreds slain on a battlefield.
Animals that face each day without caring that they just killed someone's father,
Someone's son.
And still wars are fought,
Even though we think we've learned.

But we haven't, have we?

Olivia Koski, Grade 8
Calvert School, MD

Everything in Moderation

Life is a story you can call your own.
To dream is to invent and you can only invent by dreaming.
To wish is a sin, a value that has no meaning.
Every story has a beginning and an end.
Sometimes we have to look truth in the eye and say, "We can do this, I can do this."
Motivation is the only movement that can circulate through your blood.
To be ready and brave takes much more courage than what you might expect.

Gabrielle Elia, Grade 9
Ursuline Academy, DE

Raindrops

Dropping rhythmically
Pitter patter on the roof
Thirsty flowers call to them

Tiny travelers
Silky beads racing each other
To reach their destination
Raeanna Crowe, Grade 8
Princeton Elementary School, ME

Autumn Critters

Squirrels
Energetic, jittery
Scurrying, scrabbling, collecting
Trees, nuts, fangs, wings
Flying, swooping, diving
Bugs, fur
Bats
India Pinnock, Grade 7
St Clement Mary Hofbauer School, MD

Holidays

Thanksgiving
Grateful, appreciative
Eating, gathering, giving
Turkey, potatoes, presents, snow
Decorating, wrapping, baking
Joyous, happy
Christmas
Beatrice Reyes, Grade 7
St Clement Mary Hofbauer School, MD

The Mural in the Art Room

If you can imagine it you can achieve it
If you can see it you can be it
And if you need it it's yours
These thoughts will open doors
Doors to something more
Till your dreams become real things
With happiness and much more
Sean Condon, Grade 8
Stevensville Middle School, MD

Every Day Is a Gift

Every Day Is a Gift
Even to a log set adrift
To a bee in the breeze
In fall time while you play in the leaves
Every day is a gift
Some will let your spirit lift
Every Day Is A Gift
Noah Dodson, Grade 7
Hardin Reynolds Memorial School, VA

The True Athlete

He comes from a rough neighborhood.
His dad's in jail and his mom doesn't work.

He keeps his faith strong.

He only owns one thing, a basketball,
With that one basketball he practices.
People tell him he can never make it.

He keeps his faith strong.

He plays for his high school team.
People make fun of him.
If they knew what he goes through, they wouldn't.

He keeps his faith strong.
He practices his hardest every day with confidence.
He lost a game today.

He keeps his faith strong.

He still practices even harder to make himself better.
He now has a free ride through college.
He practices even harder. He now plays in the NBA.

He keeps his faith strong.

He is humble to the game and does not gloat at the people who told him he couldn't make it.
He is a true athlete.

He keeps his faith strong.
Alex Chace, Grade 8
St Rocco School, RI

If I Were in Charge of the World

If I were in charge of the world

I would take out school and no more math problems for homework or long classes
No eating brussels sprouts at home
And you wouldn't have to walk the dog

If I were in charge of the world

I'd play video games all day
Eat pizza all day and sleep all day

If I were in charge of the world

I wouldn't take games away
I wouldn't take gum away from school
I wouldn't take iPods away from school
And we could keep our hoods up

If I were in charge of the world

Dylan Krakat, Grade 7
Corkran Middle School, MD

Riding Free
When I ride, I feel free.
In an open field is where I like to be.
My head is clear, of all my worries.
Like the sky above…
Galloping ahead over logs and trees,
It's more than enough,
To complete me.
Sierra Hill, Grade 7
Western Heights Middle School, MD

Untitled
Birds
Soft, Hyper
Flying around, singing and pecking
Nature's friendly neighbor
Birds
Dannielle Anderson, Grade 7
Wicomico Middle School, MD

Woke Up This Mornin'
Woke up this morning
The sky was crying
It's a bad day today
I'm gonna sleep the day away
I don't like rain
Sean Flannagan, Grade 7
Hardin Reynolds Memorial School, VA

The Birds
A bird sings tweet tweet
Outside my bedroom window
Roosting on the roof
Singing songs of yesterday
The zany baby Blue Jay
Bailey Damon, Grade 8
Princeton Elementary School, ME

Butterflies
The butterflies dance
Brilliant colors of rainbow
Rippling like water
Andrew Tran, Grade 7
Kilmer Middle School, VA

Sweet Summertime
Singing songs swiftly
Rolling down the clear windows
Sunbeams glistening
Sierra Barnes, Grade 8
Princeton Elementary School, ME

The Outsider in My Own Family
My stomach twists and turns.
They know.
I can feel it.
Those cold eyes.
That hateful frown.
The angle of the furious eyebrows.
They all look at me as if I'm the one who's messed up.
I'm the screw-up.
I'm the one with all of the problems in the family.
They look down upon me with that glare.
Starring at what my beautiful mother and dashingly handsome father somehow created.
Something so abnormal.
Someone who just doesn't fit.
At times I wish none of this ever happened but most of it I just couldn't help.
Not a lot of people really understand who or what I am, including myself.
I'll find out soon enough.
But for now I'm just the outsider in my own family.
Erin Eaton, Grade 9
Woodbridge Sr High School, VA

Me, a Willow Tree
I am just a willow tree,
With hanging branches and lots of leaves.
People just go to admire me,
Using me for my beauty.

What they don't see though,
Is a tear stain on my cheek, Raindrops on my leaves.
I am not happy.
My trunk is hollow on the inside,
It used to be thick, until they decided to break me,
My heart was broken so many times, it turned to dust.

They still want to break me, since I am a willow, and they are just like gingkos.
Eventually I will break down, just a leaf blowing in the wind.
Simple, ordinary, and unappreciated, so not one of them will want to break me.
But most of all, I would be,
Finally free.
Julia Zagaroli, Grade 8
Mount St Charles Academy, RI

A Long Night's Sorrow
Dark, dark is all I see staring back at me
Fleeing in the night quite an evil sight
To feast upon a gentle beast quivering in the night
Take a quick listen, my friend, and you will hear the evils surrounding me
Inside this never-ending dome I call eternity
You can feel the stretch of never-ending bars keeping me from being released

At last, day break finally releases me from this dark side,
I can no longer see the dark side that surrounded me
I am free at last! You have released me to breathe a fresh breath,
The sweet taste, the dew in the midmorning air, the sound of happiness everywhere
At last, I am free, you have detained the beast inside of me.
Eric Fish, Grade 8
Glenburn Elementary School, ME

Fertilizing the Largest Flames

It came as fire,
a flurry of flames,
small at first,
only a whisper of their names.

It was to bring them together,
to meet each other's eyes.
Now it was huge,
screaming love lullabies.

Now
when times are lame,
they look back
at that tiny flame

and think of how it gave
just a little shove,
but how it became
the largest amounts of love.

Charlotte Twetten, Grade 7
Blue Ridge Middle School, VA

Broken

There's nothing I can do
to save her.
All I can do is watch.
She sits there and
stares back at me.
Her face scarred,
she's in so much pain.
She limps,
wherever she goes.
As she watches me,
I can see her pain,
It follows her
Never to leave.
Every day I watch her
die inside.
I want to help but
nothing I can do will
be enough.
She is broken forever.

Elena Lacaria, Grade 7
Blue Ridge Middle School, VA

My Fish

I sit in the car very excited.
I walk in the store and stare.
Today I would get a friend,
From another world out there.
I look and pick the one my friend
I go home and put it in the fish bowl.
My friend was home,
My fish was home.

Justin Oh, Grade 7
Rachel Carson Middle School, VA

An Ode to Pet Rocks

When I was so tiny and young
I couldn't be found
Without my loyal pet
The stone they call
Pat or Rick or both.
Just like all the other
Domesticated rocks
Pat was quiet
And house-trained
So we could go
Anywhere we liked.
We worked together
On the coolest tricks
You'll ever see.
He sat, stayed
Or laid down
As well as any
Dog or cat.
With a little help
He rolled over too.
Good boy, Rick.

David Loftus, Grade 9
Holy Cross Regional School, VA

The Hidden Inventor

Late one night
In a room shut off from the world
Sat the hidden inventor
Hunched over his work

He sweated
As he struggled with
The last page
Of a breakthrough in science

As the clock struck three
The inventor went home
Little did he know
Men were stealing his ideas

But they took the wrong plans
They grabbed the prototype
That had many, many flaws
They were in for a big surprise
For that plan
Was known to explode

Grayson Rooney, Grade 8
St John Neumann Academy, VA

Leaf...

The leaf grips the sun like an emerald jewel
Then slowly falls in a sapphire pool
One by one, these leaves fall
Soon leaving branches with none at all.

Luke Porter, Grade 8
Norfolk Christian Middle School, VA

An Ode to Pets

Pets are very important.
They are always there,
Even if they,
May shed tons of hair.

Pets are lots of fun,
They will always play.
It does not really matter,
If it's midnight or midday

Pets are fiercely loyal,
They will always stay with you.
If you love and care for them,
They'll love you too.

Pets are spontaneous,
You won't know what they'll do next.
Pets will always confound you,
They will make you quite perplexed.

Colin O'Brien, Grade 7
St John Neumann Academy, VA

A Second

A second.
That's all it takes for your life to change.
Only a mere fraction of a minute.
And yet, it can make all the difference.

A lifetime of happiness and joy.
A life of dreams come true.
You may have it all,
But it can still end in the hands of a second.

Dread and poverty.
A life that you hate.
That can change, too.
All by the fate of a second.

This goes to show,
That as life goes on,
Enjoy every second you receive.
Because it could all flash before your eyes.

Madeline Brown, Grade 7
St John Neumann Academy, VA

My Hero

Grandma you are my fairy tale princess,
So much larger than life
You are my angel and witness
Through all my pain and strife
Now the distance holds us apart
The boundaries have no end
I hold the memories in my heart
You were my Grandma, my best friend.

Cassie Ponte, Grade 8
St. Rocco School, RI

Ode to a Gorilla

A Gorilla
Is Tarzan
Swinging from vine to vine
In the jungle
A gorilla has opposable thumbs
Just like us humans
A gorilla's chest
Is like a shield
Protecting the body
From any danger
A gorilla
Is a poodle
On steroids with black fur
A gorilla is a dog
That has a fresh haircut
And has hair in some places
But not all
A gorilla is like
A Sasquatch
That exists

Devin Franke, Grade 7
The School of the Cathedral of Mary Our Queen, MD

Ode to Annoying

My sister saw you and thought you were so cute.
Your ears pulled back and you in your spotted suit.
She was blinded by love, she had no clue.
But oh boy, did I! I wanted to sue!

You run about the house
Breaking every bit of glass
Yet at night you sleep just like a little mouse.

You bark and bark at exactly nothing.
which annoys us all, sending my father huffing.

You wait until we are all sleeping.
Listening to the sounds of the early spring peeping.
Then your bark and bark excessively!

You would never believe the uproar to follow.
the wall between us feels so very hollow.
Yet you are here, still eyeing my taco
But I still love you, my sweet little Rocko!!

Devyn Murray, Grade 8
St John Neumann Academy, VA

Me Myself and I

I am like an ocean.
Calm or fierce, soothing or loud.
Rumbling onto the shore, angry and proud,
Or sometimes offering peace quiet and beauty.
Ever changing.

Samantha Bacon, Grade 8
Mount St. Charles Academy, RI

You Are My Sun

"Words can't bring you down,"
Is your motto when I'm blue.

You smile and tease,
And my mood suddenly brightens,
For you are my sun.

Smile so bright, heart so loving,
Your friendship means so much to me.
With humor so golden and laughs so genuine,
I finally see that you are different from the others.

You can walk into a room that's dreary and sad,
And leave with everyone happy and joyful.

"Just keep believing, and you will succeed,"
You say to me when I want to give up.

Your love and care shines through the darkest times,
And I realize, you truly are my sun.

Haley Rusnak, Grade 7
St John Neumann Academy, VA

An Ode to a Smile

A smile is something great.
It's like a hug,
Warm and welcoming.
It keeps you going.
Through night and day.
A smile is laughter
In a silent way.
A smile is like a flashlight
Guiding us through the never-ending tunnels of life.
When it turns off the world turns to darkness.
A smile is a teacher
You can't push them away
They will always be there.
A smile is music
Simple but amazing
A rhythm stuck in your head that will never go away.
A dancer
Graceful but strong
It comes slowly
But lasts forever

Ivana Di Pasquale, Grade 7
The School of the Cathedral of Mary Our Queen, MD

Vile Humanity

Like a lonesome crow, I am indifferent to those around me.
Mama raised me without a care in the world.
I am orphaned from human beings.
I feel I am isolated from humanity.
I feel I am isolated from humanity.

Casey Sutherland, Grade 9
New Directions Alternative Education Center, VA

You!

When I see you my day has turned from bad to perfect, the sky turns from gray to a beautiful sunset
I can suddenly see the rainbow after the storm, my stomach feels like it has butterflies in it

I have so much going on in my life but when I see you all of those big problems fade
I start to think about little problems like how my hair looks

Your smile is the only thing that I look forward to
Except things like your blue eyes that can melt someone
I love your humor, you can make me laugh when no one else can

I like how it is impossible for me to stay mad at you
The whole world does not notice when I throw on a smile but you're not like the whole world
You can tell when my smile is fake

Sometimes I think that you are just hanging out with me to make her mad
You say you don't like her but I don't know if that is true or not
I love being your friend or even your best friend that is why I have not told you that I like you yet

I waited all my life for this moment but it will seem like torment without you
Sad with the past to be gone for we had some good times together
I am now just waiting for the future to dawn so I can be with you once again

I hope you will not forget me every time I pray I ask for you not to replace me
You will always be in my heart hopefully you will not give up on us

When you are gone there will be no one to see that can turn my day into bad to perfect
The sky will stay gray, I will not be able to find the rainbow after the storm
My stomach will not have any butterflies in

Samantha Blundon, Grade 8
Monmouth Middle School, ME

Gold

Gold is…
The delicate earrings that make you beautiful
The color of a fresh pear picked from a tree
The color of buttercup flowers that I picked from my garden
The brightest color I can think of when the sun rises and goes down

Gold is…
A smile on my face when summer starts
The school bell at 3:15
The sound of me shouting and jumping for joy

Gold is…
Pancakes sitting on the table with butter on top waiting to be consumed
The expensive food in New York restaurants
Fresh-picked fruit right from the vine with the sweetest taste
Chocolate cookies crumbling in your mouth as you swallow the sweetness stays with you forever

Gold is…
Getting my report card and seeing that I got honor roll because of my hard work
My heart pounding with joy
People cheering that the year is almost over and new things will come
Bling on my prom dress sparkling as I dance in the moonlight mist

Katherine Chung, Grade 7
McLean School of Maryland, MD

Missing You
Forget your problems
Lay them down, they stand up
Innocence is what you are
That's what I want
I've tried a million things
But my heart's been shot
I hope you try to find me
I'm confused and pacing
I know what you want to say, so say it
Forget the words I've spoken
I just want to see your face
I know the wrong I've done
Left you scared and alone
This must be the price I have to pay
I'm speechless and don't know what to say
Feverish and pinkish just want to see your face
I'm scared; I don't know what to do
I had no idea I'd go as far as this without you
I miss you I really miss you.
Thomas Counts, Grade 8
Chesapeake Alternative School, VA

Dreams
Dreams
Like an unsolvable puzzle
Speeding through your mind as fast as lightning
Day or night
Awake or asleep
Dreams are journeys of imagination
An indefinite well of thought
Dreams speak and dreams listen
Dreams create and dreams destroy
Dreams run wild and dreams command
Dreams tell who you are
Dreams are not time or number
Life is a dream
So dream big!
Steven Milner, Grade 8
McLean School of Maryland, MD

Healing
Like a clock, I am ticking time
Everything is going so slowly
Waiting for something good to happen

Mama raised me without eagerness

I'm orphaned from my past
Oh, how the days used to be horrifying and relatively long
I saw in the mirror, a brokenhearted, lost human being
I feel I was confused
I know one day I will be okay
Healing takes time
Healing takes time
Taylor Carrigan, Grade 9
New Directions Alternative Education Center, VA

The Energy That Breaks Dreams
The parasite that never leaves your being,
The very craze that sends chills down your spine,
The force that will turn your blood to ice,
That immediately transforms your legs into useless sacks of jelly,
Tying knots in your belly,
And crush your dreams at the very depths of your heart,
That will hold you back from your full potential,
When you enjoy life it lingers always present, nagging,
While you're alone it multiplies like flies,
It suffocates your breath if you give up and let it be in control,
And leaves a vile acidic taste within your mouth,
That leaves you questioning life,
That forces you into strife,
That doesn't allow pity,
And dictates all other feelings,
It is the drought that never ends,
The power to stop one's pulse dead and silent,
And turn one cornered and paralyzed,
Through the influence that creates monsters,
It seems to remain the coward behind the deaths,
Of thousands of dreams put to rest.
Kieran Kindig, Grade 7
McLean School of Maryland, MD

Sun and Moon
The sun makes me happy.
The way it shines,
Dances across the sky,
Bringing light to the world.
A brilliant star, not even close to being the best and brightest.
But closest, shining upon the Earth,
Bringing light to the world.
And the moon,
In its celestial beauty,
Showing the way to lovers in the night.
The clouds surrounding it when it's full,
And occasionally disappearing.
The orbs of light,
Shining upon our world.
We will never forget them.
Gabie Braxton, Grade 9
Holy Cross Regional School, VA

Deja
Deja
It means happy, sweet and trustworthy
It is the number 22
It is like the sky
It is like a party
It is the memory of Cortni
Who taught me to let things go and be happy
When she became my best friend
My name is Deja
It means to always be happy and let things go
Deja Witcher, Grade 7
Hardin Reynolds Memorial School, VA

In the Arms of the Ones Who Care

There were crowds of people
People waiting,
Waiting for their loved ones to arrive
Arrive home from war
War that was strenuous and long
Long time away from their families.
Families sitting around hoping they wouldn't die
Die in the war that seemed never-ending.

When the men arrived the families went crazy,
Crazy to see their loved ones alive
Alive and well and in their arms
Arms that had seen tragedy and weapons
Weapons that had killed.

All that didn't matter now,
Now all that mattered was that they were home safely.
Safe in the arms of their loved ones.

Allison Kesser, Grade 8
Norfolk Collegiate Middle/Upper School, VA

Ode to Soldiers

Soldiers have always fought for us.
They risk life and limb for what they believe in.
They never stop fighting for our rights.
They fight day and night.

They are worthy of our respect,
for they fight to protect
those they care for most,
and they never boast.

They don't get the best,
even though they fight for the rest.
Some seem to hate them,
and say soldiers start wars.

But soldiers don't start wars,
they end them.

Ransom Castleberry, Grade 7
St John Neumann Academy, VA

Hot Chocolate

Little white snowflakes swirl in the cold wind
and fall all around covering the ground.

The sky is cloudy and the ground white.
I can't wait for a snowball fight.

A little five year-old girl plays out in the fresh air
Swishing through the deep, hard, snow.

She can't wait to sit down in her warm house
To drink sweet hot chocolate after the cold winter snow.

Lissa Hilton Harrigan, Grade 7
Biddeford Middle School, ME

Upon a Rock

Water lapping up on rocks
As the current pulls this way and that
Trees and rocks tower over the banks
Like barriers against reality
Fire in the sky contrasts with soft pinks and blues shifting to night
A cool breeze picks up
Bumps rise under my thin cotton shirt
Resting loosely around my shoulders
Ducks quacking about in the river finding dinner
The only sound, shattering the silence
A sole fish jumps out of the water
Alarming me greatly
Noticing the temperature dropping rapidly
I curl up closer on the isolated rock
We've been resting on
His warmth encases me almost immediately
The world outside these rocks
Doesn't exist right now
In his arms

Lauren Heimberg, Grade 8
McLean School of Maryland, MD

Gone with the Angels

You were beautiful inside and out,
There was no doubt.
Your smile was like a ray of sunshine,
Beautiful like the May flowers,
I can't explain the pain of your death,
I'm still sad you were put to rest.
You may be far away but yet you're so close,
I miss you the most.
Even when I'm sad,
I can just be glad by thinking about our memories.
I can still hear your calming voice,
It was God's choice for you to go,
At least I know
You're with the angels now,
I love you Nana.

Arianna Conti, Grade 7
St Rocco School, RI

Love

Love is a simple word
But the power of it is treasured.
It can't be tampered with,
Nor is it a myth.
In times of trouble, it always seems to be there
Even when the world is in despair, and
even during a scary nightmare.
The power of *love* seems to be the only thing
that keeps the world together.
And at this very moment, all I can say
is that I will *love* you forever and
EVER!

Jake Pezzullo, Grade 7
St Rocco School, RI

The Least of These
Nowhere to go,
Living with nothing,
Having nothing to show,
Feeling lost in a place so familiar.

Having no voice with no one to listen,
Feeling neglected and completely forgotten,
No fine jewelry or anything to glisten,
Embarrassed for anyone to see me like this.

Having no hope for life to get better,
Trying so hard to provide for my family,
Feeling like this will last forever,
Can't afford to celebrate holidays anymore.

People sorry for me just makes me feel worse,
I want compassion not to be looked at as lower,
Someone that for once will put me first,
I hope that this will soon pass for I can't take it much longer.
Caroline Bondi, Grade 8
Norfolk Christian Middle School, VA

When 9:00 Came
A gentle touch upon my head,
I feel as if I were dead.
I had heard a big, loud bang
Until the sirens in the background sang.
Broken bones and sorrowful cries,
I want to believe that it is all lies.
Shattered windows beneath my feet,
I could see my sibling in the next seat.
They touched his head and looked in his eyes,
But all I wanted was to say my goodbyes.
And when 9:00 came,
I would never be the same
Because I had to hear them say,
I'd never see my sibling another day.
Natalie Batzel, Grade 9
Norfolk Collegiate Middle/Upper School, VA

Friends 'Til the End
She could tell I was country,
On the first day of school…
I had a pair of torn jeans and cowgirl boots on,
She knew we would be friends,
As she has told me before,
She then noticed my southern style,
The way I was raised and born…
Then I realized we could be friends…
Friends until the end…
It's only been two years,
But it feels like forever
I have never felt this close to someone,
I have never felt any better…
Cassidy Hartless, Grade 7
Rockbridge Middle School, VA

Piano
Pianos are a quick way to escape
Pianos let you express your feelings
Whether they are sad or horrible
Whether they are happy or excited.

When I am happy
You are an option
To express what I feel.

When I am sad I go to you for advice
You are like a wise monk
You tell me what I know but can't think of.

Pianos have all of the keys
That any musician will ever need to have
You give so many opportunities
Whether they are good or bad.

You are also like the devil
You make the pianist over-think the simple
With one slip of a finger your beautiful song
Is a terrible waste of time.
Charlie Seerden, Grade 8
Norfolk Collegiate Middle/Upper School, VA

Firefly Night
Tiny twinkling flashes of light dance
as the orange glare of the setting sun fades.
The stars of the growing dark are no match
for the heavenly show upon the earth.

Yellow sparks of flitting radiance
alert other glowing bodies to illuminate.
No artificial light is needed
when nature's flashlights waltz across the sky.

The waving grass brushes scampering barefoot toes
as eyes round with wonder follow the vanishing lights.
Soon, feathery legs tickle the hands of their captor.
When the cage doors open, the fireflies erupt and flutter away,
becoming part of the sparkling dance once more.
Reilly Geritz, Grade 8
Trinity School, MD

El Yunque
Extremely lush and green
An incredible scene
Over the rock wall
We caught our first glimpse of the waterfall.

The canopy of leaves keeps the water mostly in shade
The memory of swimming in a freezing cold waterfall will not fade
Swimming in the waterfall was really fun
I just wish there was more sun!
Rachel Wade, Grade 7
St Rocco School, RI

Feasting Scenes

I may starve in Africa
but these scenes are food to my eyes

the moon glows
like goat cream soup
the stars glint
like Momma's spice, salt

the sun rises slowly
like the bread at the bakery
the mud is smooth
smooth as good butter

the music here is sweet
like the fresh fruit
the clouds are white and soft
like mashed potatoes

the sky is blue and clear
like awaited rain after summer

now I am stuffed from
the feast my eyes indulged
I may starve in Africa
but these scenes feed my eyes
Christine Pantangan, Grade 8
Norfolk Christian Middle School, VA

Basketball

The screech of sneakers
Slamming down
In all this excitement
I could drown.

The championship game
The end is near
All this practice
And it's finally here.

We work together
We are a team
Almost move as one
It would seem.

Down by 1
10 seconds remain
One more shot
To win this game.

The ball goes up
The buzzer screams,
It is in…
We lived our dream.
Ariana Ciunci, Grade 8
St Rocco School, RI

A Perfect World

I wish there was a world
where things were always right
where everything was perfect
and peaceful every night

where birds could fly free
and plants grow everywhere
fish swim in the sea
with great nature and care

where war did not exist
but love and peace ruled the night
friends and family were never missed
no one had to run in fear or fright

I wish there was a world
where things were always right
where everything was perfect
and peaceful every night
Sydnee Burnette, Grade 7
Hardin Reynolds Memorial School, VA

My Turtles

I have two turtles, one is Todd,
He's a little shy and quite odd,
The other one's name is Jello.
They're cute like two peas in a pod.

Their colors are brown and yellow,
They make my heart sing like a cello,
Every feature on them is small,
When you walk by they say hello.

They are clumsy and always fall,
They're noisy too, if I recall,
Well at least they're not in my hair,
They are pretty good overall.

I wish they could always be there,
I hope they know how much I care,
Cause when they go my heart will tear.
Cause when they go my heart will tear.
Grace Rogers, Grade 7
Trinity Lutheran School, MD

Snowball Fight

Snow is fluffy.
Snow is white.
If it is a lot,
We will not,
Have school today.
In the snow I will play,
A dancing, playful game.
It is called a snowball fight.
Damian Montgomery, Grade 7
Rockbridge Middle School, VA

Hypocrite

You say what's on your mind
pour it out
onto the floor
into my brain

Why don't you do it
just go through with it
cause you're a hypocrite

Stitch him up
take it out
watch it go down
I don't care

Pour it out
onto the floor
out of your heart
you hypocrite
Brandon Shanahan, Grade 8
Stevensville Middle School, MD

A Place to Get Away

After a restless day,
of schoolwork,
friends,
grades,
and pure drama,
one begins feeling,
like nothing matters.

The only remedy,
for me,
is the gentle sway,
of the top,
of a pine tree.
Something about,
these giant gifts of nature,
makes living life,
perfect, clear,
and understandable.
Jacob Keith, Grade 8
Blacksburg Middle School, VA

Hurley Rebels

Here we come state championships
We're halfway there watch us whip
Semifinals piece of cake
Pass goes over watch the fake
Waynick will dunk over a punk
The other teams defense is worse than junk
Hurley Rebels all the way
We could beat you any day
Grundy, Twin Valley whoever you are
We can beat you sure as far
Justin A. Daniels, Grade 7
Hurley Elementary/Middle School, VA

Beach Bliss

The magnificent golden sun shines down on the ocean,
as turquoise and cyan waves rush to the shore like race cars.
The snow white foam bobs above the swells
while patient surfers catch a perfect wave to shore.

Tan colored sand tickles my feet as I walk back,
hiding between the toes of daily beach goers.
The miniscule grains create a golden array,
shining as the bright summer sun beams down on the shore.

The seagulls flutter with their cream colored feathers,
swooping down to pick up leftovers and say hello.
They are out all day, even if I'm not,
walking and talking across the sandy shore.

The sound of the ice cream truck
swirls through my ears like a gust of wind.
Little children race up the sand,
hoping to be the first one in line.

Delia Burl, Grade 8
Trinity School, MD

Heart

My beat is very low…
My size will eventually grow…
Sometimes I'm in pain…
A numb feeling I can't explain…
The walls are forever cold…
For my soul has been sold…
You can see how I throb…
All my happiness has been robbed…
You can feel my fear…
But I still do not shed a tear…
Pain is throughout my life…
'Cause love is the pain that cuts like a knife…
Sometimes I am pulled apart…
For I am called
THE HEART…

KC Chaffin, Grade 7
Corkran Middle School, MD

Me, Myself and I

Abigail
It means outgoing, loving, and cheerful
It is the number 28
It is like a beautiful blooming rose
It is a trip to the Caribbean
It is the memory of my Mom
Who taught me to always follow my dreams and never give up
When her beautiful green eyes first looked into mine
My name is Abigail
It means to be yourself.
Being someone else doesn't get you anywhere in life.
If people don't like you, oh well. Being yourself is all that counts.

Abigail Lange, Grade 7
Hardin Reynolds Memorial School, VA

Ode to the Teddy Bear

Hearts are filled with bliss at the sight of you
Whenever you are hugged
A feeling of warmth is reached
You are so soft and cuddly
You are like chocolate
Giving people happiness
Except you last forever

You are always there to comfort the hurt
You represent a fearsome, great animal
But while you may be great
You are not fearsome
Both kids and adults love you
People can never grow too old for you

You can stay with people for many years
Just like a loving friend
You are even there at night
A time when people are alone
You are light keeping dreams alive
You replace loneliness with a sense of welcome
For you are the great Teddy Bear.

Maria-Alejandra Radiguet-Correa, Grade 8
Norfolk Collegiate Middle/Upper School, VA

Being Human

I am vulnerable,
I am scared,
I make mistakes,
I don't always do what I'm told.
I can't do everything right.
I live the only way I know how,
I regret things that shouldn't have happened,
I can't be perfect.
But I am a good person,
And I do try my best,
I do all I can.
And I hope it's good enough
For those who matter most
And I'll try to be perfect,
But I'm only human.

Maddy Reed, Grade 9
Norfolk Collegiate Middle/Upper School, VA

The Candy Princess

I found the Candy Princess; big green apple eyes,
Bubble gum pink lips, Hershey brown hair,
Skin like butterscotch candy,
Head like a watermelon sour patch,
Dress wrapped in a red fruity fruit loops,
Crown like a white chocolate pretzel,
Shoes shiny like blue jolly rancher,
I found the Candy Princess swimming in a chocolate pool
With trees of dangling oranges around it.

Kimberly Munoz, Grade 9
William E Tolman High School, RI

Kony 2012

What does it mean to have power?
Does it mean you have control over someone?
Or someone else is your property?

Innocent children
Taken from their homes
Stripped of their identity
Turned into soldiers at 10 years old
Forced to kill
Their cries are silent
And they need our help

This has been going on for 26 years
And is just being noticed now

"Nothing is more powerful than an idea whose time has come."
This is what needs to bring the world together
Bond as one
Make Kony famous
Not to praise
But to find him
And bring the children home
Our time is now

Carter Kennedy, Grade 8
Norfolk Collegiate Middle/Upper School, VA

Hunting

The sun reflects the morning dew…
Crystals and diamonds, soft shades of blue.
Tall brown reeds sway in the breeze,
Thin knifelike slivers of the bay that freeze.
Rafts of birds that float on top
Held by a rope in hopes that others will stop.
Steamy breaths from coffee hot
Warms the boys as they wait their shot.
Soft whispering commands for dogs to sit
Like statues of marble barely lit.
It is work and waiting at best.
Warm layers of clothes and perhaps a vest.
Players appreciate the nature of this game,
Knowing another day is never the same.
Pack it all at the end of the day,
Reliving the tales of a hunt on the bay.

Hunter Lee, Grade 9
Norfolk Collegiate Middle/Upper School, VA

Hockey

Hockey is loud, fast, and joyful.
The ice is nice and slippery.
Snowflakes falling softly onto the frozen ice.
I see my cousin sprinting down the long icy road.
Firmly grasping his stick and ice skates.
His face red, and puffing the cold air.
He says, "Want to play some hockey?"

Ricky Ruck, Grade 7
Biddeford Middle School, ME

Was It Worth It…?

You look at her with your stone-cold eyes…
laughing about what clothes she buys…
You poke her ribs with your manicured nails…
Laughing at her flaws and fails…
She grabs her books as she walks by…one trips her
She doesn't cry out in pain…she doesn't stir…
I feel my anger…
It is hot and on fire…
Your "crew" strolls out of the hall
And kicks her hard and sharp like she is a soccer ball.

In the next few hours…
She is cleaned with a few good showers…
The hospital tells me that she may not live…
But why??? I wonder…
You caused her body a pain like thunder…
She dies…
All because of the clothes she buys…
Her hair wasn't silk, but a knotted mess,
No one will bug her now when she is at rest…

Now you tell me…was it worth it?…Was it really worth it?

Ashleigh Miller, Grade 7
Massabesic Middle School, ME

My Dog

Just you and the beach, two lovable things.
The beach can be bad with all of the sand.
The hard sand pelts me as the rough wind sings.
And the sand is coarse, leaves red on my hand.
The waves can be rough they're really bad.
Also beaches' sand can be oh so hot.
And the rowdy teens really make me mad.
And I ignore the trash, I simply cannot.
But you, unlike sand, are not at all rough.
And the white spot on your head is quite cute.
And even though you are cute, you're still quite tough.
My friend, I would never give you the boot.

Holly, my friend, you are the cutest thing.
And when I see you I just want to sing.

Tae Bogan, Grade 7
Trinity Lutheran School, MD

Valentine

V isualizing the snowfall of February
A s I listen to the sounds disappear as winter comes
L oving the symbolism of the holiday
E xcited about the upcoming dance
N ever know who will have a crush on you
T iny Conversation Hearts
I n this holiday we celebrate love
N ow is the time for love
E nding the loving holiday with a kiss

Kayla Coleman, Grade 7
Rockbridge Middle School, VA

Papa

I miss your smile, your kindness, your heart. I miss the fun times, memories, and stories, but mostly your love.
You were more than just my grandpa. You were my best friend, my hero. You were the person I looked up to.
You were the bravest man to walk this earth.

A is for the amazing times together.
B is for you believing in me.
C is for the courage you had.
D is for the determination you had.
E is for everyone who loved you.
F is for being the biggest football fan I know.
G is for the best Grampy ever!
H is for the hero you were.
I is for the ice cream we ate every night when I was there.
J is for the funny jokes you told.
K is for the kind heart you had.
L is for the love you had for your family and friends.
M is for making bread together. Just the two of us.

N is for never giving up.
O is for the outgoing man you were.
P is for Papa, the one and only.
Q is for the quiet thoughtfulness you had.
R is for the biggest Red Sox fan I know.
S is for the amazing stories you told.
T is for the games of Trash we played.
U is for understanding me
V is for your very gentle spirit.
W is for all the TV shows we watched together.
X is for the x-ceptional way you cared for your family.
Y is for you, who will always be in our hearts and will never be forgotten.
Z is for sneaking in all those ZZZZ's you took when we weren't watching!

We love you and you will always remain in our hearts.

Marissa R. Pond, Grade 7
Sanford Jr High School, ME

An Adoption Story in the Voice of a Child

When I can taste the tears rolling down my face it's always bad.
The smiles of other people leave me when I walk away, faces I can no longer grasp in my fingers.
The family that stays behind while I go on.
Some people think that adoption is always a horrible thing; they think it's like a death in a kid's and/or parent's soul.
Adoption is not always a bad thing, there is always something better around the corner.
The tears ran down her face as she said. "I will see you again. I love you and you." — I never saw her again.
I was scared because they said I had to live with different people, people I didn't know.
I was mad because in my mind they were taking my mother from me.
I was suspicious because I was nine and didn't understand why they were doing this to my brother and I.
I was untrusting because I don't trust anyone until I know them, and they were strangers to me.
I moved to about five or six different houses before we got to stay permanently in one for two years.
After school we went to daycare. Bam! That's when we saw our future brother and family.
There is always something better around the corner, the better was a brand new future.
A future that didn't involve moving from place to place.
A future that didn't involve living with strangers.
A future that saw us with a family
I am thankful now more than ever that they chose to adopt us.
It was a life changing experience for me and changed the way I think about many things.
I love the family I have now more than anything I will ever love; Now, I feel loved and happy.
Adoption is not always what it's thought to be like.
There is always something better some for somebody, and that just might be adoption, like me.

Briona Godbolt, Grade 8
Rodney Thompson Middle School, VA

Beauty in the Sunlight

Beauty is seen, in the sunlight, the waves, the monkeys, coconuts falling and people relaxing, or swimming in the water.
Beauty is heard in the night, the wind gushing, the sun shining, or a bird calling anything in peace.
Beauty is me, good deeds, happy thoughts that relax themselves, in your dreams, on the beach, and even in your rest.

Andrew DeMatteo, Grade 7
Massabesic Middle School, ME

The Seaside
As I sit on the dock,
Watching the clouds float by,
I don't worry about the clock,
Or the world bustling by.
I float on the water,
My head to the sky,
I enjoy the beautiful weather,
And the clouds floating by.
When it's time to depart,
I don't hang my head and cry,
I keep this time in my heart,
The seaside, where nothing is awry.
Daniel Casker, Grade 9
Holy Cross Regional School, VA

Basketball
Basketball is fun
You're always on the run
Sometimes   you   fall
But you get back up and steal the ball
I   go   back   down   the   court
'Cause   I   show   a   good   sport
So   I   need   a   Gatorade
I'm   starting   to   dehydrate
Basketball   is   fun
'Cause you're always
on the run
Wanda Murray, Grade 8
Corkran Middle School, MD

Squirrel in a Tree
Squirrel, squirrel in a tree,
Climbing high as eyes can see.

Jumping from the highest twig,
From tree to tree, 'cross gaps so big.

Climbing down, down toward the ground,
Making very little sound.

Squirrel, squirrel in a tree,
Climbing down in front of me.
Douglas Dubosky, Grade 8
Mount St Charles Academy, RI

Winter Skiing
I can feel the powder under my skis
The snow behind me is white
Crystal clear ice on the trees
Snowflakes falling softly to the ground
A white rabbit hops across the trail
I pass over the small tracks
Happiness fills me for the ride down
I had a great day
Noah Morin-Roy, Grade 7
Biddeford Middle School, ME

Surprising Emotion
What is this feeling?
It only happens at certain times,
times when I really need it, and sometimes unexpected.
Sneaking up on you out of nowhere, giving you a surprising shock —
but also giving you a boost, a new sense of courage.

It overcomes you, and over-joys you.
Makes you feel like you're a part of something.
Lets you know that you are in a good place —
surrounded by people who care,
and knowing that good times are happening.

You look back at memories, and know that it was present.
You see the look upon your face, and your friends' faces.
Somehow you just know.
You just know that then, at that moment,
it is there.

The emotion some try to conceal,
others embrace.
Most greet warmly, some push away.
The feeling everyone deserves…
…happiness
Christa Craighead, Grade 9
Franklin County High School, VA

The Ocean
Quiet. All you hear are your thoughts and the waves.
Calm. Everything is still.
Peace. It's like the world is at peace.
The ocean.

It's like dogs lapping up water.
But it is only the waves lapping up against the shore.
Higher and higher they reach.
Then lower and lower they creep.
They loosen the sand,
And leave little shells behind.

Little creatures stir below me.
They come close to observe me,
But back away quickly if startled.
Back and forth they come.
Back and forth, back and forth.

It's so calm in the ocean
So quiet you can hear the beat of your heart.
It harmonizes with the waves.
It's almost as if you're lost in time.
You're still, but everything around you still goes on, outside the ocean
Jennifer Hansen, Grade 8
Holy Cross Regional School, VA

Three Wishes

The days I go back,
And put them on a note with a tack.
Knowing that I miss the green leaves,
Or how I would climb the trees.
If I just had three wishes one would be,
For spring to stay and always be.
If I had 3 wishes it would be great,
I would use them wisely or so I think.
I would wish that I could see the ones I love,
After they have vanished when their lives just begun.
Three wishes what a great idea.
I wish the things that no one would,
I would wish these because I could.
The last wish you see.
Would be the hardest for me.
No it is not world peace.
But for people all to be free.
No more people without homes.
No more people abused and hurt.
These three wishes would be amazing.
If only I had three wishes to be.

Stacia Brant, Grade 7
William S Cohen Middle School, ME

Don't Be Someone You're Not

If you try so hard to be like someone,
  it can be frustrating,
especially when you're the victim
  awaiting.
Jealousy can get into the head
  and control you to be that "someone."
I'm the kid finished with her lunch;
  seriously done.

My head just might explode —
  you're as difficult as an access code.
I don't get fake people sometimes,
  but I know you won't be copying me on my time.
I've learned I must just ignore.
  It's not worth it anymore.

Amanda Tansill, Grade 8
Mountain Christian School, MD

OTF, Only the Family

Like a soldier, I am fighting for my family
And for the world to know who I am
I WILL BE FAMOUS
Mama raised me without guilt
I'm orphaned from some of my family
That lives somewhere else
A boy that wants to make it is what I see
in the mirror
I feel I am the heart of my family
I feel I am the heart of my family.

Jordan Smith, Grade 9
New Directions Alternative Education Center, VA

Beauty

Is beauty like a diamond?
Perfect and clean.
Shining upon a plush pillow in a glass case.
Not touched, only seen.
Is beauty like a diamond?

Is beauty like a rose?
Clean and fresh.
Growing alone in a flower pot.
All alone, never changing.
Is beauty like a rose?

Is beauty like a dove?
Dainty and cute.
Always kept in a cage instead of soaring.
Held back, always watched.
Is beauty like a dove?

I say beauty is none of these things.
So keep your diamonds, roses, and doves.
To me, beauty is freedom to be who you want to be.

Marissa Liotta, Grade 8
Mount St Charles Academy, RI

Imperfection

Too fat, too thin
Too short, too tall
They judge no matter what
Even when they don't know you at all
Too quiet, too loud
Too small, too big
You may not be perfect
But heck nobody is
Too weird, too normal
Too ugly, too hot
They'll judge you for what you lack
They'll judge you for what you got
Too different, too similar
Too unique, too true
They might always judge you, but at least you are you

Alexandra Miernicki, Grade 8
St. Rocco School, RI

Cyber Bullying

A text message sent, like flying through the air,
One minute or the next, you get a feeling of despair.
The wicked words sent from your hand,
The Sunday news at eleven,
You heard that he had fallen; —
Fallen because of you,
Fallen because of what you said,
Fallen because he was hurt,
Fallen because he was "bullicided," —
Fallen because he committed suicide.

Raleigh Thomas, Grade 7
Homeschool Plus, VA

Still Standing

In this Life
So far I've learned
People can be cruel enough
To break you down
Make you cry
Make you lose faith in yourself
Turn your world inside out
Throw dirt on your name
Push and push you
Until you're on the edge
Then they throw you off
It's a long way down
So you begin to recollect yourself
So when you hit that ground
You land on your own two feet
Then the pain is gone
So you're titled champion in the game
Because smiling
Is the only reason I'm
Still standing
Dasia Bailey, Grade 7
Sudbrook Magnet Middle School, MD

Two Spring-Green Trees*

In a tangled embrace, the boughs
Exchange their loving spring-green vows.
The bond that's granted to each tree
Is the closest nature allows.

"I love you," spoke one spring-green tree,
"And I cannot live without thee!"
"For we are entwined together,"
The other tree cried happily.

But in the bitter dark winter,
For the hearth that lacked a cinder
An ax brought one tree to its death,
And took it away for tinder.

But in its place, to stop and rest,
A planter dropped a seed, his best.
That seedling with a spring-green crest,
Lived with the tree 'til its last breath.
Eleanor Donohue, Grade 7
Rachel Carson Middle School, VA
*In the style of Robert Frost

Riddle

The rich need
The poor have
Beyond space
Before earth
In dead skulls after years
Around the moon
Tommy Caldwell, Grade 8
Stevensville Middle School, MD

Imagination

Our eyes roam
Throughout endless space
Where time is meaningless
And reality is warped
Truly seeing how infinitesimal we are

The mind scorns comprehension
To that of logic and reason
The idea of thought travels faster than light
And arrives instantaneously

Like a veil drawn away from eyes
What was once thought to be fantasy
Now proven to be truth
You can still believe

That there is fact in the unknown
That unknown does become fact
It is just this hunger
That creates this desire
For this journey
Nick Sarris, Grade 8
Norfolk Collegiate Middle/Upper School, VA

Forget You Not

I couldn't forget you if I wanted,
        if I tried.
I couldn't forget you if I wanted,
        if I cried, cried, cried.
I couldn't forget you if I wanted,
        if I smiled every day.
I couldn't forget you if I wanted,
even if there is nothing left to say.
I couldn't forget you if I wanted,
        if the days turned into years.
I couldn't forget you if I wanted,
        if I stopped counting the tears.
I couldn't forget you if I wanted,
because of all that you have done for me.
I couldn't forget you if I wanted,
        it is quite easy to see.
I couldn't forget you if I wanted,
        whether you are near or far.
I couldn't forget you if I wanted,
because forgetting you isn't possible;
        you will always be in my heart.
Emily Merchant, Grade 8
Admiral Byrd Middle School, VA

Peace

Peace is what the world needs,
        Peace should be in society.
Peace should be present every day,
A place where citizens can live in harmony.
Jacob Ritmiller, Grade 7
St. Clement Mary Hofbauer School, MD

Fourth of July

As I delicately dangle my feet,
I craft soft ripples
In the cold water
Of a placid lake.

A rocket of white fire
Whistles above my head
And brightly bursts
Into countless white sparks.

The lustrous lake
Mirrors the beauty
Of the glorious glow,
The radiant light show.

White, blue, and fiery red missiles
Shoot upwards into the black,
Creating a thunderous crackle
And illuminating my night sky.
Kate Maguire, Grade 8
Trinity School, MD

The Invisible Girl

Look at the invisible girl in the corner
The one that nobody likes
She always seems to get laughed at
And is always afraid of a fight.

Will they punch her, or kick her,
Or call her a name
That poor, lonely girl
Always covered in shame.

No one to talk to
And no one to share
Dripping down her cheek
Looks like a tear.

Someone should be her friend
Someone should set her free
Someone should rescue her
That someone is ME.
Alisha Ciunci, Grade 7
St Rocco School, RI

Spring Fever

The sun shone upon the earth
And the flowers were filled with mirth
The animals came out of their dens
And danced around with their friends
Warm is the weather
But now it's getting wetter
Rain hits the window with a ping
I guess that's just spring!
Jillian Barnabe, Grade 8
Mount St Charles Academy, RI

Tippity Tappin' our Toes

I go over my steps.
Try to get them right.
Step toe, step hop, step hop, step, out in,
Butterflies join together
In my stomach.
What is the next step?
Flap heel, heel spank, heel, toe, heel.
I glance up at my sister
On the other side of the stage.
In her sunrise leotard, and matching skirt
She looks like a nervous butterfly.
I give her my confident smile
And mouth, "Don't forget the arms!"
She smiles.
The music starts
Without my permission,
But I know what to do.
Jump, shuffle, jump, toe shuffle, ball change.
Soon we finish,
Big smiles on our faces.
Tippity tappin' our toes

Mia Burgess, Grade 7
Blue Ridge Middle School, VA

Searching

Where do I turn now?
I tried to go up, but they pushed me down,
And many times I just ignore it,
But this time I could not endure it.
I hate being alone, I have this fear of being on my own
So who do I turn to now?
Because I don't know at all,
Everyone I leaned on let me fall.
Tell me......
Who do I talk to now?
Because everyone I confided in turned my words around.
Who do I go to for a shoulder to cry on?
You know, when you're on your own, it's harder to be strong.
Somebody tell me, where do I go?
I used to have all the answers but now I don't know.

Devine Booze, Grade 8
Charles Carroll Middle School, MD

Life Is a Battlefield

Life is a battlefield
The ones you know will die
The world will burn around you
Bombs will burst wherever you look
But never look down
For you cannot stop moving
Or you will end yourself
For you must do everything to survive and thrive
For you must accomplish your goal no matter what
For life is a battlefield

Zachary Stump, Grade 8
Stevensville Middle School, MD

Ode to a Crayon

Bittersweet,
like a hot cup of chocolate
warming you on a cold winter day.
Aquamarine,
like a mermaid
splashing in the Caribbean water.
Maize,
like the fall cornfields
blowing in the cool autumn wind.
Dandelion,
swaying in the summer sun
I make a wish
hoping summer will last
forever.
Tickle me pink,
like bubble gum
waiting to be chewed
at the candy store.
Fuzzy wuzzy brown
like a child's teddy bear
warm and worn

Lauren Rudolphi, Grade 7
The School of the Cathedral of Mary Our Queen, MD

Tranquility

When he holds me
in his arms
the rest of the world goes away
vanishes
and there is only him
surrounding
encompassing but not
crowding
as the thoughts slip away
back into the recesses of my brain
and there is peace.
not just in my head
the tension in
my muscles
ebbs away

Madeline Bartley, Grade 9
Western School of Technology & Environmental Science, MD

Cooperstown

Located in a rural town
Hides a magical place that deserves a crown
It holds store fronts, museums and fun filled facts
Visited by friends, families and all types of acts
The children go to play on the field of dreams
They try to hit the ball with seams
Their parents take the stands with joy
As they watch the bases covered by their boy
A place where I would like to be
The Hall of Fame is filled with history

Kyle St. Germain, Grade 8
Mount St Charles Academy, RI

Ode to the Shelter Cat

Oh Cat, you are the true embodiment of grace,
Tiny yellow lanterns blazing on your fierce face.
Oh Cat, you were worshiped in faraway lands.
You were a goddess surrounded by Egyptian sands.

Now, as I twitch the feathery ball,
Out from your metal cage you crawl.
And when you catch it in your claws,
I admire your jet-black paws.

When playtime comes to an end,
I smile at you, my new best friend.
And when into my arms you leap,
You snuggle in, you snuggle deep.

Oh shelter cat, I love you so
(that's why I volunteered, you know)
And as I fill your water cup,
I think, "How could anyone give you up?"

Emma Nelson, Grade 7
Kilmer Middle School, VA

AAP <3

God I know you had a reason
To take him from his Earthly home
You could have given us forewarning
That you would take him to his Godly form
You didn't mean to hurt us I know you didn't
But think about the living.
        The hurting mother.
            The aching brothers.
                The pained father.
                    The tormented friends.
                        This longing little girl.
                            Those are the ones who hurt.
Plus imagine the pain of that mother
No pain is close in comparison.
Not even a major wound.
Losing a brother, sister, parent, or spouse
No it's not the same as losing a child.
Not the same as having to lay your child down in a casket…
    No it's not the same.

Gabriella Greco, Grade 8
Holy Cross Regional School, VA

The Wealthy Are the Poor

Rich
Greedy, Selfish
Spending, educating, powering
Your outsides are different, the insides still count
Saving, begging, working
Needy, run-down
Poor

Alexandra Wilder, Grade 8
Stevensville Middle School, MD

Ode to a Snail

The gentle
snail
is a slow moving train,
always staying on the right track
reaching its destination,
like a rain drop falling to the ground.
With focus
the snail
with its tunnel vision,
has its sight set on one place,
like Tim Tebow
looking towards the sky
praising the Lord.
A snail can't be a snail without stress,
always on the lookout
like mother watching her child,
fearful of getting stepped on
and becoming a pancake on someone's shoe.
As the day ends
hopefully all went well,
so the snail can go to bed in its shell.

Tommy Murray, Grade 7
The School of the Cathedral of Mary Our Queen, MD

Sweet Loves End

Roses are red
Violets are blue
I never knew love until I met you

The lemons turned sweet
The sun started to shine
Our love oh so innocent was a beautiful sign

But the sun went away
The lemons turned sour
And all that was left was a dead little flower

Now no more roses are red
No more violets are blue
The skies turned to gray
And I'm without you

Hannah Dewberry, Grade 8
Stevensville Middle School, MD

Summertime

Summer is a time
With pools and fun
You can run all around
Barefoot and hot
You run inside and have a nice lemonade
And then go back outside to swim some more
Having fun all the time
Summertime is a time for fun

Amber Joyce, Grade 7
Hardin Reynolds Memorial School, VA

Love

Love is like an illness
That we all have shared one time or another
Love is a cold
Something that is hard to get rid of
Something in the pit of your stomach
Something you feel deep down in your core
A lot of people don't want it
A lot of people say they don't need it
Once it's gone
You want it back
Once it's back
You want it gone
The people together
Holding hands
There for each other
Wishing that they would
Never be separated never be alone
But not me
I will be forever alone
I embrace the loneliness

Felicia Pyle, Grade 7
Corkran Middle School, MD

Gray Matter

Gray is a haze of mystery,
It mimics beings,
Following in their footsteps,
It looms over earth bringing blessings,
And answers to millions of pleas,
It is the screams from the victims of a disaster,
And the empty, care free,
Echoes of steps from their grieving loved ones,
The bitter-sweetness of the clear liquid savior,
As it trickles down one's throat,
It doesn't take sides,
But chooses a path in between,
It fades into the background,
Helping everything else to shine,
It is the hollowness of a broken heart,
And the fog of stress clouding one's head,
The sorrows at the loss of a battle,
And the shadow hiding the tears,
Helping, protecting the treasurable belongings,
One loves most

Noa Steiner, Grade 7
McLean School of Maryland, MD

Unexplainable

Like a tiger locked in a cage, I have no freedom
Mama raised me without any problems
I'm orphaned from trust because people have
Broken the trust with me
I feel I am too much of a forgiving person
I feel I am too much of a forgiving person

Ashley Alvarez, Grade 9
New Directions Alternative Education Center, VA

Ode to an Iceberg Lettuce

On Thursday morning
Sat an iceberg lettuce
Same as the rest
In its clean coat sat coolly
Surrounded by cold air
She saw it near the carrots
Gave it a disgusted glance
The lettuce ignored
And dreamed of sailing
Past the shore its coat solid ice
And bigger than Captain Crunch
Its dreams were interrupted
It had been chosen for a delicious meal
And for the first time was bought
Months later it sat there
In the fridge
Near the neglected tartar sauce
Its coat turned brown and started losing leaves
Just like the lettuce
It had lost its dreams

Amanda Sessa, Grade 7
The School of the Cathedral of Mary Our Queen, MD

Shark Attack

The shark
Is a magnificent creature
With its rough, gray skin,
It protects itself as if it
Were holding a shield
The shark's
Teeth are like knifes
It acts like
A murderous person
The shark is
The deputy of the sea
It is as fast as
Usain Bolt
When it kills,
The shark shreds things to pieces
Like a meat grinder
When you see the jagged fin,
You'd better leave because
You are in the shark's
Territory

Lauren Lavelle, Grade 7
The School of the Cathedral of Mary Our Queen, MD

American Soldier

Never fear or fright,
A hero is protecting you day and night
Standing tall and strong
Hoping to never do their country wrong
Yet never caring what they rank,
Just to know they have American soldier strength

Michaela Gamache, Grade 8
Mount St Charles Academy, RI

It Took Experience

It seems that sometimes,
everyone that you love slips away.
Just like water in your hand,
they fall to the ground,
further and further from you until
they splash against the cold, hard dirt, gone forever.

But then, somewhere down the road,
another rain cloud appears and it rains.
Some people will just fall past you and
hit the ground without coming near you,
while others will fall onto
your fingers, then slip down to the earth.

Then those very special few
will land on your palm,
there to stay with you longer.
But one day, they too
will slip down, then the
vicious cycle will start
again.

Kendra Arnold, Grade 9
Woodbridge Sr High School, VA

Ode to Food

Ode to food so yummy and fun.
I like it all, I'm not fickle.
A juicy cheeseburger on a bun.
With ketchup and a pickle.
And crinkle cut fries on the side.
From a garden potato.
Who doesn't love a hot dog.
And a sausage link that is fried?
Or spaghetti and meatballs with a sauce of tomato.
And cranberries from the bog?

Ode to food, a hungry boy's dream.
Love those vanilla milkshakes!
Peanut butter pie topped with whipped cream.
Chicken legs and crab cakes.
You need to try Savannah rice.
My dad makes it — he's a cool dude.
I'll eat all the strawberries I can find.
And on a cold day soup is nice.
Ode to glorious, wonderful food
Of each and every kind.

Alexander Gillespie, Grade 7
Rockbridge Middle School, VA

Don't Forget Me

Don't forget me when I'm old,
don't forget that I'm here,
please don't forget that I have been here for you,
and don't forget that I care.

Rissa Scholes, Grade 8
Biddeford Middle School, ME

A Good Idea...

A good idea:
Like a light bulb in my head,
Flickering off and on,
Sometimes failing to even light.
But sometimes, and only sometimes,
It sparks alive, alight with brilliance,
Dancing throughout the dark.
A good idea:
It stands out among the other thoughts in my head,
Pushing and shoving its way to the front of my mind,
Somehow it gets through the crowd of feelings.
Climbs out of its home and perches on my ear,
Until it feels I'm listening and it whispers to me.
A good idea:
Its message comes through my ear again,
And the idea runs to catch up with it,
Its journey is almost over, but not quite yet.
The message sometimes gets lost in the wind,
And all the idea can do is hope it will come back,
But sometimes, and only sometimes,
It catches up, and something beautiful, like this, is made.

Corinne Williams, Grade 7
Rachel Carson Middle School, VA

White Is...

White is...
The flag symbolizing surrender, the moon's light in the darkness
Marble statues and grand buildings.
Clouds dancing in the sky, shape-shifting all the time
Snow, a blanket that's made for skiing,
Sand on a Caribbean beach,
The paper with the homework assignment.

White is...
The sound of smashing waves on a beach
A wonderful spring breeze

White is...
Vanilla ice cream on a hot summer day
Cream cheese on a poppy seed bagel
Sugar cubes on anything you like
A sprinkle of salt or sugar on anything imaginable

White is...
Peace, serenity, dreams, calm
White can make the world a better place

Stefan Abarbieritei, Grade 7
McLean School of Maryland, MD

My Family Is Seasons

My mom is winter, cold and sad with a few nice days
My dad is fall, mostly pleasant with a few cool breezes
My dog is spring, always perfect and just right
I'm summer, excited and fun until the hose gets turned on you

Hollyann Wettstein, Grade 7
Western Heights Middle School, MD

My Name

When I was born my name was Scott
My parents liked that name a lot
My birthday is St. Patrick's Day
So then my great aunt came to say
"Patrick should be his name; not Scott"
So Patrick is the name I've got
That's what I'm called to this day
And with me, that's just OK
If you call me Scott, I will not mind
But Patrick is the name that's signed
On my certificate of birth
I've got the best name story on Earth

Patrick Horsky, Grade 9
Delaware Military Academy, DE

February Vacation

School vacation is entertaining
(just as long as it's not raining).
Having no homework
is really a nice perk.
I'm off on my snowboard.
There's no chance to be bored.
The hot chocolate's poured —
it's an awesome reward.
We hang out with our friends.
Have fun till it ends!
DRAT! It's Sunday.
Back to school Monday.

James Del Bonis, Grade 8
Mount St Charles Academy, RI

Silvery Frost

Silvery Frost
sparkled in the moonlight glare,
silver shot with white-like-snow.
A perfect figure
gliding through the night,
and though it is cold to the touch
inside it burns with the heat of the sun.
Singing of kindness and joy and light,
carrying on till night is done,
then slowly, slowly, sinking down
deep into the soft powder-snow,
radiant to the end.

Fiona Polk, Grade 9
Woodbridge Sr High School, VA

Frogs

Their once was a frog named sock,
Who jumped from rock to rock.
Went into the wet grass,
With only a big splash,
And back to the end of the dock.

Caryn Boutaugh, Grade 9
Stearns High School, ME

The Awakening

A singing mocking bird serenades the awakening life all around
A tiny glittering dewdrop falls from an intricately woven web
A freshly grown green blade of grass takes it safely in its arms
The rich soil thinly veils the restless animals under the earth
The first ray of sunlight shines across the newly dampened land
The entire meadow seems to finally arouse from its deep slumber
A lingering leaf falls from a lone oak in a sea of flowers
Bee's bustle from one golden station to another gathering pollen
In hopes to be done before darkness settles over them yet again
And yet the valley lulls itself back to sleep once more to its softly whispered lullaby,
only to be awakened again to the sweet songs of the mockingbird

Claire Albright, Grade 8
Mount St Charles Academy, RI

A Ball of Thunder

I felt like there was a bomb going to explode any minute, tic tok tic tok
How much longer can I wait?
She told a lie, one I cannot forgive
This feeling balls up inside of me, I am in the hall…
WAITING…for something or someone to come
TIC TOK…TIC TOK
Five minutes
Ten minutes
NOTHING!
I cannot wait much longer. I am…
FRUSTRATED

Arielle Ungar, Grade 7
McLean School of Maryland, MD

Sin

Sin is like a knock on one's door.
Once you open the door, sin consumes you, attacking you at your core.
Sin tempts you to come its way.
When you start down the road of sin, death awaits you every day.
As you walk towards sin and you are about to take its hand,
God's Spirit comes bursting through, giving you strength to withstand.
God always delivers you when you battle against sin's way.
For God's child, sin does not have the final say!

Stephen Bullock, Grade 8
Westminster Academy, VA

Pool Side

Sitting, looking, watching.
Sitting by the pool side…
Watching others swim
Hear the water glide
Watching the sky dim
Just jumping in
Having fun
Splashing everyone
All over you see water
Like it had rained for days
Wet, wet, wet
Water world.

Madilyn Cronin, Grade 8
Corkran Middle School, MD

My Cat

I have a cat
As a matter of fact
She gets very lazy
And sometimes crazy
She tears up the couch
Scratch, scratch, scratch
When she's awake it all goes south
But after it's all over
When asleep
She sits close warming our feet
But the next day it starts again
Like a bad rerun all over my friend

Nathaniel Whittaker, Grade 8
Corkran Middle School, MD

Silent Is She

To sit with no words.
There is so much to say, yet too much to speak.
Silence deafens the ears of the shy,
And makes the air heavy with breaths from the unspoken.
No words, but only thoughts through the mind.
The world may speak, but silence is all that is heard.
Her dreams are her world, her noise, her voice.
The darkness forecloses to let in the light of belief.
Silent she is, but she speaks inside.
Fear leaves her silent…
Of what, she does not know.
So scared of life, of love, of trust, of everything.
Life beats from within her,
Though she appears to be dead.
Words are thoughtless, mischievous, dangerous sounds.
Can spread love, or hate.
Say hello, or goodbye.
Words are not needed to be spoken
When all that is left is noise.

Hannah Tibbetts, Grade 9
Narraguagus High School, ME

Where I'm From

I am made from summer,
From my birthday and going to the beach.
I am made from the shells that I collect,
And the place where the sun shines all day long.

I am made from chocolate,
Ice-cream sundaes too.
I am made from candy canes,
And Jolly Ranchers blue.

I am made from music.
Headphones in each ear.
I am made from Radiohead.
Playing for all to hear.

I am from many things,
And that is what makes me,
Me.

Saahithi Budharaju, Grade 8
Stone Hill Middle School, VA

Books

Mothers read for their children
the thin perfected pages
with written words in cages
of spines and tough covers.
Every single rendition
is a blossoming seed
that starts out quiet, still, and calm
until a different, fully opened flower
is in one's palm.

Kelsey Crawford, Grade 8
Trinity School, MD

If Joy Was a Color

If joy was a color,
It would be bright yellow
As luminous as a topaz.
If joy was a taste
It would be just like honey on a cool windy day.
If joy was a feeling
It would be as charming as a picnic on a emerald covered hill.
If joy was a smell
It would be as lovely as a fountain made of glass
If joy was a sound,
It would be as peaceful as a relaxing day near a river.

Aaron Zhang, Grade 8
Mount St Charles Academy, RI

My Next Life with You

Whenever they ask me —
Where would you like to be in your next life?
I would always say
Right next to my beloved Isaiah.
They would ask me again —
Why do you want to be right next to your beloved Isaiah?
I would say because
Without him I'm nothing;
Without him my happiness is gone;
Without him I have lost everything.
With him I shall be in my next life.

Tolulope Ademola, Grade 9
William E Tolman High School, RI

Determination

I look around,
And see what I see,
There are a lot of guys,
Taller than me,

Pay attention and listen,
The coach yells to us all,
He's not here to joke,
It's about playing ball,

Your team is your family,
So never forget,
On and off the court,
Treat them all with respect,

Never think I can't,
Always say "I can,"
Step up and take the chance,
Be the first to raise your hand,

Hard work and determination,
Will give you power and strength,
So never give up on anything,
You can always do more than you think!

Joseph Torti, Grade 8
St Rocco School, RI

Chance
I've given you
One too many
If it's too much to count
That means
I've given you plenty
Plenty of chances
I gave out
That means I do not have
Time to hear you out
Hearing your lies and cries
As if you meant it
A thousand times
As if I was being tormented
I'm done I can't take it
I give my heart to you
And you break it
That's it I'm truly done
This was the last chance
You will ever get from me
I'm done
Ashtyn Bennett, Grade 9
Rivermont School-Tidewater, VA

I Am
I am the almighty all powerful
I wonder if I can fly with God
I hear voices calling me
I see angels beckoning me to come
I want to stay not go
I am still alive and still breathing

I pretend that life is perfect
I feel as the world suddenly stops
I touch the soft grass and dream of hope
I worry about life and the earth
I cry rivers to make the pain go away
I am alive and still breathing

I understand I will die one day
I say not today I will live on
I dream of a better day
I try to dream of peace and love
I hope I can live till the end
I am still alive and still breathing
Catera Moore, Grade 8
Corkran Middle School, MD

My World Is Finally Right
My heart is filled
With love and joy
He makes me feel
Complete and alive
My world is finally right.
Bre Thompson, Grade 7
Hardin Reynolds Memorial School, VA

Fire and Ice
Frost turns to ice,
and embers turn to fire,

The ice runs into my veins,
and the fire burns in my heart,

But I know I can't stop,
I have to see this through.

The challenges are tough,
But life just isn't enough.

Unless it's lived to the fullest,
After its run its course,
Your heart will be full of remorse.

Pour into life your heart and soul,
Give it all the time you have,
Even though it could take its toll,
That's life.

Frost turns to ice,
and embers turn to fire,

The ice runs into my veins,
and the fire burns in my heart,

But I know I can't stop,
I have to see this through.
Elizabeth Taylor, Grade 8
Holy Cross Regional Catholic School, VA

Funny or Serious
Some people think
that poetry is
funny
and sometimes
it is
but not always
sometimes poetry
is serious
like this poem
is not supposed
to make
you laugh
it is
supposed
to make
you think
about how
not all poetry
is funny
some is very
serious.
Pearl Nissen, Grade 8
Thomas Pullen School, MD

Shoreline
Meet me by the shoreline
Where waves roll in like thunder
Crabs click across the rocks
And the air is full of harsh seagull cries
Meet me where treasure winks at the sun
Dark ocean water gracefully arcs overhead
Footprints and memories wash away

Meet me by the shoreline
Where salty wind bitterly whips skin
Cool spray kisses sun-touched burns
And foamy ocean water feels your toes
Where we explored sand dunes as kids
Laughed as teens, and when we grew,
Took our steps a bit slower

Meet me by the shoreline
Where we loved to walk for miles
Where you found that sea glass
Finished your precious collection
Discovered happiness in chipped glass
Meet me one final time, everything is fine
Right here along the beautiful shoreline
Maya James, Grade 8
Oakland Mills Middle School, MD

Mother
Mother, I am scared.
Mother, hold me tight.
Please do not leave now.

Mother, I am sorry.
Mother, must we fight?
Please do not cry now.

Mother, I am safe.
Mother, you're my knight.
Please do not die now.

Mother, I am a seer.
Mother, grant me sight.
Please be with me now.

Mother, I am sacred
I shall soon take flight.
Please come teach me now.

I am here.
Yes, strong is my might
With my wisdom here.
Aliya Hochstadt, Grade 7
Kilmer Middle School, VA

Believing in You

Believing in you,
I thought was right.
Believing in you,
I thought was safe.
Believing in you,
no more because
believing in you,
was the wrong thing to do.
Believing in you
was hurtful too.
Believing in you,
no more because
of you.
Kristina Wade, Grade 7
Hardin Reynolds Memorial School, VA

Battlefield

Life is a battlefield,
hard and dirty. It can
bring you pride or
tear you apart.
Joyful days are
limited and horrifying
days are endless.
You give it your all
and get what you
put in. You don't
know why you're
there but you know
to give it your all.
Kevin Wolbart, Grade 8
Stevensville Middle School, MD

Dishonesty

Dishonesty is a minefield
Dangerous and wrong
A chain reaction that goes on
And on
Hating justice and fairness
Killing a person
deadening their senses of reality
And right
Deceiving,
Leading you into an ever-deepening
Pit of consequences
This is what happens when you walk
On the minefield of dishonesty.
Daniel Russell, Grade 8
Stevensville Middle School, MD

Dreamworld

I'm in a dreamworld
Where nobody can find me
Where nobody looks
Brooke Valentine, Grade 8
Holy Cross Regional School, VA

Picture Perfect Myrtle Beach

I stand calf deep in the cold, calming water
While the large golden sun melts into the deep blue ocean like hot wax.
Various shades of purple and orange paint the dusk sky.

Salty ocean air races towards me before sundown.
The faint squawks of seagulls float into my ears.
Delicate ivory sea shells decorate the darkening sandy beige shore.
Clear white foam, blossoming like flowers,
forms on the edges of ink blue waves.
The waves climb up the shore
To wrap their ice cold fingers around my ankles.
Soft sand squeezes its way between my toes.
Clean and crisp ocean air floods my nose, dances across my skin,
And weaves through my hair.

Every detail from the watercolor sky
To the shimmering deep blue ocean
Creates a picture perfect sunset.
Kira Zarzuela, Grade 8
Trinity School, MD

Freedom

I look up and cry out in anguish
The curling tendrils of the sun's light have yet to kiss my battered skin
I long for the embrace of light and warmth
Yet I stay here bound to the wall by heavy chains
The darkness is falling on me like a thick blanket
I am ready to give up and surrender myself to the suffocating black
Then I look up and see a single drop of pure light fall from the sky
It is a teardrop from the sun's amicable face
The drop spatters to the ground
I see the blinding light spread out from the place where the tear dropped
Like a wave the light runs out making the darkness black wisps of smoke
My chains fall at my feet and run away with the darkness
Who now must flee to avoid destruction
I now am free in the pasture
Holding hands with the light of the sun
Only this darkness returns every day
Only to be defeated once more by the sun
I am the moon
Alexander Brinkley, Grade 8
Norfolk Christian Middle School, VA

Yellow

The sun beating down on the hottest day of summer
Sand tickling my toes, fish scales reflect under the water surface
Dandelions' waking up with buzzing bees flying around them
Monarch butterflies with dots like eyes looking at you
The glowing yellow school bus that takes me to school every morning
I hear the song of the goldfinch in the big oak tree
The taste of cool lemonade sliding down the back of my throat
My hard teeth sliding into a soft mushy banana
The ridges on the pencil I pick up every day
Sleep, the whisper of my mom's goodnight
Sam Rappaport, Grade 7
McLean School of Maryland, MD

The Hopes and Dreams of Many

Thousands of leagues under the sea lie the hopes and dreams of many.
Crushed by thousands of pounds of water weighted down by hatred and unkind words.
The water is pounding down upon the hopes and dreams of many.
All that is left is darkness.
Sunlight is completely blocked out by the evil ones.
They are who sank the hopes and dreams of many.
They now lie thousands of leagues under the sea with not even a glimpse of light.
All of the sadness and darkness I now look down upon, high above the clouds.
The angels come down from Heaven to fight the evil darkness
and to rescue the hopes and dreams of many.
Few are still held captive by the evil ones waiting to be rescued.
One day I will become an angel, the angel to save the few hopes and dreams still held captive by the evil ones.
On that day a light will shine through the darkness with its warmth comforting the hopes and dreams of many.

Michael Knowles, Grade 7
Most Blessed Sacrament Catholic School, MD

Black

When the lights come on and shine down onto the stage the Adidas shoes move to the music
Ta Ta Ta Taaaaaa Ta Ta
Until the lights shut down and the sound of applause is heard
Black is the smell of a hot dog roasted on the grill for too long being defeated by the charcoal
The hot dog lost
The sound of thunder rumbles, rumbles as if someone was being chased by a humongous black giant
Black feels furious, depressed and angry all at the same time.
Feeling frozen wanting to stare into space and get lost in a dream
Far in the distance a puff of black smoke appears as if it's coming to get me and that it wants something from me
I stand there and a whip of smoke overtakes my face making its way into my mouth it tastes bitter
Black can be anything you want
It can be anger, exuberance, or sadness, but black is something that you create on your own

Taylor Forbes, Grade 7
McLean School of Maryland, MD

Winter

The taste of hot chocolate and the smell of pine sometimes send a shiver down my spine.
Snowplows roaring and people singing, sometimes I can hear those sleigh bells ringing!

On the ice people are fishing, fish are flopping and kids are hopping!
Chipmunks stop and watch, then drag their food away, safe at home so they don't have to roam.

Animal prints lead into the woods and snowmen watch, taking in the scene.
A flag goes up, a fish has been caught only to be released to another day.

Wintery air sweeps over the ice, it's kind of nice!
Now I know that winter is here.

Sarah Mason, Grade 7
Biddeford Middle School, ME

My Family Is a Plot

My Mom is the Exposition, the one who wakes up everyone and shows us new people,
My little sister is the Rising Action, always crying for attention,
My step-Dad is the Climax, he gets frustrated when my little sister starts crying and screaming,
    and he is not sure how to console her,
I am the Falling Action, I calm my little sister down and get her to take a nap,
Lastly, my Dogs are the Resolution, they show us how to always be happy and upbeat just like they are.

Kendall Bartle, Grade 7
Western Heights Middle School, MD

The Creek

In the cold of the night, animals run about in fright
For they cannot compare
To the creature over there
The one with the quick claw

So many great warriors
Scream out "He is invincible!"
To turn the terrible tide
And claim the bountiful prize
Covered by a tarp something beyond anything ever
Witnessed by a pair of eyes

No one can beat the one, the one with the quick claws
'Til one brave peasant walks up "The Creek!"
Holler the haughty losers
As the rabbits cackle and the cats snicker
The creek drowns out the unbeatable dog with quick claws

They watch in silence as the creek lifts the tarp
The bountiful prizes' home turns out to be a bone

"It is a fix!" shouts a smaller dog
"A scandal!" croaks the frog
"A scheming twit though with admirable wit"
Says The Creek the now respected Creek

Rehan Madhugiri, Grade 7
Rachel Carson Middle School, VA

Space

Space is where we put things in need of rest
It is filling what's not there
Holding spot for items like crates and boxes
We place wooden chairs in its spot so we can sit
We put desks in its spot so we can write great books

Space is where rockets fly and where mice crawl
Silent as a picture,
As tasteless as a cold empty plate
It feels like what it is as calm
It smells like what was there before

Space when filled replaces the hole
When your back is turned it can mimic your movement
It keeps you company when you're alone
Runs away when tried to be caught

There is always enough when you look for it
There is never enough when it's found
At times it can be difficult to find
It's an unlimited natural resource

It can whoosh without making any noise
It's always there, it's always there
If we know where to look

David DiBari, Grade 8
St Jane De Chantal School, MD

Oh Pencil

Oh pencil, oh pencil,
My stubby little pencil.
What great times we've had,
From writing letters to solving math problems.
I remember when you were big, smooth, yellow, and perfect, pencil.
But, like Benjamin Button, you slowly became
Smaller and smaller.
By the start of the second quarter,
You were having a mid-life crisis,
About getting younger.
You may have been getting tinier,
But also more experienced.
Oh pencil, oh pencil.
By Hanukkah you were a frail old lady, beaten up and small
By Christmas you were on your last lead,
And by New Years, it was time for you to go.
Oh pencil, oh pencil.
The trash can will be your grave
With all your brothers who have shared your fate.
Rest quietly, dear pencil.
I will miss you.

Ben Manning, Grade 7
Blue Ridge Middle School, VA

Success

When I am successful
I will be in the MLS
CBS will be looking at me
saying I am the best
I will trick all the players
schooling them up
I will be the next star
my nickname will be Messi the Messer up
I will win the next world cup
for my team U.S.A.
I will look like the player Pele
This is my story
of being a star
Maybe one day
you will also go far

Jeremy Mattanah, Grade 7
Baltimore Montessori Public Charter School, MD

The Spelling Bee

My heart was beating like the sound of a drum
With this last word to spell I could not act dumb
I was at the Spelling Bee in grade six
If I lost this Bee it would hit me like bricks
It was the final round with one word to spell
When I got it right I heard a bell
I heard a choir of angels singing a song
My confidence level grew so strong
My family hugged me with all their might
I won the Spelling Bee so I guess I did all right

Daniella Ferranti, Grade 7
St Rocco School, RI

Strong

I'm strong as a rock
but on the inside
I'm soft like a pillow on a winter's night
I hear people laughing
people pointing
so I know
I know people are talking about me
I don't yell, I don't pout
if you try to break me
it's going to take a lot
when times get hard I hang on tight
because at the end
I'm soft like a pillow on a winter's night
but strong as a rock!

Tranae Henderson, Grade 8
Corkran Middle School, MD

Death

I love my life too much to lose it
I'm not ready for my life to come to an end
Not now, not ready
Not ready for my story's finale
For my world to be ceased
For my heart to conclude
For my brain to stop thinking
For my eyes to close forever
For my wings to be destroyed
For my family to sob
For tears to stain my grave
For my afterlife to arise
I'm not ready yet for
Death

Shannon Garmer, Grade 8
Stevensville Middle School, MD

Guilt

Guilt is a metal chain,
Keeping you from telling the truth
And from any trouble.
You sit there,
Full of rage and anger,
Yanking harder and harder
Trying to break free
As it laughs and clutches you tighter
Even when you scream
Here and there.
It plays with you,
Hearing you moan in frustration
And finally lets you free from the torture
When everything comes spilling out.

Subul Malik, Grade 7
Rachel Carson Middle School, VA

A Flame Within

Focus,
Steady,
Aim.
I'm more than just a piece in their games.
Draw back the bow,
Kneel on one knee,
Running quickly through the trees.
A distant buzz,
Wind in my ears,
Facing all of my biggest fears.
Make a difference,
Take a chance,
They left it all in my hands.
Stories unfold,
Filled with lies,
It's all about saving his life.
Broken dreams,
A work of art.
I fire the shot,
Straight through the heart.

Dalianna Vaysman, Grade 8
Norfolk Collegiate Middle/Upper School, VA

Ode to Summer

Bright orange sun
Heat radiates down
Cold sunscreen mists the air
Dark skin,
Light hair
Warm days and cloudless skies

We count the days until you arrive
A precious three months
Of tropical vacations
We praise you every day that you are here

Cold salty water
Hot sand burns my feet
Brightly colored umbrellas for miles

You give me long days and cool nights
Barefoot in the grass
We run through sprinklers as cold as ice
And cannonball into pools.

Zoe Papadopoulos, Grade 8
Norfolk Collegiate Middle/Upper School, VA

Till You Stand Up

The stars
The moon
The sun
Space
You'll never reach it
Till you stand up

Bradley Gorman, Grade 8
Stevensville Middle School, MD

Skating

Grab my skateboard
Rush out the door
Sun is setting, orange and pink
Cold air, fingers numb
Drop down my board
Push off, once, twice, again
I'm off, wheels spinning, wind blowing
Heading to the ghetto skate park
Friends waiting
Pop up the front of my board
Rolling, turning, stopping
Trying to do a trick
Failing, crashing, tripping
Instant pain
Get back up
Trying again
Getting colder, darker
Had a blast
Going home

Ben Pufahl, Grade 7
Rockbridge Middle School, VA

Black Friday

It's a mad rush
Floods of people crowd the store
Never ending, non-stopping
They just want more, more, more

They don't care about anyone else
They just care about themselves
Grab and buy as much as they can
Everything flying off the shelves

It's best you not go
You really should stay home
It's the day after Thanksgiving
I'm surprised they're all still living

If you stay home,
You better hide, and right away
Because that time of war is here
It's Black Friday

Annamarie Hadley, Grade 8
Norfolk Christian Middle School, VA

Clouds

Flying so high in the sky
Bright as day
Dark as night
Cover the sun
Bring out the shade
Illuminating love
Sharing cheer
Holding pain

Carissa Rizzo, Grade 7
Western Heights Middle School, MD

Spring Dancer
Dress of sunflowers
Hair of roses
Eyes of cherry blossoms

She steps to the sound
The sound of the wind
The sound of the stream

Flowing with the flowers
Each arm moves
As if they were blades of grass

Leaping over meadows
Twirling in plains
Bowing to bushes

She respects the nature
The newly born nature
Which caresses her face

She represents spring
Its freedom and life
Its new beauty
Autumn Silvious, Grade 8
Lindale Middle School, MD

Unwise Decision
The vagueness in your voice
How shallow can you be?
You think you're royal
you think you're better than me?
I think you think you're the king
But I'm the queen
You think you can dictate me
Your actions are unwise
I think you need to revise
I see you changed your mind
You made the right decision
But you still need supervision
'Cause your on the path to collision
Nicole Sensabaugh, Grade 7
Rockbridge Middle School, VA

America
We came from far to be free.
We sailed across the dreadful sea.
When we landed, things got rough.
But we stayed strong and we were tough.
We built towns, we built cities.
We created 13 colonies.
The British tried to take our freedom.
A war happened and we beat 'em.
We are free still today.
We are free to roam and play.
Jacob Mallar, Grade 7
William S Cohen Middle School, ME

I'm Supposed to Be in Love with You, After All
Brown hair and hazel grey eyes,
a slab of skin,
neither chiseled nor soft
just there, existing.

That soft Mormon held my hand
and watched me cry
saw me spill my bowl of secrets everywhere.
He never forgot what they were.

That Mormon boy held my hand
and wrapped me in his arms.
He whispered scriptures from Nephi
and made me laugh.

That Mormon boy sang me songs
and played me music on his piano.
He understood what made me tick,
and looked past my outside
of one hundred and sixty-seven tired brown scars
and rat tail ribs.

I forgot every soul in the world,
but I don't need to remember the Mormon one.   He's still here.
Emma Desrochers, Grade 9
Appomattox Regional Governor's School for Arts and Technology, VA

Favoritism Bought
Equality is talked about but never really sought
What the people really want is favoritism bought
The feminists, for example, call for equal opportunity
But it doesn't seem that what they want is very equal to me.

If you don't want to be held back from financial transaction
Just because you're a woman, and you take action
Prepare to be paid more, but pick up the check on dates
Carry around our stuff while we hang out with our mates.

Equality is talked about but never really sought
What the people really want is favoritism bought
The black activists, for example, demand retribution
For the slavery to which no one alive today has made a contribution.

You speak of equality, and people being changed
But the change has already happened, and you just look deranged
You don't get special treatment because your skin is dark
Let all children equally wait in line for the highest slide in the park.

Equality is talked about but never really sought
What the people really want is favoritism bought
Embrace the past, and learn from it, remember your history
But just drop it like everyone else has and there's your equality
Paul Redling, Grade 9
Appomattox Regional Governor's School for Arts and Technology, VA

Ode to a Tiger
A tiger is fierce,
a powerful wave
knocking you down
A tiger is as fast as the speed of light,
nothing stands in its path
The tiger stalks his prey,
similar to a soldier
moving swiftly in tall grass
The tiger pounces forcefully
with no mercy
The tiger rips into the flesh,
its claws and teeth sharp like knifes
piercing through skin
The tiger tugs and pulls on the meat,
like a savage man
eating a drumstick
Once the tiger is done,
it licks its teeth and prances away
Its fur is a painting
shimmering in the night

Abby Fisher, Grade 7
The School of the Cathedral of Mary Our Queen, MD

Fire
Taste the beauty of dancing fire.
Flying high in the sky like a phoenix reborn.
Brilliant hues, all colors of the rainbow.
It dazzles those who gaze upon.

Feel the crackle of mighty fire.
The thunderous roar, you cannot ignore.
A boisterous bomb of energetic sound.
It grabs the spotlight for miles and miles.

Hear the echo of faded fire.
Drifting down like leaves during Fall.
Faint sparks, reminders of a fiery display.
The smell of smoke and ash, lingering still.

Connor Ryan, Grade 9
Homeschool Plus, VA

All or Nothing
Dribble, dribble, I charge down the lane for the foul.
I hear the whistle blow,
The ref gives me the ball for my free throw.

Coach called a time out and said I want the ball,
We need a steal on the throw to win it all.

Running back and forth…bouncing a ball,
Taking the shot or taking the fall,
The crowd looks grim, as the ball rolls around the rim.

Swish the ball is in, two points the team wins.

Samantha Loffredo, Grade 8
St Rocco School, RI

I Am This Person
I am a swimmer and 13 years old.
I wonder what life is like as an adult.
I hear I'm good with cooking.
I see my bakery opening in the future.
I want to achieve well.

I am 13 years old and a swimmer.
I pretend everything in life is ok when something is not.
I feel life is like the never ending road.
I touch chalk and get the chills.
I worry I'll fail in high school and not achieve as much as I want.
I cry when I'm disappointed in myself.

I am a swimmer and 13 years old.
I understand that life comes with challenges.
I say I want to be 27 because that's my lucky number.
I dream big and come out strong.
I try to impress people to show that I can achieve without help.
I hope for everything to fall in place in the future.
I am a swimmer and 13 years old.

Alexis Uffer, Grade 8
Mount St Charles Academy, RI

I Am a Blanket
I dream about being in a warm house.
I try to keep people warm.
I am a blanket.
I wonder if people will like my style.
I hear tapping.
I see people walking past me and talking about me.
I want people.
I am a blanket.

I pretend to dance.
I feel people touching me.
I touch peoples' hands.
I worry that people won't like me.
I cry when people ditch me.
I am a blanket.

I understand that the blanket keeps people warm.
I say people like to cuddle with me.
I hope to last forever.
I am a blanket.

Ashlee Woodward, Grade 8
Western Heights Middle School, MD

Spring
The rain starts falling the leaves start to come back
and all the animals start to come out and play.
It starts to get warmer as the seasons start to come
again. Soon it will be summer and be hot then next
year spring will rise again but soon it will start to
hibernate like a bear in the winter.

Austin Labbe, Grade 7
William S Cohen Middle School, ME

Summer Swim Team

Summer is for swimming.
It's the escape from the heat.
Every morning bright and early,
Swimming calls us to meet.

We practice hard and it pays off.
We are getting ready for our Saturday meets
To go undefeated and win our league.

Swim meets start at the crack of dawn,
With everyone looking half asleep.
But warm ups come very quickly;
The thrill of swimming is about to begin.

Hours and hours in the heat,
Laughing with our friends,
There is no end to the fun.

The relays show we are near the end;
We are all screaming, cheering, and wild.
Our relay is up the adrenaline pumping;
We swim as fast as we can from beginning to end.
We are done for today…
Until the thrill of next week.

Hayley Tate, Grade 9
Norfolk Collegiate Middle/Upper School, VA

Into the Darkened Doors

Eyes look into the darkened doors
Rumors paralyzed the young mind
Forgotten love, dreadful memories
Light fades into the dark walls
Water fills the eyes as they drag them away

If only they knew it was true
If only they knew of the love
They would not have changed
They would have kept their strength

But society changed them
Their hearts drift away from the truth
If they were told of the love
It wouldn't be like this

They would be carefree as children
No worries of the future
But their hearts stray away
Away to the darkened doors

If they were told like others, about everlasting love
They would choose to never look
Into the darkened doors

Maren Jackson, Grade 8
Norfolk Christian Middle School, VA

My Help

There is a whisper in me; it's my foe.
Battling; it is hard, but I have light.
Choice is always mine — will I stay or go?

In temptation, my resistance is low.
Though, my Father cares for me on dark nights.
There is a whisper in me; it's my foe.

The world has it and says "follow the flow…"
Blocking this is the Savior cloaked in white.
Choice is always mine — will I stay or go?

In my acquaintances, evil does show.
Whenever I see my Savior, joy ignites.
There is a whisper in me; it's my foe.

I get down too much to the last row,
Where's the hope that I can survive the night?
Choice is always mine — will I stay or go?

Where will I be when the earth stops to glow?
My father has given power to fight!
There is a whisper in me; it's my foe.
Choice is always mine — will I stay or go?

Priscilla Lee, Grade 7
Trinity Lutheran School, MD

My Favorite Game

Arms slick with perspiration
Mind distraught in concentration
Weary eyes scan the play
Hoping for a skillful relay

Then a crack rings through our ears
Our brains replay all our fears
These crucial seconds pass like hours
Over our heads, the ball does tower

Soon the ball is not so high
Plummeting down from the clear blue sky
Hearts racing with hope and suspense
Our outfielder's back is now to the fence

And then the ball's in the player's possession
And it's as if there were no recession
Cheerful yells and cries of relief
Replace the noise of fear and grief

We run to the dugout with grins ear-to-ear
In the coach's eye rests a joyful tear
And we all chant that outfielder's name
Yes, this is why softball's my favorite game

Kaitlyn Graham, Grade 7
Lake Ridge Middle School, VA

Ode to the Moon

You sit up there in solitude
Like a single leaf upon an old tree
Ready to fall and be replaced,
You seem so sad and cold all alone up in the night sky
Abandoned and sentenced to live alone in an empty world
Where your only company is the few that visit
Some are enemies that pound away at your surface mercilessly
Leaving scars that resemble that of a veteran soldier's,
The friends that do come stay for no time at all
And leave only strange symbols to remember them by,
You are like an abandoned soul longing for freedom
Striving to leave your once-great home,
But even when you are cold and alone
You still shine bright and always come back almost every night,
You change your face and color to suit your mood
From white happiness with a full bright shine
To sad darkness with no shine at all,
Even though you might be scarred and bruised,
You are soft and beautiful
And you will rule the night forever
As the bright star you are moon.

Cammy Melchiorre, Grade 7
The School of the Cathedral of Mary Our Queen, MD

Ode to Fuzzy Socks

The humble pair of fuzzy socks sits
At the top of the heap of socks within the sock drawer
Waiting and wanting to be worn,
The soft warm fabric is comforting, like a baby's blanket
The smell of fabric softener lingers on them,
Taking anyone back to childhood memories.
Blue and pink stripes jump up the sides
Inviting someone's foot to stop by for a while
And enjoy the comforts of the sock's interior.
These socks are as glorious as hot chocolate on a cold day,
And yet, no one wants to wear them.
They feel unwanted, a waste of space,
The person no one wants to partner with for projects.
They are a beet, the awkward vegetable that nobody knows
What to do with.
While the socks mournfully cry out their tears of lint,
And pray for a better future, they come to a realization
They
Have
A
Hole.

Anne Melia, Grade 7
The School of the Cathedral of Mary Our Queen, MD

All United

You know that feeling?
You get it when they come close
So close you feel their breath
Trickling down your spine
Like rain on the window of your room
Down. Down. Down.
When you get that gut feeling
Like a weight just dropped down your throat
This is the adoration everyone desires
The passion that all long to possess
The affection one aspires
It's also a need.
Not to be happy,
To be united
Together
This is love.

Gabby Cleaver, Grade 8
Sandusky Middle School, VA

Basketball

Four years ago I started to play
I wasn't quite sure on how long I would stay.
I kept trying and trying to get a shot in
Because I know my team was determined to win.

Four years later here I am in eighth grade
Thinking about all those shots I have made.
Thinking about all the practice we've done
And thinking about all the games we have won.

Here I am now my last game to play
Listen to all the fans how they shout hooray!
Seconds count down till the final seconds end
Here's to all our fans the message we'll send
"We are now the basketball champions."

Miranda Jacavone, Grade 8
St Rocco School, RI

From Hope to Despair

Hope
Optimistic, bullish
Living, breathing, standing
Filling the soul with hope, draining the soul with fear
Dying, backsliding, unreforming
Incorrigible, chronic
Despair

Aaron Grzymkowski, Grade 8
Stevensville Middle School, MD

Winter

Winter is crisp and sharp
The black ice covers the road
People slip on the ice
The ice cracks under them
I slip and fall
I can see the deer in the corner looking at me crazily
The deer feels like laughing because everyone is falling
He knows he shouldn't laugh

Erica Leland, Grade 7
Biddeford Middle School, ME

My Anna
Anna, a pale wispy blue,
Floating away, smiling askew,
A reaching hand,
Pulls away,
Silently she fades to gray,
Away she goes, adventures near,
A dream drawing fear,
The fear that came,
The fear that lost,
Anna found what she had sought,
The light had touched the blue…
Felicia Tan, Grade 7
Rachel Carson Middle School, VA

Sly Cat
Death is a sly cat
waiting, waiting, waiting
for just the right moment to strike
to catch you off guard
to attack the center of your heart
watching, watching, watching
for the moment when you turn your back
to kidnap someone you love
to see the tears fall from your eyes
Death is a sly cat.
Catherine Sherman, Grade 8
Mount St Charles Academy, RI

The Beginning of Accomplishments
I first came to kindergarten
My first experience in school
I first started learning the alphabet
And shapes like triangles
Squares and circles
I was getting smarter
Someone fell in love with me
But I was too young
Kindergarten is where all
Of my accomplishments started
Javon Sankoh, Grade 7
West Frederick Middle School, MD

Peace
Peace, peace,
What it means to me.
Peace is what the world needs to be.
Peace is happy, loving, and kind.
Peace is a beautiful state of mind.
We need peace in this time and place.
We need peace, just in case.
For in this world, you can see,
Peace, peace
There needs to be.
Keelin Kernan, Grade 7
St Clement Mary Hofbauer School, MD

Black Women
Black women are beautiful in their own way
Black women get mistreated every day
Is it our color or the way we act
One thing black people got is each other's back
Black no matter if you big small tall
Or larger we should be respected by all
Black strong beautiful women we are pain hatred take that and make something out of it
Don't just be about it
Why don't daddy or mommy love
Why do they just thug me
Never kiss or hug me
Mom and Dad I just want you to love me
Why why why is the question
Black women always stressin'
Let this teach you a lesson
And just be the best from now 'til then
Bri Reynolds, Grade 9
Excel Academy @ Francis M Wood High School, MD

Kahlil Should Rule the World
If I were in charge of the world
I'd make sure that everyone was a Detroit Lion's or Detroit Tiger's fan.
I'd lower gas prices to a nickel.
I'd give you $500 each month as your pay.

If I were in charge of the world
There'd be one day of fun school each week.
There'd be free pocket rocket razors for kids only!
There'd be no school forever when you turn ten years old.

If I were in charge of the world
You wouldn't have to go to work you automatically get paid!
You wouldn't have to wait to get a license at 16 years old.
You wouldn't have to buy things at all! Everything's free!!
Or spend a lot of money on food, cars, and clothes.
Kahlil Hasty, Grade 7
Corkran Middle School, MD

River
The river runs deep through my soul.
without a sound I quiver, shake, and moan.
I lived here once long ago with my mother, sister, and father.
I remember nights long ago on the prairie dancing, singing, and singing.
Our laughter settling in the air.
I loved them all so.
The river runs deep through my soul.
But, soon the prairie air turned to cold and sickness settled into my home.
Mother's warm smile soon faded into cold, depressed, and pale.
I soon started to despond for there was no hope on the prairie.
For the sickness had killed my fair, fair mother.
So, I lay there moaning, moaning, and moaning as my heart throbs.
I have no more.
The river runs deep through my soul.
Taylor Bradley, Grade 7
Rockbridge Middle School, VA

Your Blossom

Your petals bloom wide,
Colors so bright like rainbows,
Vibrant reds, like blood.

Rosy pink, like cheeks,
The sunbeams so perfectly
Right on your tall stem.

From winter to spring.
April showers bring May flowers,
On the grassy field.

Skylar Roberts, Grade 8
Norfolk Collegiate Middle/Upper School, VA

The Women in Gray

Though lost and confused,
They cannot be shaken.
Though mocked and ridiculed,
They cannot be broken.
Though they hide under cloth that masks,
They are brave.
They stand up for their beliefs,
And they stand tall.
They will not be unnerved by the note
That some angry Taliban man wrote
They are Afghan women, and they vote

Kristina Wise, Grade 8
Norfolk Christian Middle School, VA

Winter

I lay there in the cold winter snow
Ice melting all around

Sun shining
I can hear the birds chirping

"Chirp chirp"
"Chirp chirp"

The yard is turning green again
I wish the cold, winter snow would stay

Marisa Holzworth, Grade 7
Rockbridge Middle School, VA

Let Them Run Free!

To know them
Is to understand them
Trying to run freely
Free as the wind blows
Gazing at the moon
Howling at night
Singing the sweet music
In the midst of the night
Wolves!

Ciera Hubbard, Grade 7
Rockbridge Middle School, VA

Bruises

I bruise so easily
my mom used to hold up bananas in Safeway and joke,
this is your skin Chloe
because there are marks all the way down
My body reads like a story book
my arms yell easily with dark brown marks and ink stretches
spaces on my chest are like battlefields
my thighs are cellulite and blue veins like tattoos
and long scars on my legs prove that I'm a soldier, a warrior
my ex used to make fun of me for them,
how he could hold me and I would flinch and then wake up with bruises
upon bruises
upon bruises
but I would never laugh
I just cradle them and pray for myself, pity my marks
the way a single person could open my cover and flip my pages
my paper skin, crumpled

Chloe Thompson, Grade 8
Stevensville Middle School, MD

Dreams

I have had a lot of inspirations in my life.
One inspiration has actually changed my perspective of dreams
I have learned that even if everyone turns on you and tells you no over and over again,
You never want to give up; you have to have hope
Everyone has a dream to overcome and fulfill inside of them
Some give up but some fight for their dreams and achieve
Those who give up, live with regrets for the rest of their lives with no answers
But those who fight for what they believe in achieve further as champions.
I have gone through tough decisions in my life but I still keep walking with my head up
Even with regrets in my decisions
But I have a life ahead of me with those there to support me
Although there will be people that will envy you.
I have had hard times in life in which I wanted to quit and scream
But then I listen to my heart and realize that I have to accomplish not quit
Mistakes in your past make you stronger not weaker,
Overcoming them is what makes you a better person.

Nicole Leal, Grade 8
Holy Cross Regional School, VA

7th Grade

Looking back how seventh grade started…
How nerves cause stomachs to toss and turn.
Hoping you will be in your best friend's class.
Wondering if you'll get the teacher you hope for,
While losing sleep over grades and assignments.
Thinking will this be the best year ever?
Then you realize you're walking in
To a place of memories and the same old things.
The people, lockers, books, uniforms are all familiar
And give you comfort, but
You still wonder if what everyone says is true.
Will seventh grade be the hardest year?
Only time will tell if you'll now, but for now you're putting in your all.

Isabella Montecalvo, Grade 7
St Rocco School, RI

All I Live For
I live for the long bus rides,
I live for the uniforms that give me pride,
I live for the friendships that are made,
I live for the memories that will never fade.

Basketball is all I do
There's nothing else I want to do.
I always practice more and more,
Because basketball is all I live for.

The feeling of the crowd cheering my name,
Makes me feel like I have so much fame.
To make the winning shot,
Or block my opponent's shot,
Makes me feel like a celebrity
And gives me another memory.

Basketball is more than a game
It's the reason I have a name
All day every day is when I play
Basketball is what I live for
And absolutely nothing more.
Ariel Endicott, Grade 7
Hurley Elementary/Middle School, VA

Happy Place
Every river
Is my happy place,
The place I dream of.
The small sand mounds,
With grass growing on top,
Are where I rest my feet
After a time without the glittering waters
I call home.
The green trees around me,
Along with ferns and brush,
Hang over me.
Only slivers of sun show
In the shallow waters
Of the river.
As clouds hover under the sun,
The light disappears,
And it is a green dim.
Then the clouds pass,
And the streams of light come back.
I know this far too well.
Is this my heaven?
Ross Hession, Grade 8
Blacksburg Middle School, VA

Leaves
The leaves are changing,
They fall off and go soaring,
The wind is their guide.
Katherine Foley, Grade 8
Mount Saint Charles Academy, RI

Time Is a Beautiful Butterfly…
Time is a beautiful butterfly
That soars in the deep night sky
Its wings will never falter
And its soul will never die

Each beat of a wing is a second
Each day is a bright new flower
Every wave is a sign of strength
Every flap is a sign of power

Dancing among the winds
And soaring among the grass
Time flies when you don't want it to
And quickly does it pass

A part of its soul in every clock
And also in our hearts
And even when we are gone
Time will never part

Yet time is a beautiful butterfly
That we have only made
And forever in our humans minds
Forever it has stayed
Sneha Ravi, Grade 7
Longfellow Middle School, VA

Game Time
Passion, burning inside you
Like a fire engulfing a forest

Anxiety, slowly eating you away
Waiting for the moment you shine
Until you can't take it anymore

Excitement, flowing through your body
Giving your body the energy it needs
Pure adrenaline

Nervousness, flush it all away
Don't think about losing
That is useless
Only think about one thing, winning

Pump yourself up
Before you go out
Give yourself
The emotional advantage

I can't say anymore
Because now it's your time
It's game time
Akhil Madhugiri, Grade 7
Rachel Carson Middle School, VA

If I Were in Charge of the World
If I were in charge of the world
I'd get free video games.
I'd get free food.
I'd get free drinks.

If I were in charge of the world
There'd be no homework.
There'd be no chores to do.
There'd be no rules.

If I were in charge of the world
You wouldn't have to mow the lawn.
You wouldn't have to clean your room.
You wouldn't have to wash the car or
Eat corn, broccoli and cauliflower.

If I were in charge of the world.
Jordan Waddell, Grade 7
Corkran Middle School, MD

True Love
Let love go on forever
Because you are mine
Now that I have you
I will never let you go

I never thought
I would fall in love
With you like that
There is no one in
In this world that
Will take you away from me

Would you die for the
One you loved?
Would you cry if you
Saw me crying? Hold me in
Your arms tonight
Sara Mejia, Grade 7
Hardin Reynolds Memorial School, VA

If You Forget Me
I want you to know one thing
If I look at the crystal moon
I know our time will come soon
If I touch near the fire
You would have known my heart's desire
If little by little you stop loving me
I shall stop loving you little by little
If suddenly you forget who
I will already have forgotten you
Go ahead and forget me
Forget all the memories we once shared
Forget the fact that I even cared
Lauren Laabs, Grade 7
Rockbridge Middle School, VA

I Am a Picture Frame

Each month I possess a new memory
A memory of you and your friends,
Even your family.

I become dusty;
You have grown older.
It seems as if I have been forgotten;
I haven't been changed in months.

Soon enough I am packed in a box,
A box filled with memories.
I am taped up,

Stored away.
I will wait;
I will lie here until a new memory comes along,

A memory good enough to replace the others.
I waited and eternity for you.
When I am pulled from the box,
You place a new picture inside me.

I am here on your shelf once again,
Hosting your happiest moments.
They say a picture is worth a thousand words,
But what does that make me worth?

Megan Stracener, Grade 9
Norfolk Collegiate Middle/Upper School, VA

Where I Come From

I come from the playground,
Running and chasing others on the mulch.
Always first one picked, last one out.
Searching for others,
Pretending to have my eyes closed.

I come from first generation immigrants
Hard work is treasured.
Rice one day, noodles the next
Chinese proverbs recited around the dinner table.

I come from a family of happy endings
Happiness cannot be bought, but
Teasing and joking and laughing
If only a snapshot of our faces could be taken
Priceless

Scattered across my room
A living timeline,
A living reminder that
Although time flies and
Although I have changed,
Never will I forget;
Where I come from

Andrew Wang, Grade 9
Poolesville High School, MD

I'd Rather Be...*

Let them be as parakeets,
always fed, watched, and adored,
but contained to a cage.

I'd rather be a hummingbird, flying free
moving from one flower to another, never stopping
wind beating against my face as I fly where I desire.

To break out of the bars of my cage
to fly, exposed to the dangers
of the wide, beautiful, world.
To be beaten side to side by the wind of reality
carrying my thoughts, my differences, beyond my times of despair
or into the forest of society.

I'd rather be unnoticed, and
then ignored by everyone
than to be a bright, noisy parakeet,
growing up in captivity
where it is loved, admired, and spoiled by needy, childish hands.

I'd rather be scarred with the cuts from the trees
then to be pretty and spotless.
If I could fly, wild and free,
I'd rather be an independent hummingbird.

Melanie Foster and Katie McCarthy, Grade 8
Mount St Charles Academy, RI
*Based upon "Identity" by Julio Noboa

What Matters?

When you look at a picture do you see the frame?
When you look at a cross do you feel any pain?
When you touch cold water does it have a sting?
What matters to you?
What matters to me?

When you drop a pebble in water, what do you see?
You see, but do you think?
In the spring, flowers bloom,
And bugs come out under the full moon,
As a symbol of the love we know,
The sun's rays begin to show,
Do you see any of those?

When you catch a leaf, do you see the veins?
Or on a muddy lake full of cranes,
The clouds with their eyes full of rain,
What matters to you?
What matters to me?

No matter what tribe, country, or what we have done,
We are all humans and we should run,
What matters to you?
What matters to me?

Grace Bland, Grade 8
Westminster Academy, VA

Life Before Death*

Life is something that doesn't last forever,
You can try to make it last forever.
No matter how much medicine,
or how many machines you have,
life can only last for so long.
With the time you have left
spend it wisely because before you know it
your time will run out.
When death arrives
it makes us feel sad and upset,
because there is nothing that we can do.
When we know that the victim is out of her pain
in a better place,
looking down on us,
watching us and guiding us.
We feel better
knowing that after death…
comes life.

Taylor Conrad, Grade 9
Cab Calloway School of the Arts, DE
*In memory of my Grandmother 1944-2012

Mother to Daughter

Listen daughter, friendship for me hasn't been baking a cupcake
It has been scorched many a time
Mistaken ingredients combined together
And boy have I baked a bare cupcake,
Tasteless
But, that doesn't keep me from baking
I experimented with new recipes
Questioned a professional on why this was happening to me
Or taking a break from baking and trying something else
So don't you give up now, daughter
Keep mixing those fine ingredients
Cracking those raw eggs
And pouring that smooth batter
For friendship hasn't been baking a cupcake for me

Michelle Curtis, Grade 9
Worcester Preparatory School, MD

You Are Beautiful

How do I love thee? Let me emphasize.
I love thee even more than a bouquet.
The cars always give you the right-of-way.
In beauty contests you attain first prize.
I love you even more than the sunrise.
Plus I love how your teeth do not decay.
I love how you don't rub down the wrong way.
You are more beautiful than butterflies.
I love how you are not a wall flower.
I love how you are not very uptight.
I love how you are both sweet and sour.
You are still pretty without makeup on.
And you are even cuter than a fawn.

Emma Williams, Grade 7
Trinity Lutheran School, MD

Seasons

The season of winter is cold & blue.
The year like the fallen snow: new.
The nights are cold dark and long.
Not one bird sings its song.

The season of spring is warm & green.
Flowers begin to make themselves seen.
The days are long, the trees awaken.
Those cold winter days have all been taken.

The season of summer is hot and bright.
Every living thing basks in the light.
When the sun goes down, night is still warm.
But soon this nice warmth shall be torn.

The season of fall brings in a chill.
Slowly but surely we know it will.
Animals try to fill their den.
As the cold blue winter begins again.

Sarah McCormack, Grade 8
Holy Cross Regional School, VA

The Question

The question of life
Is the question of death
That vital moment when you take your last breath

Some believe we cease to exist
While others see our spirits in the mist
We ponder and ponder
Some forever will wonder

But really we should not worry
We are all in too much of a hurry
For whether heaven or hell
Reincarnation or nil
The answer is inevitable

Brittny Meeks, Grade 9
Warren County High School, VA

Sugar, Spice, and Everything Nice

Little girls —
The perfect little angels.
Playing with dolls and dressing like princesses
Dressing in blues, purples, pinks, and reds
Giggles and big smiles.
Smells of new Rose Buds.

Little boys —
Trouble-making little rug rats.
Playing with dirt and monster trucks.
Always making messes.
Always screeching and making noise.
Smells of dirt and the outside world.

Kennedy Gerow, Grade 8
Glenburn Elementary School, ME

Ode to the Feather Friends
Thanks for the music that fills the air.
It lets me know that you're always there.
Even if my day is bad,
Your sound of hope makes me glad.

I know I can't catch you 'cause you fly,
But that makes more color fill the sky.
If by luck you color falls to land,
Your surface feels like silk in my hand.

Your eating habits change each time.
That doesn't stop you from eating mine.
Still, thanks for getting rid of the bugs on my skin,
I think their existence is one of sin.

The presidents had a scuffle over you long ago.
To pick the one that's brave or tasty, they didn't know.
All I know was that it's your type that found,
The land to which my life is bound.

Thanks for your place on this Earth.
You have given my life all of its worth.
Morgan Kent, Grade 8
Norfolk Collegiate Middle/Upper School, VA

Stuck in the Middle
Stuck in the middle
Everyone is watching
And everyone is expecting.
They're expecting greatness.
The only thing is I can't deliver.

When I ask for help, they ignore me,
When I do badly, they wonder.
When I try, they put me down.
The good I bring isn't recognized.

In the morning I wake up put on my clothes, and my smile.
At home I change and hang it up for the next day.
I feel like it's just me, but the good news is,
I know today was today and that's done and
On the bright side tomorrow is tomorrow and that's a fact.
Christian Rodriguez, Grade 9
Norfolk Collegiate Middle/Upper School, VA

God's Love
The spirit that gives a special bond
Its love takes you above and beyond
Trials and tribulations he brought you through it
Just put your trust and love in him, that's all to it
He sacrificed his son to pay for what we've done
Do you know a friend that would do that? He's the only one
That joy and good feeling that I put nothing above
Is the comfort and protection of God's Love
Jordan Williams, Grade 9
Bladensburg High School, MD

A Day During the Harlem Renaissance
I look outside and see the city lights,
and I know that it will be a great night.
I hear people having a blast,
finally, peace at last.

Harlem is the best place for us, African Americans to be,
this is where we finally get to be free.
We play and play our magical instruments,
which show that they are magnificent.

Africans and Americans are all the same yet very different,
but all this time we were always dormant.
All we hear is jazz and good news,
which is something that we could all use.

It makes us feel happy and blessed,
and lets us all rest.
and finally comes night,
where we can all sleep tight.
Leela Ekambarapu, Grade 8
Rachel Carson Middle School, VA

47 Chromosomes of Kindness
I watch her and sigh.
I sigh because she doesn't know how to be mean
I sigh because she doesn't know how to lie
I sigh because she only knows how to love.
But no one else knows.
They don't know that her favorite food is macaroni and cheese
They don't know that she loves listening to music and dancing.
They say such cruel things
But she forgives them
She always does.
I'm not as strong as she is though.
She tells me not to worry about it
But deep inside, I wish they would know.
I wish they would know that Down Syndrome
Is the best thing to ever happen to the world.
So innocent, pure, honest, caring, kind.
If everyone had an extra 21st chromosome
The world would be a much better place.
But I stopped telling people that long ago
They never understand
Until they meet her.
Maddie Curtis, Grade 7
Rachel Carson Middle School, VA

The Zoo
The birds in the sky cry and cry,
The bears in the caves roar and roar,
The monkeys in the cage swing from tree to tree,
Until finally the day is at an end.
Jessica Turner, Grade 7
Western Heights Middle School, MD

Be the One to Listen

You all know a girl
Always a smile on her face
You never see any sorrow
Not even a trace

She's always there to comfort you
To see if you're all right
You have no idea what she deals with
What she has to fight

You treat her like she's invisible
Like an empty space
You treat her with no respect
It's written on her face

Maybe it's time
Time to change
You could make the difference
Just have your thoughts rearranged

Next time you see her
Ask if she's okay
Be the one to listen
To what she has to say
Amber Derosier, Grade 8
Admiral Byrd Middle School, VA

The Less

Life like ours is easy
But living like them is hard
We have everything we want
But they don't have what they need

We have wealth
We have clothes
We have all we desire
But what do they have

Starving, hungry, and scared
They wait for something new
Waiting for help
But it never comes

We go on and not even think
About the ones who have less than us
We have the best
And never think of the less

Maybe one day we'll think of them
Maybe one day we'll care
But that day doesn't seem soon
It never does
Jessica Beamon, Grade 8
Norfolk Christian Middle School, VA

A True Love for Bacon

It's not possible to live without you
I gave you up, it was my worst mistake
I couldn't stop because my hunger grew
A bite out of you I wanted to take

So a bite I took and it tasted good
I ate you whole, then I wanted you more
I didn't feel bad, but I know that I should
My craving grew so I went to the store

You look so gloomy, popping in the pan
I can picture you crying greasy tears
I will make it up to you if I can
I have wanted to speak to you for years

I love you so much and won't let you go
I wrote this poem just to let you know
Mitchell Baki, Grade 7
Kilmer Middle School, VA

Searching the Endless Road

Life is a mystery.
We wander through the streets,
Not knowing where we're headed
Or where this path may lead.

Young and old are on a search,
A search deep within the soul,
Looking aimlessly ahead,
For something to make them whole.

Is it love or is it peace?
The answer; no one knows.
I look and dig and scavenge,
But still I have not found
The path I'm meant to take
Or the road of which I'm bound.
Alexandra Cook, Grade 9
Norfolk Collegiate Middle/Upper School, VA

Pushed Around

Shoved, kicked, pushed around
The pain, it sends bullets through my chest
Shatters my heart into a thousand pieces
The insults that pierce through my skin
Those demons that control my every move
I am a puppet
Hanging from a string
Having no freedom
It's like being trapped inside a box
The tears flow out of my eyes
Like a waterfall
I never show the fear and pain
But inside, my heart slowly bleeds to sleep
Randy Wang, Grade 7
Rachel Carson Middle School, VA

Springtime

Dandelion fuzz drifting about,
all their seeds coming out.
Apple blossoms, bright and merry.
Lots of fruit; my favorite's cherry.
People already work with lawn tools,
while some leap into their swimming pools.
Pretty spring clothes,
big pink bows.
People jump rope,
and eat cantaloupe.
Glistening, green grass,
hopefully it will last.
Spring is my favorite season,
for millions of reasons.
Micaela McCann, Grade 8
Admiral Richard E. Byrd Middle School, VA

Chaos in the Middle Kingdom

So long ago
The dragon flag fell
And the red and black of anarchy rose
The land divided
Greed and chaos against order and virtue
Ancient unity abandoned
From east to west
North to South
No one was safe
Old foes came to seek revenge
But one day
The Middle Kingdom will again be united
By force or by speech
One day peace will return
Nick Weissman, Grade 8
McLean School of Maryland, MD

Laid to Rest

As she is laid to rest
I keep saying it's for the best
But as they lower her in the cold dirt
My heart begins to hurt
It weeps like a small dog
As gloomy as a heavy fog
Now looking around seeing sad faces
Tears running down in the same places
And as those tears hit the floor
I can't help but go to the door
Now my heart is ready to burst
As if I have been cursed
With a forever sadness
Along with some forever madness
Reece Kinsey, Grade 8
Corkran Middle School, MD

My First Love

My first love is oh, so sweet

I think he's really neat
I don't think he knows
How much it hurts when he goes
I think of him all day
I wish I knew what to say

Why do I daydream of him every night
In the bright moonlight?
Why does my heart ache
Every time I wake?
Why is it when I'm alone
I'm always reaching for my phone?

When I'm with him
I can't help but grin
That way he makes me smile
Every once and a while
When I'm at his house
I can't help but want him to be my spouse

I love him with all my heart
I hate it when we part.
Savannah Ford, Grade 7
Massabesic Middle School, ME

Broken

Shattered, our mirror lies on the ground.
Ever so silently we hold the pieces
Of our once beautiful mirror.
Could it ever be repaired?

Time after time again
We softly look at the pieces,
Not saying a word,
For it is not time.

Slowly we mend the mirror,
Hoping not to break it
Into tinier pieces.
Is it possible?

On the surface it is fixed,
But when we look into it,
The long line dividing us appears thicker,
Longer,
Harsher
Than before.
It will never be,
The mirror we once knew.
Sarah Green, Grade 9
Norfolk Collegiate Middle/Upper School, VA

Buried Alive

They sit
with muddy crucifixes
in puddles of their own
discolored saliva
Their empty, black eyes
resting comfortably
in my ocean gray ones
Through the dark, they're all I see
but they are the dark
that keeps me from the surface,
the dirt surrounding my casket,
the mud that initially dragged me below
This place has buried me alive
and the dirt is leaking into my coffin
I can feel the tons of earth above
pushing me farther down
I know there is no escape
Still, I'd rather suffocate
in my own familiar air
than with a mouthful of
old mud.
Hayley Phillips, Grade 9
Tunstall High School, VA

Mental Cage

Trapped forever, in a mental cage
There is no escape
The pain, the suffering
Of such a feeling
Full of rage
Struggling to break free
Free as a bird
To see the light
The light of freedom
But all there is
Is a dark gray
What keeps you from friends
A beckoning whisper to give up
And surrender
The feeling of gloom
Of fear
Escape from this cell is impossible
Unless you stand up
Stand for yourself
Or you feel the need to retreat
Back into the mental cage
Conall Rubin-Thomas, Grade 7
McLean School of Maryland, MD

Butterfly

Butterfly, butterfly so delicate and free
Fluttering your wings all through the trees
Your intricate designs are a sight to see
Butterfly, butterfly so delicate and free
Sienna Lee Silva, Grade 9
Charles Shea Sr High School, RI

Me, Myself, and Silence

Silence arrives
on soft
padded paws

creeps up
behind
enveloping me
in darkness

I do not run
it is too late
maybe I wouldn't
even if I
got the chance

silence is golden
so leave me be
I will stay here
in this spot

for eternity
in the silence
with the thoughts
of the world.
Mary Kate Gunville, Grade 7
Frank H Harrison Middle School, ME

Dogs

Some dogs are yellow,
Some dogs are white.
Some dogs are black,
Some dogs are bright.

Some dogs are dumb,
Some dogs are lazy.
Some dogs are smart,
Some dogs are crazy.

Some dogs are friendly,
Some dogs are mean.
Some dogs are fat,
Some dogs are lean.

My dogs hunt,
My dogs sleep.
My dogs play,
Hide and seek.

I love my beagles when they're happy,
I love them when they are sad.
I love it when they jump on me,
It makes me very glad.
Chris Cutler, Grade 8
Salem School, MD

Don't Turn on the Light

Demons in the closet,
Flashlight's in pocket,
Ghosts all in the attic,
I'm not a big fanatic,
Don't turn on the light.
Something under the
Bed, Screams in my
Head, the only sound
Are the cries of a wind
"Don't
turn
On the
light"
A shriek
from the hallway
Lights flicker and
Everything's quiet

Emily Smith, Grade 8
Stevensville Middle School, MD

I Am Sociable and Crazy at Times

I wonder how space looks in person
I hear garbage trucks and ambulances
I see sand rocks and streets
I want a dirt bike
I am sociable and crazy at times
I pretend to not be crazy sometimes
I feel good about myself
I touch my desk at school
I worry about my family
I cry when I lost my grandfather
I am sociable and crazy at times
I understand how people talk
I say nothing
I dream about going into the NFL
I try out at sports
I hope I go to college
I am sociable and crazy at times

Cameron Queen, Grade 7
Corkran Middle School, MD

I'll Always Remember

I'll always remember,
When I was a child,
The way you used to treat me,
The way that you smiled.
I'll always remember,
The way you used to guide me,
And through all my struggles,
You'd always be beside me.
And now that I'm grown,
I've turned into a young man,
And it's been because of you,
Since the second I began.

Michael Bittner, Grade 7
St Rocco School, RI

A Crush

The sweet smell of flowers
Which Ernie gives every hour
Ernie is as sweet as the sound of a dove

Mentally challenged, Ernie is
But with the help of his mom
Ernie finds Dolores at the hardware store
He falls in love
Almost every morning

With the help of Jack
Ernie's flowers grow
It takes a very long time
But finally they are left in the door crack
In Dolores' heart you hear a chime

Until his mom dies
So Ernie cries
He gets sent to another home
To find love

Kaitlyn Barnes, Grade 7
E Russell Hicks Middle School, MD

Ode to America's Game

As the fall goes on,
Tensions mount.
As two teams look ahead,
To the game that truly counts.
Army and Navy,
Two special schools.
They both want to find out,
Who truly rules.
Once the game kicks off,
They battle between the lines.
But after the final whistle,
The two sides align.
Army and Navy,
While opponents on the field.
Know their true calling,
Is to protect the country's shield.
Cadet and Midshipmen,
Forgo the fame.
To bring the country together,
Making it America's Game.

Reid Wilkinson, Grade 8
Norfolk Collegiate Middle/Upper School, VA

Elvis

Elvis is the King.
And I love to hear him sing.
You should watch him dance.
He sure can shake in his pants.
His shiny stones on his clothes.
Wish I could have been at one of his shows.

Keisha McCoy, Grade 7
Hurley Elementary/Middle School, VA

I Wish I Were a Fly

I wish I were a fly,
I could fly high,
in the sky,
but if I were a fly,
I would stink,
and that would be the link,
to my demise,
as a fly,
and if I didn't stink,
it wouldn't be the link,
to my demise.
as a fly
it would be the beginning
to the winning
of how far you could fly
high in the sky
as a fly

Dominick Lizotte, Grade 7
William S Cohen Middle School, ME

America's Heroes

Remember the long trip home
The golden torch carried by Lady Liberty
Welcoming you home
After your long struggle.

Hold your family close
And swear to never let go.

Watch the tears fall down your face
As memories flood back.

Know that you have served your country
In a way like no other.

Smile to yourself
Knowing that you are
America's heroes.

Emily Baer, Grade 8
Blue Ridge Middle School, VA

Veterans Day

V arious
E ndless
T ours of duty for
E very well
R ounded
A merican that
N ationally
S erved

D ay by day
A warding American people
Y oung and old, the privilege of freedom

Nathan Poole, Grade 8
Rivermont School-Tidewater, VA

I Am a Beautiful Butterfly
I am caring and helpful
I wonder what people think of me.
I hear whispers of my name in my mind.
I see people talking about me.
I want to go to my own world at times.
I am caring and helpful.
I pretend not to hear them.
I feel sad and upset.
I touch beautiful butterfly wings.
I worry what people think of me.
I cry when I think of the loss of my favorite Uncle Scott.
I am caring and helpful.
I understand I am a beautiful and cute girl.
I say I just wish I could be in heaven.
I dream that I could fly like a free beautiful butterfly.
I try to ignore the rumors at school.
I hope someday I can fly like a beautiful butterfly.
I am caring and helpful.
Arielle Nicole Halsey, Grade 7
Corkran Middle School, MD

Pain Is
Pain is
A feeling that is physical
You sometimes suffer

Pain is
Caused by injury and illness
It could be emotional or mental suffering

Pain is
Distressing sensation in a particular part of the body
It is a hurtful feeling

Pain is
Like pouring rain of sadness on you
Like a thunderstorm

Pain is
Everywhere
Shelby Fairchild, Grade 8
Corkran Middle School, MD

Accents
I have a teacher from New York
She's a Yankee
Talks more weird than anyone I've ever seen

She says things like
"May-o-naise"
"South Ah-mer-uh-cur"

She says "four-wheelin'" instead of
Riding four wheelers
Where is she from?
Who talks like that?
Ryan Chittum, Grade 7
Rockbridge Middle School, VA

Winter Day
The vast plain is covered in snow,
the fierce wind has continued to blow,
a storm is coming.

I see the snowflakes spinning round,
watching the wind push them down.

I'm sitting by the fire trying to warm my feet,
when I see a little boy start running through the sleet.

He's having so much fun just playing in the snow,
As I just sit and watch from my small window.
Hunter Strom, Grade 7
Biddeford Middle School, ME

Sledding
Crisp wind chills her rosy cheeks,
Powdery snow spraying at every move.

Snowflakes, blinding her,
Landing softly upon her lashes,
Knotting her wet, tangled hair.

Kids, running up the path sealed with black ice.
Parents, trailing behind, pulling worn toboggans.

A smile is plastered upon her face,
Hitting a jump, feeling triumphant.
Lauren Girard, Grade 7
Biddeford Middle School, ME

I'm Free
Like a tennis ball on a field, I'm free
The feeling of being captive is no more

Mama raised me without problems

I'm an orphan from Washington DC, for I know where I come from
And when I look in the mirror I see all the pain in my body

I feel I am free to express myself

Cause I'm like a tennis ball on a field
Cause I'm like a tennis ball on a field
Juan Carlos Sorto Bustos, Grade 9
New Directions Alternative Education Center, VA

I Miss You

I miss you
You slipped away.
And now,
I can't say all the things I want to say.
I'm sorry I didn't realize it sooner
'Cuz now it's too late.
I'm sorry for any pain I made you feel.
I messed up real badly.
I shouldn't have hesitated,
And told you how I felt.
'Cuz now there's this aching.
I was always happier when we talked.
I wish I could see you, or tell you how I feel,
'Cuz I'm dying keeping all this emotion inside.
My friends think I'm crazy for having these feelings,
But I just want to see you, or even talk to you
To tell you how I feel.
But I missed my chance because I was stupid
And acting like a snobby brat.
And now it's to late.
I miss you.

Shellby Pucci, Grade 9
Gloucester High School, VA

New Beginning

A blossoming rose is like a new beginning;
A black rose is the end.

Clouds of gray form and cry,
With a sky so sad with dripping eyes.

Rain falls softly with a steady calmness,
As the sky above is filled with darkness.

When the drops of rain hit the ground,
The sound is empty silence.

Buildings and homes are soaking wet.
Children watch the sun stretch and rise from their windows,
As everything has a golden glow.
Glitter and fallen leaves are swept and caught in the wind.
Puddles and dampened sidewalks sit in awe,

For the storm is over,
And a red rose has just begun to blossom.

Ashanti Damique Brown, Grade 9
Norfolk Collegiate Middle/Upper School, VA

Poetry Is…

Poetry is like the flow of water, the breeze in my face.
So quickly written or thought out deeply.
Poetry is the sweet smell of flowers in the springtime air
It flows out of you like a stream of thought, so easily expressed.
Most poets express love or just the beauty of life as it is.

Erin White, Grade 7
E Russell Hicks Middle School, MD

Ode to a Snake

The snake
as agile as a hawk
and become shadows as they stalk their prey.
They are like ninjas,
quick to strike.
When they strike
they are a deadly bullet.
Some are poisonous needles,
graceful enough to make a clean kill
then swallowing their meal
like a garbage truck does its own.
Some choke the life out of their prey,
as does the vacuum of space.
They are unseen.
They clothe themselves in black.
The snake is clever when it talks.
The snake is decisive.
The snake is strong.
The snake is an assassin,
silent but deadly.

JD Martinez, Grade 7
The School of the Cathedral of Mary Our Queen, MD

Pollution

Do you know what smog is?
It destroys our atmosphere,
Letting in the sun's rays, strong enough to fear.

Do you know where the forest went?
It was cut down, you see,
Scaring the animals, far away from thee.

Do you know where the stars disappeared too?
They blinked out of here,
Scared of the light pollution, that made them all clear.

Do you know what you've done to our world?
You've destroyed it,
For the money and the power, but the pollution,
You weren't able to avoid it.

If you take a step back and see what you've done,
Will the money and the power be worth it,
When we're all dead and gone?

Sarah Sallee, Grade 8
Blacksburg Middle School, VA

Waves

Waves flow all day and night
They swim through your feet
They may look small but beware their might
They keep you cool in the summer's heat
In the winter they make you cold
Waves, yes, waves are very bold

Kyle Sonneveldt, Grade 8
Stevensville Middle School, MD

Departure Day

Once upon a summer's day,
There was a man, who walked away.
When he would return, he did not say.
Where he went, I cannot say.
Oh why, oh why, that fateful day,
Did my father walk away?
With the army, he walked away.
Nothing more than goodbye to say.
Oh why, oh why, that fateful day,
That day, nothing I could say,
Would stop my father, from walking away.

Ari Goldman, Grade 8
Norfolk Collegiate Middle/Upper School, VA

Colored Glass

Through the colored glass,
I see your face,
with the tears that flood your eyes.
I know your feelings located inside,
and your pain.
I understand your cries,
and your pain.
I know your feelings located inside,
with the tears that flood your eyes.
I see your face,
through the colored glass.

Melina Marks, Grade 8
Norfolk Collegiate Middle/Upper School, VA

The Rock

I am here
I was here
Time can't destroy me
It only lets me wither
I am big
And I am small
I am short
And I am tall
Planets, galaxies, everything
I am
Rock

Dennis Engebrigtsen, Grade 8
Norfolk Collegiate Middle/Upper School, VA

Smile

I try to smile and act like everything is okay
I don't think I can do this everyday
I think I need help I just don't want it
It's my downfall
I hide under my smile
Sometimes I think I should disappear
Why can't everything just be simple
It's complicated at times
But sometimes I just need to smile

Raul Tello, Grade 7
Wicomico Middle School, MD

Ode to the Great Mountain

The great, gorgeous mountain stays strong,
While the whistling mountain grass makes a melodious song.

The great, gorgeous mountain provides cooling shade,
Over the frosty glade.

The great, gorgeous mountain is a place for a flock of migrating birds to take Flight,
Outlined by the luminous moonlight.

The great, gorgeous mountain dotted by refreshing springs,
Which have frozen due to the cold that winter brings.

The great, gorgeous mountain is a gift from the earth,
For the tiny creatures that roam its turf.

The great, gorgeous mountain is a place to share,
By humans, animals, and plants that bear,
Nothing more than a simple joy,
As they deploy.

The great gorgeous mountain will remain tall and strong,
As it should and will always belong,
To the small people below gathered in song.

Andrew Roberts, Grade 7
Cape Henry Collegiate School, VA

You

You with your messy, curly brown hair
You have those blue-green eyes and that half smile that makes me blush
You with the guitar and the notebook sticking out of your back pocket
Your hugs make my day
Boy, you are so amazing in every way
I wish you could see that
Your voice enchants me and I feel like we're the only people in the room
I know you don't realize it
But I love everything about you
I love how free-spirited you are
I can tell you everything and you always listen to me
I love spending time with you
You're the best thing that's happened to me in a long time
You light up my world
Thank you.

Kaleigh DePetro, Grade 9
Woodbridge Sr High School, VA

Words

Words are like blades
They can hurt you, or heal you
Your words can hurt someone else
If you don't watch your words you can loose someone you care about

Watch your words, and in life you will go far
Respect others, and respect what people have to say
Watch what you say to others, and others will watch what they say to you

Rebecca Elliott, Grade 7
William S Cohen Middle School, ME

Wolf

Wolf
A hunter
Silver and silent
howling at a silver sphere
running like a madman
silent and alone
unless in a pack
mean and lean
vicious sharp teeth
razor like claws
sharp attuned hearing
enhanced sense of smell
Wolf
hunter in packs
warrior without armor
carnivore
howling in the wind
faster than coyote
enhanced senses

Aden Knott, Grade 7
The School of the Cathedral of Mary Our Queen, MD

Me, Myself, Not I

I turn to the sun and see the light
But I always turn to face the shadow
The shadow of darkness

I fear the darkness
I seem to cheer up when going into the light
But it still follows me; that shadow

I will never know how this shadow
Goes into darkness
And follows me to the light

The light will always shine
As the shadow of myself follows in darkness

Faith Rush, Grade 8
Norfolk Collegiate Middle/Upper School, VA

A Permanent Mark

I am the wind. Softly singing dreams to trees.
  Driving them to deep sleep before
  Winter creeps in.
Changing the weather by moving clouds
  of feelings.
I am a pen, leaving a permanent mark
  wherever I touch. Always a reliable tool
  to keep beside
I am the moon. Reflecting the shining light of others.
  Opening a path of happiness in
  the dark, sad night.
  Leading other stars
  to do the same.

Hayun Chong, Grade 7
Kilmer Middle School, VA

Life Is a Roller Coaster

Full of twists and turns
You never know what's next
You might go up, you might go down
It might even spin you around.

Full of terror and excitement
It makes you scream and shout
You must be ready for anything thrown your way
And never have a doubt.

As you roll up the hill
The fear grows inside you
But what goes up must come down
Once you're on, you can't get off.

Conquer your fears, it will make you stronger
Face the challenges,
Don't wait any longer
Life's a gift, enjoy the ride.

Carly Porter, Grade 7
St John Neumann Academy, VA

Airsoft

Airsoft is cool because you shoot
Airsoft is fun because of friends
The smell of gas smells really bad
The sound of gas makes a big bang
The bullets are like little guys
They hit miss and sometimes even spit

Airsoft is cool because you shoot
Airsoft is fun because of friends
Out of BBs
Throw a grenade and it will make a big bang
Then you run like a man

Airsoft is cool because you shoot
Airsoft is fun because of friends

Hunter Tereyla, Grade 7
Corkran Middle School, MD

Constellations

Lying in a field, looking at the stars,
You see many heavenly bodies, even the planet Mars.
Wondering what's really up there, how pretty it must be,
You start to see an eye-opening, figure-filled sea.
Off in the very distance, you start to see a bear,
Looking at his size, you start to imagine hair.
Then what is right above you, you see a handsome satyr,
And how good of a shot he is, he could probably kill a gator.
Soon there stands a tall, firm man, suited in a robe,
Guarding the whole world below, guarding the globe.
These are some figures you may see, with your imagination,
Once you find one, give it a name, now it's a constellation.

Zachary Wheeler, Grade 7
Rockbridge Middle School, VA

Blue

Blue is...
The sky, gasping for an opening in the clouds to show the world its beauty
Rain plummeting to the ground, curious about how the world feels
The ocean, some days calm like a sloth, some days fierce like a lion
An iceberg, no destination in mind but nevertheless pushing on

Blue is...
The calm singing of a mother, luring her child asleep
An orchestra, playing one of their calmest pieces
Boat gliding in the water, making nothing but a gentle splish splash
The breath of a man, calm, relaxed, but slightly cautious

Blue is...
Tea, cool, calm, refreshingly perfect
Water, clean, clear, and necessary for the body
Seaweed, slithering down your throat carefully like a snake after being gingerly prepared to please.

Blue is...
The soft pitter patter of tears, sometimes of happiness, other times of depression
The gentle sea breeze, trying to calm a person down and let them relax
Being held by a mother like a baby and feeling safe, secure

Blue is...
A mentor, able to teach people to remain calm

Scott Dranginis, Grade 7
McLean School of Maryland, MD

Ode to the Clarinet

Oh clarinet, I see you peek out of your case, your silvery buttons polished and your bell as slick as ever.
How I long to take you out of your case and to put you together, as I gaze at your parts disassembled.
I pick you up and walk into the room, the room where I play you every week.
I pause before I gently touch my lips to the reed and blow, not too hard and not too meek.
I place my lower lip in perfect alignment with the bottom half of the reed and play an open G.
The feeling I have missed and longed for all week bursts inside of me.

I play a scale pushing my fingers down one at a time on the newly polished keys.
As the lesson ends, it breaks my heart to take you apart, I can't wait until next week.
At my next lesson, I press down the register key and put all of my fingers down, and out comes a squeak.
Not a rich, creamy sound, but a high pitched squeak.
A thousand thoughts race through my mind as I play that squeaky note. Will my teacher be irate?
Was it my clarinet's fault or was it simply mine? I'm sorry, it could never be your fault.

I see your partly open case outside the music room, your bell glistening, your barrel gleaming, and your
silver buttons shining as bright as the sun.
As I walk by you, I see you open your case just slightly more and just enough for you to smile at me.
As I leave, I see you turn around and talk to your best friends, flute and oboe.
They're left out in the hallway alone and unplayed as well, just sitting there waiting to be touched by a musical hand.
I look back and sulk about the times I've thrown your case or ripped my music because I was so mad the
sound wouldn't come out perfectly.
But it was never your fault, it was mine.

Leeann Soyka, Grade 7
Kilmer Middle School, VA

Ode to a Honey Badger

The Honey Badger
With a fiery braveness
Went out for food
Scanning the area like a hungry shopper
He found his prey,
The cobra
And as fast as a jet
The Honey Badger went into battle
They took turns striking each other
First the Honey Badger
Then the cobra
And back and forth
As if they wanted to still fight fairly
In the end the winner was clear,
The Honey Badger
Don't we all wish to be as brave as the Honey Badger
Knowing that he could die
He still does as he wishes
Like little kids when they have no fear
And they just jump in the face of danger
Just as a Honey Badger would

Jenna Notaro, Grade 7
The School of the Cathedral of Mary Our Queen, MD

The Seasons Are Forever Changing

The seasons wax and wane their way through life.
The seasons are forever changing.
Autumn sweeps in donning a dress of gold.
The seasons are forever changing.
Winter gusts bring frozen crystal and merriment.
The seasons are forever changing.
Then she swaps her robe of icicles for a
Gown bursting with daisies and tulips.
The seasons are forever changing.
The gown blossoms into fields of flowers
With the smell of fresh cut grass in the breeze.
The seasons are forever changing.
The seasons twirl as we grow old.
The seasons are forever changing.
There is one thing we know for sure.
The seasons will be changing forever.

Beverley Guay, Grade 9
Stearns High School, ME

Seasons

The rain falls like tears
Flowers bloom like a new beginning.
Sunshine shining bright in my eyes,
Breeze blowing makes me want to fly.
The wind whips, bringing joys of autumn,
Leaves falling in pretty colors.
The snow falls gracefully like a swan.
The fire burns, brings joy of winter.
Soon, this all will happen again in the New Year.

Cassandra Seifert, Grade 7
E Russell Hicks Middle School, MD

I Am Me

I am mischievous
I wonder about the kids on the streets
I hear monsters in the closet
I see ghosts in the dark
I want a tiny giraffe
I am me!

I pretend I can fly when I ride my bike
I feel the wind in my face
I touch the handlebars on my bike
I worry about what people think
I cry when I'm scared of the dark
I am me!

I understand why some people are different
I say the world needs to change
I dream that one day everyone will change for the better
I try to be nice but I just can't
I hope people like me for me and don't want me to change
I am ME!

Hailey LaFon, Grade 7
Corkran Middle School, MD

New Best Friend

I was new in school
Had a lot of friends and then it was time to move onto seventh grade
This year I got a new best friend
Her name is Brionna
We hang out all the time
We got our nails done for the first time
We went shopping by ourselves
We talk all the time
We play fight
We do basically everything together
We do stuff we're not supposed to do and get in trouble
We get mad at each other for dumb stuff
But at the end of the day
I guess that's why we're best friends.

Dejah Hawkins, Grade 7
West Frederick Middle School, MD

Innocent Lives Wasted

War is not glamorous
War is not even heroic
When there is war
All is calm and all is fine
Then the bombs, they come down unnoticed
By the poor, poor people
That disappeared in the flame
Why would a man be as vicious as this?
The differences that make me, me and you, you
All of this carnage is because someone wants the world his way
That is war
Not a fun game

Warren Chen, Grade 7
Kilmer Middle School, VA

I Am

I am a boy who plays basketball
I wonder what happened to my friends
I hear noises through the court
I want a lot of money and a small-sized bunny
I am a teenager who plays basketball
I pretend something happens that is impossible
I feel what can be felt, like skin
I touch an invisible word in the world
I worry about the dangerous fears of life, like dying
I cry about things to be cried about, like failure
I am a boy who plays basketball
I understand that life isn't fair
I say things that have to be said when needed
I dream about great things that are rich, like gold
I try not to be too bold or get old
I hope to never fail on the way through the life trail
I am a boy who plays basketball

Keontay Stewart, Grade 7
Corkran Middle School, MD

The Oak Tree

The clouds are rolling through the sky
And the bees are buzzing free
But I am laying here still looking at this lonely oak tree
Why does it look so dreary, and wood so moldy and thin?
Why have the leaves fallen off, and no birds to play on it?
I wonder about its past, and what it has seen
The pain it went through still inside; buried

I feel the power of its roots deep under the ground
And I feel the grace and beauty that is lost but can be found
Sometimes we face hard times, kind of like this oak tree
It goes dormant in the winter and then rises in the spring

We may not know what life may throw at us
But we have to find a way,
To be like the oak tree
And live another day

Eric Sisco, Grade 8
Norfolk Christian Middle School, VA

The Daydream

Summer heat finds me
sun rays gold and peach
on a heated day in summer
spent at the beach
as waves clap against the shore
the salty sea mist scatters galore
the tiny grains of sand sparkle and illuminate
as piles for my sand castle begin to accumulate
summer days seem to last forever
worries seem to be as light as a feather
as the wind whips through my hair
how I'd love to be there

Brigid Murphy, Grade 8
Mount St Charles Academy, RI

What's Love Like?

Love is like a song
It makes you happy all the time
Love is like a bird
It sings the happy song with rhyme

Love is like a riddle
You solve it, then you shine
Love is like a number
It's a ten, or sometimes a nine

Love is like an accident
You don't mean to find your perfect dime
Love is like a mistake
It happens all the time

Love is like an alarm
It wakes you up, when it's time
Love is like that bad feeling
You'll have them, they'll go, and you'll be fine

Kaelyn Thompson, Grade 7
Hardin Reynolds Memorial School, VA

Ole House

Here I stand sturdy and strong
I don't know what went wrong

Paint and flowers were always at their finest
Now I'm embraced with bushes and vines

Laughter and happiness filled these walls
Today stillness is all that answers the calls

No one will use my windows and doors
Critters are all that walk my floors

Oh how I wait for a gentle embrace
To give me back my wonderful grace

Rebekah Berry, Grade 7
Rockbridge Middle School, VA

Self-Reliance

Blindly walking
We have to trust our own instincts
We should rely on no other
Neither brother nor mother
Because until we learn to do that
We will forever be dependent
There will come a day when we have to cross to the opposite side
And there is no hand around for a guide
Then we will ponder
How is it that I do not know how to do this?
But the answer will hit us
Square in the face
You were carried through the whole, entire race

Joanna Olaoye, Grade 7
Samuel Slater Jr High School, RI

Flash of Hope

Ba-boom.
The clash of lightning, the streak of hope,
whose wind went whistling way, way west.
Best time to run, best time to try,
I ran like a fox, soared like an eagle,
let the wind carry me away from shackles of fear.
Ba-boom.
That flash was all I needed, needed,
a sign that the spirits were at my side.
If only my Pa could see me now,
doing what he had dreamed of doing,
what all of my kind had dreamed of doing.
Ba-boom.
I could hear the clatter of hooves behind me,
ca-clomp, ca-clomp, ca-clomp, ca-clomp,
but the spirits and I were too stealthy,
as I ran straight north to heaven,
as I ran straight north on the runaway train.
Silence.
The hooves had stopped, the lightning had calmed,
I was here, I was at heaven.

Justin Turner, Grade 7
Rachel Carson Middle School, VA

Day Dream

As she looks out the window
She loses her grip on reality
Her mind wanders to a place
Where she has dreams she can chase
It is too hard for us to find
She has almost forgotten the world she has left behind
It is her fairy tale
Her own story
The way she wants it to be written
Here she is in her glory
But this is not real
No matter how true it does seem
This is all a figment of her imagination
A world of her own creation
This is just a day dream

Sofia Cadden, Grade 8
St Rocco School, RI

Two Foods I Like

One of the foods I like is cake, my favorite treat.
After supper, that's what I'd eat.
I would find one in my lunch box,
and I'd eat it faster than a fox.

Another food I like is pizza.
It's so tasty, mama mia!
With some pepperoni and cheese.
Now I'm hungry, so can I have a slice please?

Caleb Estep, Grade 7
Hurley Elementary/Middle School, VA

A Soccer Field Is a Battlefield

A soccer field is a battlefield.
The midfielders and forwards go to battle at the start of the game.

The goalie is their leader and commander.
The refs make sure everyone is safe.

You face off against the other team to see who is victorious.
Strategically, your team has to break down their defense to win.

Every shot on goal is a bullet just barely missing its target.
Punting is sending a volley of arrows back at them.

If their goalie lets a goal slide in, it's a little skirmish won.
Being ahead is momentum for your team to keep on pursuing.

Every substitution is reinforcements.
Having an all-offense strategy is a suicidal or successful mission.

When you win, you know you have accomplished your mission.
Losing is defeat.

Inessa Cooper, Grade 7
St John Neumann Academy, VA

Music

Music is such a beautiful sound
Some instruments are straight and some are round
Some music is very loud
But that is what pleases the crowds
Music can even be when a rooster crows
Tubas can hit notes that are really low
So many sounds to choose from
I don't know which is my favorite one
Music can be delicate and sweet
Just as candy is a sweet treat
Some people like to learn how to play the drums
People sing the blues when they are glum
I am learning how to play the guitar
And guitars are mainly used by rock stars
When we hear of rock stars
And we hear their music from near and far
Don't forget how they got where they are today
They practiced music most of their days
So remember to try really hard
And maybe one day you could be a famous rock star

Bryan Cotellese, Grade 7
St John Neumann Academy, VA

My Family Is a: Flower

My mom is the stem: keeping us up high
My sister is the leaves: giving us support
My dad is the roots/soil: making us shine bright
My sister is the center: holding us together
I am the petals: showing the love and beauty in my family

Carmela Gerlach, Grade 7
Western Heights Middle School, MD

Beach

I shuffle towards the water,
It covers my feet,
Then slips away only to return again.
The sand is soaked,
And as I walk my footprints form little puddles,
Then become erased by the persistent waves.

I look up to see the sunset.
I stare at it in awe of its beauty.
The sky is shades of pink and orange,
Brushed on the sky,
As a painter would brush paints on a canvass.

I inhale a breath of the salty air,
And a smile forms on my face.
Awestruck,
I stand there,
Basking in its beauty.

Courtney Hodge, Grade 8
Blacksburg Middle School, VA

The Hunt

As I looked, I could not believe what was in sight;
It was two male deer in a fight.

Their horns were gripped tight;
Their legs continued, always a flight.

One deer had lots of fear,
But one was graceful and queer,

Then the gun lead into thunder,
As the deer descended struck with wonder.

The fierceness flowed out one deer's eyes,
As he left him meek and large and wise.

Gentleness relaxed his head,
As the twelve point deer fell over dead.

Bryce Rolfe, Grade 7
Harrington Elementary School, ME

You and I

You have always made me laugh and smile
I have always made you go the extra mile

You will be there in everything I do
Also, I will always be there for you

You and I have been friends from the start
That means you have a special spot in my heart

You and I have had the best of times and
Nothing can break us apart

Ivorie Dickinson, Grade 7
Massabesic Middle School, ME

Ode to My Heart

My heart, so near, so dear to me
Keep me alive and we shall see how well this poem turns out to be.
Now listen to me and stop what you are doing.
NO! NOT LITERALLY!

You are here with me by day.
You are here with me by night.
When I am happy, you beat with delight,
But when I am scared, you stop with fright!

When I walk, you are at a steady beat,
But when I quicken my pace and my feet,
You beat like the heart of an athlete.

My heart, you beat so loudly.
You beat very loudly.
I'm proud that you are my heart,
And I really hope we never part.

Anna Mishoe, Grade 8
St John Neumann Academy, VA

Memoirs of Those Passed

Hell was once a cat,
But no longer lives he here.
Now it is the rat,
Of Doomsday drawing near.

Those days once so clear;
Forgotten
All we see is fear,
Kings of men now rotten.

To Hell, march our kin,
To war, this faint, dull star of Hope.
Break to freedom, out of this skin.
Life ends; there is no time to either change or cope.

Darkness comes behind the mourning dove,
Our only hope, of what we once called love.

Lauren Pettit, Grade 8
E Russell Hicks Middle School, MD

The Great River

I am a small creek burbling down a slope.
I reflect whatever looks at me, only distorted,
So that nobody can quite tell exactly what they are looking at.

I am a stream running down a mountain.
I quickly flow to wherever I am going.
And it takes a lot to shift my path.

I am the great river gouging a canyon into the earth.
Unstoppable, my waters toss and turn,
As they flow down, into the future.

Champ Dietzel, Grade 7
Rachel Carson Middle School, VA

Months of the Year

January is the month for hot cocoa, snow angels, and snowmen, and when it's over, I wait anxiously for it to come again.
February is the time for valentines, chocolate, and friends, and when we have fights, we must make amends.

March is the month of poems, softball, and warm weather, and when we all have troubles, we should all help one another.
April is when the sunlit spring truly starts, and when you can go to a museum and look at the arts.

May is Mary's special month, when we crown her with blossoms, every time I see her with the crown, she looks respectfully awesome.
June is when we all leave school and go to the beach for laughs, because school to us kids is a snooze and a half.

July is my birthday; it's on the very last day, all of my best friends come to play.
August is when school starts up, oh yay! But at least my next homeroom teacher is Mrs. K.

September is when the weather starts to get chilly, and at night it's usually rainy.
October is full of ghouls, pranks, and treats, but then you get sick because of too many sweets

November is a time to be grateful for everything we own, it's a time to be with family, not alone.
December is Jesus' birthday to celebrate with great happiness, because He brought the light that shined on our darkness.

Angela Aleman, Grade 7
Most Blessed Sacrament Catholic School, MD

Sounds of the Game

In the distance rings the encouraging almost musical chants, from the sideline.
As the ball is tipped the crowd roars to life.
Bounce, bounce, the ball in constant collision between itself and the floor.
Listen closely for the squeaks of colorful leather shoes as they dance across the shining floor.
As a deep voice rained from above over the crowd, announcing the players and the statistics.
As you hear the abrasive whistle blow, it signifies a change in the game.
And the slap of the ball and the yell of break to start the play.
As the ball then flies over the outstretched hand of the defender and gracefully falls into the net.
And finally as the buzzer rattles it signifies the end of the game.

Daniel Allen, Grade 7
Rockbridge Middle School, VA

Zipper

You might like it
Or you might not like it
It's okay to be scared
Just ask a friend to get on with you
So it's less scary
You hear the people screaming
You see it spinning around
It's not as bad as the Samurai
It's not so bad
Try it out
It's okay
You may not feel good when you get off
But it's okay
You'll have fun
You see the people on the ground
You hit your head on the seat
You feel it spinning around
When you get off you feel a little dizzy
But at least you had fun

Kayla Fullerton, Grade 8
Corkran Middle School, MD

The Darkness Inside

I'm caught in darkness
It is tearing at my mind
I cannot break free

Noah Mata, Grade 8
Holy Cross Regional School, VA

Spring

Spring is here at last
Birds in the sky are chirping
I am so happy

Lane David, Grade 8
Holy Cross Regional School, VA

Flower Bud

flower bud will grow
little baby inside it
still has far to go

Lily Finch, Grade 7
William S Cohen Middle School, ME

At the Beach
Waves crashing down,
People all around.
Seagulls squawking,
Children gawking,
Sand in my toes,
Sunscreen on my nose!
Saltwater spray,
We're not at the bay!
Footprints going on and on,
Swimming and surfing all day long!
Maybe build a sand castle,
Enjoy relaxing without a hassle.
Seashells, dunes, and jellyfish,
If I could just have one wish,
I'd ask for something in my reach,
A family trip to the beach!
Gabriella Barbieri, Grade 7
All Saints Catholic School, DE

Geometry
You are composed of many pages
Pages that read terrible things
Things unknown to all who've tried
Who've tried to conquer your evil ways
Ways that have torn down many
Many brilliant-minded individuals
Individuals who never speak
Never speak of their experiences
Experiences of grief and paralyzing horrors
Horrors of epic proportions
Proportions too epic
Too epic for faint-hearted fools
Fools who have attempted and failed
Failed to unlock your secrets
Secrets known only to you
Bailey Jones, Grade 8
Norfolk Collegiate Middle/Upper School, VA

Moonlight Walk
They Walk
down to the river
under the moon.

The bright moon
covers the secret walk,
to the dark mirror-like river.

The shimmery river,
reflects nothing but the moon;
hiding the strangers walking.

The strangers walk
under the moonlight to the river,
in the dark of night.
Tyler Smith, Grade 8
Norfolk Collegiate Middle/Upper School, VA

Football*
Football is fun,
Even though the season is done.

The immense pressure,
Of winning or losing,
So others don't think
Our skill is reducing.

All of the eyes on us,
Wondering if we will win,
Doubting our strength
Our strength from within.

As our adrenaline rushes,
Our hearts pounding,
And because we won,
People call us astounding.

Football is fun
Even though the season is done.
James Georgieff, Grade 7
St Clement Mary Hofbauer School, MD
Inspired by Rose Fyleman

Forgiven
I forgive you for the pain that may transcend the years
I forgive you for causing those sorrows and fears
And though sometimes we shattered apart
Calluses were cut away from our hearts

And after the fight came the redemption
As sunshine follows the storm
We drew together and it knit us close
But scars were left on our hearts

What doesn't kill you makes you stronger
What doesn't destroy preserves us longer
Though marks from the fight make bands 'round my heart
Trust can be built and we'll have a new start

For time is a balm and God a healer
And together we will mend
Scrubbing away the hurt and the pain
A family, always forever
Megan Pierce, Grade 9
Home School, VA

Gold Fever
Cities of dust lay still.
Gold's mission, temptation,
Leading man's soul to damnation.
Evil deeds both lost and forgotten.
Sunny Cushing-Spiller, Grade 9
Lee High School, VA

February Wonderland
Sugar crystals
Rain from the sky
Clear and cold and crisp.
They catch the pale sunlight,
All fluffy and white,
Whispering with a lisp.
An icy wind guides them
As harsh as a whip
Between snowy, smoky clouds
Down toward land
Where skiers have the upper hand.
They stop
And resolve instead to swipe a snow angel
To send back to the pristine ivory sky.
Gladly do the heavens
Welcome new additions;
And in return, they sigh,
Releasing their polar flurries
Unto those who love them most,
Those who hail the frost,
Those who love the slopes.
Maria Bernal, Grade 8
Trinity School, MD

Lost

I see hundreds of students
different sizes, shapes, and colors
but no one looks like me
everyone is walking around to their classes
but I don't know where to go
I here the late bell ring
I see the hallways clear
I'm so lost and don't know where to go

Daejah Melara-Keels, Grade 9
Bladensburg High School, MD

Grades 4-5-6 Top Ten Winners

List of Top Ten Winners for Grades 4-6; listed alphabetically

Ashutosh S. Bhown, Grade 5
Duveneck Elementary School, CA

Ashley Chou, Grade 5
Bowen School, MA

Valerie Ho, Grade 5
Dingeman Elementary School, CA

Sierra Kolodjski, Grade 4
East Bethel Community School, MN

Layla Razek, Grade 6
The Study School, QC

Niyati Shah, Grade 6
PCrossRoads Middle School, SC

Michael Shragher, Grade 5
Our Lady of Mount Carmel School, PA

Crista Thyvelikakath, Grade 5
White Eagle Elementary School, IL

Olivia Wagner, Grade 6
Jefferson Middle School, PA

Madelyn Wolf, Grade 6
Mount Nittany Middle School, PA

All Top Ten Poems can be read at www.poeticpower.com

Note: The Top Ten poems were finalized through an online voting system. Creative Communication's judges first picked out the top poems. These poems were then posted online. The final step involved thousands of students and teachers who registered as the online judges and voted for the Top Ten poems. We hope you enjoy these selections.

Aunt Faith

Aunt Faith I adore you.
It was sad when you died.

I talk to you every day now.
Jessica is sad with out you.

Grandma takes great care of them.
Jessica looks at your pictures all the time.
Josh misses you…I miss you.

We all miss you.
Ashauna Boykins, Grade 4
Featherbed Lane Elementary School, MD

Holocaust

When I sadly look out the window
I see the world
but it seems like only
yesterday
I was frolicking with my family
And now we're separated
but I get a sigh of relief
When I live to see tomorrow
then when it's my time
I know that
I was good
Tyrone Word, Grade 6
Monelison Middle School, VA

Beauty

Mirror, mirror for what do you see
but that's not your choice
It's really for me.

This is what I think
That the beauty within
Is the one that will truly win.

Again, and again
The beauty that wins
Is the one that comes from within.
Rodrigo Ibanez, Grade 4
Hebbville Elementary School, MD

Nature as I See It

A dark, murky puddle
Small, lonely and undisturbed
Calm in the cool breeze
Long, wide, deep black lake
Waves at me in the strong breeze
Many kinds of colored fish
Grass sways in the breeze
Full of life in the open meadow
No trees, lots of space
Zachary Wilkins, Grade 5
H M Pearson Elementary School, VA

Love

love is love meant to be shared
love is a rose waiting to be found

love can be at any moment for love is love
love can be at any second for love is love

love is love meant to be shared
love is a rose waiting to be found

love can be at any moment for love is love
love can be at any second for love is love
Aria Jarsocrak, Grade 4
Featherbed Lane Elementary School, MD

What Do You Do in Your Spare Time

What do I do in my spare time?
You ask,
I journey to a distant planet,
Protect the universe,
Ride my bike,
Play video games,
Fight for justice and freedom.

How do I do these things you ask?
I'll tell you,
Another day
Anthony Johnson, Grade 6
Magnolia Elementary School, MD

Friends

Friends can be mean.
Friends can be nice.
Friends can be sad.
Friends can be glad.
Friends can be bad.
Friends can be good.
Friends can go over the hood.
Friends can always work it out
Like Trinity E. and me do now
Trinity E. and me are friends
And always will be
Rebecca Frazier, Grade 4
Courthouse Road Elementary School, VA

Colors

What are colors?
Colors are feelings
Colors are symbols
Red is angry or love
Blue is sadness or sky
Green is jealousy or grass
Orange is a warning or fall
All the colors in the sun's rays make white
White is peace
Hank Valentine, Grade 4
St Christopher's School, VA

Environmentally Safe

Recycle everything you can,
Cardboard, boxes, cans, plastic,
Paper, bags, and glass,
That would be fantastic!

Reduce air pollution,
Use public transportation.
Walk, carpool, or bicycle,
Bypass the gas station.

Reduce water pollution,
Keep toxic chemicals out of a stream.
Use natural and eco-friendly cleaners,
That should be everyone's dream.

Reduce soil pollution,
Limit use of fertilizations in your yard.
Use organic alternatives when possible,
It's also safer for your St. Bernard!
Cassandra Thompson, Grade 4
St Clement Mary Hofbauer School, MD

Scuttle

I scuttle
I scurry
I leave in a hurry
To get to the prey
In the saltwater spray

I snip
I snap
But my arms flap
With the weight
Of my
Claws going
Snip snap snap

Lobstermen hate me
Because I get in the way
Of their fine fishing day
But in the end
I always get away
Hadwin Belcher, Grade 6
Hebron Academy Middle School, ME

Rose

I may not be the one
You've been looking for
For, I am not a rose
Beautiful and strong
I am a dandelion
Made for dreams
No, the sun doesn't shine for me
But I don't ask it to
Marina Seibert, Grade 6
Mortimer Y Sutherland Middle School, VA

River
White river rapids
Flowing, gushing, paradise
Fast paced place to live
Jack Thompson, Grade 5
St John Neumann Academy, VA

Home
A country with pride
Flag glistening in the sun
Our troops guarding us
Asa Castleberry, Grade 5
St John Neumann Academy, VA

The Tree
The humble tree sits
Shading the people below
Helping, not trying
Everett Aguirre, Grade 6
Immaculate Heart of Mary School, MD

Test
Test day butterflies
Shaking, twisty in my seat
Bubble what I know
Bengatha Dugueh, Grade 6
Magnolia Elementary School, MD

Butterflies
Butterflies flying.
Pretty colors everywhere.
Landing on flowers.
Yasmine Ward, Grade 4
Hebbville Elementary School, MD

Nature
Emerald green leaves
Glistening in the bright sun
Very beautiful
Farida Abubakar, Grade 6
Magnolia Elementary School, MD

A Pleasant Change
Falling to the ground
I watch a leaf settle down
In a bed of brown
Scott Mason, Grade 6
Magnolia Elementary School, MD

Me, Myself, and I
Me, myself and I
Standing straight, in my own world
Independent, free!
Vanessa Koroma, Grade 6
Magnolia Elementary School, MD

My Cut Head
My cut head, it's so fragile.
The reason it's cut is because I'm not agile.
When I tripped, my head ripped.
And when it ripped, I flipped.
Now every time I peered in the mirror,
I feel like I'm feared.
So now all I can think of in my life,
I'm glad it wasn't cut with a knife.
In the ER I didn't whine or cry much;
That day I realized it's just like a car, the doctor pulled the clutch.
From now on I'm a lot more careful and cautious, but when I got to the ER I felt nauseous.
My cut head is not a treat, but it's a hard story to beat.
Cody Ferguson, Grade 4
Tazewell Elementary School, VA

White
White is such a beautiful color!
You can hear the soccer ball being kicked!
Hear that baseball being smacked.
But don't forget those bowling pins being knocked down.
You can feel the gliding and scraping on that ice rink!
White makes you feel the freezing snow.
Just taste those squishy, white marshmallows!
You can't forget the cold milk splashing down your mouth.
Take a moment to just relax and watch those puffy, white, slow moving clouds!
Lets take a trip to Alaska and feel the snowflakes dancing down the sky.
Don't you think white is such a beautiful color?
Lauren Dohoney, Grade 4
Immaculate Conception Catholic Regional School, RI

My Wish for the World
Wishes for world peace can be hard when there is no one there to support it.
Don't let people tell you what to do and what not to do.
Out in the open you hear people cry but why?
They should be full of joy.
Not sad tears but tears of joy.
Run away to a place far away.
People can be happy with little to spare.
Love is in the corner of the world but some not as much as others.
People run with joy only to see the sadness ahead.
Dive into it without a sound trapped in a place where all around laughing every day.
Samantha Focazio, Grade 6
Floyd T Binns Middle School, VA

7 Special Days
Long, long ago God created the world we know.
First, He created the light, with all his might.
Then He made the stars, moon and sun, and boy it looked like fun!
Next He separated the sky from the land and made them all by hand.
Then He made the fish and the birds and made them in herds.
Then He made the animals the same and created Adam who gave them a name.
On the 7th day the sun had shone and God said my work here is done!
Andrew Barrios, Grade 5
Church of the Redeemer Christian School, MD

Ballin'
Coming down the court
Just past LeBron James
I jumped in the air

It's a bird
It's a plane
It's Superman

Going in for the dunk
I'm F-L-Y-I-N-G
Uh, oh, BOOM, threw it down.

Three seconds on the clock
Sailing up the court
My team passed me the ball

They've left me open for 3
I couldn't have done it without my TEAM!
Anthony Davis, Grade 6
Magnolia Elementary School, MD

Painting
I have my brush
I have my paint
And the board
I'm ready to start
Brush, brush, brush
I paint and paint
A sun, clouds, grass and a house
I mix and match colors
What a masterpiece
It is cool, awesome
I show it to Mom
It's wonderful
I show it to Dad
He said it's great
I say it's good
Because I painted it
For you and everybody
In the world
Keyon White, Grade 4
Featherbed Lane Elementary School, MD

The Laundry Mistake
One day I made a laundry mistake.
I put the whites and pinks together.
When I put them out to dry
They did not look right on the line.
My mother's best white shirt
Looked like a pink shirt.
My dad's best vest looked like a pink dress.
My parents weren't happy with me
So I had to sleep in the dog house
For a week!
Magdalene Meek, Grade 4
Greater Portland Christian School, ME

My Cat
My cat is fat.
My cat is lazy.
All my cat does
is sleep and eat.
My cat is really
out of shape. I
really think my cat
ate my old cat.
Lilly Marie Peveto, Grade 4
Courthouse Road Elementary School, VA

Birthdays
B elieve in yourself
I ce cream is yummy!
R eceiving gifts
T ime to eat cake!
H aving fun,
D ancing to music,
A wesome presents!
Y ears pass quickly by.
Katy Hernandez, Grade 5
Gaithersburg Elementary School, MD

Who Are You?
I know you're there
I know you see me
I hear you're laughing through the air
Why do you watch my pain and tears
As if it is your holy thing?
You enjoy my pain, blood and tears
You love when I cry, and laugh when I do
Who are you; are you even human?
Xavier Sparrow, Grade 5
Rosemont Forest Elementary School, VA

Moises
Moises,
Kind and helpful,
Loves video games
Hard working
Student
Likes Legos,
Loves pizza, tacos and hamburgers
Enjoys Harry Potter and *Star Wars*.
Moises Zelaya, Grade 5
Gaithersburg Elementary School, MD

Skittles
Skittles are good
And they are sweet
They really are a tasty treat.
They come in many different flavors,
They're a candy that I favor.
They have a sweetness that I savor.
Shylvine Nchang-Lum, Grade 4
Gaithersburg Elementary School, MD

The Huge Dog
There once was a huge dog
But we called him a hog
He slipped on ice
And fell twice
When he couldn't see in the fog.
Rhoedane Simpson, Grade 4
Hebbville Elementary School, MD

Family
Relation
Loving, crazy
Annoying, caring, trusting
Always there for you
Family
DaiJordan Brown, Grade 6
Floyd T Binns Middle School, VA

I Feel
I feel pain when I fall or get hit
I don't care
Because I don't feel the pain
I don't feel anything
But my heart and soul aches.
Courtney Gibbs, Grade 5
Rosemont Forest Elementary School, VA

Love
Love is the sun
Love is the cool breeze
Love is the summer fun
Love is always not due
Love makes you freeze
Alexandra Epstein, Grade 5
Rosemont Forest Elementary School, VA

Soccer
Soccer
Athletic, lively
Kicking, sprinting, laughing
Love it so much!
Sport
Jacqui Taff, Grade 6
Immaculate Heart of Mary School, MD

A Boy from France
There was a boy from France
Who had trouble wearing his pants.
He went to the outlet
To buy an outfit
And that's what made him dance.
Ralph D. Carter, Grade 4
Hebbville Elementary School, MD

Angels in Heaven

I was in heaven
I was one of the angels
We play music for the Lord
The doves are listening to our music

Our Lord is always happy with us
He loves all His angels
We worship Him and praise Him
We love Him with all our hearts

We are glad that He made this wonderful heaven
It's a wonderful place that is amazing
We thank the Lord and we love Him dearly
We will be there for Him like He was for us

Everyday I sing to Him and play music for Him
He always cares about us
Our Lord is our Sovereign Savior
We are His angels always

Alexis Rae Antola, Grade 5
Church of the Redeemer Christian School, MD

Where Beauty Is

After a hard day of work
I hang up my dirty apron
I need to find something
Something called beauty

When I rest my stiff body
I think and think
Finally I decide
Where beauty is

It is where grass sways carefully
Where vivid colors surround the setting sun
Where twinkling stars begin to shine
Where I can sit and rest my body

Where the soft breezes awaken the moon
Where the earthen ground is soft with moss
Where a sweet tune can come out from a bird
Where beauty can grasp me there forever

Jessica Shi, Grade 4
Matoaka Elementary School, VA

If I Could Fly

Sometimes I wish, in the air I could fly,
like a bird, with my wings, I would soar through the sky,
I would leap with my might and fly straight through the air,
the wind would go by while blowing right through my hair,
I would feel a pumping, coming in through my heart,
faster and faster, going fast like a dart,
I would land on the ground knowing that I am new,
but that's only if my wish would forever come true.

Kyle Mendez, Grade 6
Paul L Dunbar Middle School for Innovation, VA

Beach Days

Beach days are fun, the waves are fun.
The waves go crash, smash on my toes.
My younger brother screams "Aaaa" and I laugh.
My family is happy and I enjoy that.
While the day lasts I sit in the sun, climb on the rocks
After that I take a swim the waves swish over my head
I see a fish and swim with it.
The day goes by fast and my family laughs.

Lydia Espling, Grade 4
Greater Portland Christian School, ME

Courage

Everybody has courage
They just don't know where it is in them
For some people it's easy to find but others it's difficult
People think it's just some word
All courage is being brave without having fear
Everybody has fear in them but there are different fears
Bottom line: we all have it and big or small
There is courage for all

Ford Burke, Grade 5
St Christopher's School, VA

The Big Game

The big game is about to start
Fast beats coming from your heart

The ball tips off and the crowd goes wild
This is no place for a young child

You think to yourself, who is going to win?
But all you know is it's going to be close in the end

Alex Vaught, Grade 5
St John Neumann Academy, VA

Bold Cold

I've got a cold.
It's very bold.
It's not leaving me.
I take medicine you see,
But it's never leaving me.
So I've got to cough every day and sneeze for awhile.
But somehow, I still have a smile.

Adam Dillon, Grade 4
Appomattox Elementary School, VA

Life

Life is like a young child
Trying to draw a spiral
Each curve different from the next
For life, though worthy
Is only a fleeting illusion
Forever unsure whether to repeat good or bad
So forever changing, forever unsteady.

Heather Parkin, Grade 5
Woodlin Elementary School, MD

Urban Rhythm
A song
sang through the night
violins wailing
trumpets roaring
pianos screaming

structures shook to the beat
cars drove to the rhythm

day after day
verse after verse
the flawless song played on
shiny cars kept driving
skyscrapers kept shaking

then
it stopped

one day
it will start again
Connor Galardo, Grade 6
St Brigid School, ME

Love Story
We laughed
We cried
We loved each other and
We promised to stay together until we died
But then one day
It all became strange
She left me alone
And she said I had changed
I didn't understand
It all happened so fast
I was sad because
I knew it wouldn't last
I came down the street
Then I saw her walking
With her new boyfriend
Laughing and talking
But that was 2 years ago
Now I've found true love at last
I am happier than before
And I never think about the past
Devin Austin, Grade 6
Monelison Middle School, VA

Planet
P laying kids
L oaded with wonderful people
A lways spinning
N ot perfect
E verlasting
T he place I call home
Ben Stephenson, Grade 6
Floyd T Binns Middle School, VA

Candles
Candles are bright
Candles are for when
Your electricity runs
Out of energy.
Candle, candle, candles.
Karianna Carcamo, Grade 4
Featherbed Lane Elementary School, MD

Beach
B eautiful weather.
E normous waves.
A t the water's edge I sit.
C louds are fun to watch.
H aving lots of excitement.
Jaquelyn Ruiz, Grade 5
Gaithersburg Elementary School, MD

Unique
I am a person who defines unique
I have eyes as blue as the sky
I am thin and have freckles who am I?
I am Mercedez with a z not an s
A person you can call unique!
Mercedez McMillin, Grade 4
Featherbed Lane Elementary School, MD

Skate
S kate parks
K ids having fun
A wesome tricks
T ony Hawk is one of the best
E ngaging in trick to trick
Ikem Okoro, Grade 4
Gaithersburg Elementary School, MD

School Is Fun
School is fun!
School, I like school!
My favorite part of school is lunchtime.
And when I see Mrs. Nettles,
I know I'm going to have a great day!
Hunter Pugh, Grade 4
Courthouse Road Elementary School, VA

Batman
Throughout the shimmering gold,
There once lived a man who was bold.
He fought for the good,
As I guess that he should,
Fighting for justice for young and old.
Kevin Truong, Grade 5
Gaithersburg Elementary School, MD

Honor
A convoy of trucks
Lines up at the school

Support American pride
Honor fallen soldiers

Kids from all around
Different elementary schools
Gather

The trucks will bring wreaths
To Arlington
One for every grave

To honor
To mourn
To believe
Patrick Griffin, Grade 6
St Brigid School, ME

Friends
Friends are enjoyable.
Friends are like stars,
Making their own light.
They care for you,
Like I take care of my pet.
They help you,
Turn the worst times to good times.

They make you happy,
Like a sunny day.
They are like a bunny,
Hopping in the sun.
Friends make you happy,
Like getting straight A's.
They listen
To every word you say.
Jozie Wilson, Grade 5
Tilghman Elementary School, MD

Pools
Boy do I like a big pool.
So much room to play.
When swimming I feel like I'm flying.

We're having a pool duel.
Hitting and swimming.
Thrashing and lashing.
Fighting like people in the UFC,
But still love each other as deeply as can be.

After swimming and fighting,
All tired and wore out,
Me and my brother worked it all out.
Clayton Tyler, Grade 5
Tilghman Elementary School, MD

My Cat Is Like a Car
My cat is like a car,
running and sleeping,
running in the wind,
sleeping in the dark.

A car is like my cat,
sitting in the park,
waiting for someone,
to take them before dark.

My cat is like a car,
loves to get all dirty,
before they get all pretty,
in the rain and snow.

A car is like my cat,
a fun time all the time,
a fun time here,
a fun time there,
the cat and car are similar.
Joel Van Tassell, Grade 6
Massabesic Middle School, ME

The Dictionary
I have a lot of words for nerds.
I am as thick
as a brick.
I define a line and time.
I am stuck on a shelf
all by myself.
Not your average book
But I can be on a Nook.
I am a valuable resource
for every college course.
I am found in a school
sitting on a stool.
I am filled with facts
not snacks.
You can study with me
before every spelling bee.
There is no hope that
I will fit in an envelope.
It could take ages
to flip all my pages.
Jacob Winkler, Grade 6
Archbishop Neale Elementary School, MD

Hearts
H uge and red
E asy to break
A lways beating
R eady to love
T rue love
S trong and safe
Demetrius Powell, Grade 5
Rosemont Forest Elementary School, VA

I Am
I am a girl
Who loves kittens
But hates green beans.
I am a person
Who likes to swim
But hates to snowboard.
I am a pet owner
Who likes to read
But hates homework.
I am a human
Who loves to dance
But hates the color black.
I am a child of God
Who likes to sing
Who dislikes writing.
I am Malika Okot.
Malika Okot, Grade 4
Greater Portland Christian School, ME

Thanks Be to God
Have mercy on us,
Mercy for all.

Thanks be to God.
Please pray,
For the homeless.

Thanks be to God.
Help all out,
Even the ignorant.

Thanks be to God.
Please be thankful,
For all we have been given.

Thanks be to God.
James Bush, Grade 5
St Clement Mary Hofbauer School, MD

Grandma
I wish you were standing near,
next to me right here.

but you are in North Carolina,
I miss you more than kinda,
and you know how much you're dear.

I wish I could write you a letter,
thanks for the jacket of leather.

we would make cupcakes,
and design them with snakes.

I wish you were here.
Davida Wilson, Grade 4
Featherbed Lane Elementary School, MD

What Is Poetry?
Poetry is the tamer
of the beast within you

It is the glue
that holds life together

It is what you see
when you look deep into your soul

It makes you think so hard
that you can't think at all

It is an open door
to a world that is
and
to a world to come

It is the dream
in a dreamer's eye
and
the holding of hands
of a friend
for you
Anna Garrett, Grade 6
St Brigid School, ME

Winter
W hite, wonderland.
I gloos are everywhere.
N ice fluffy snow.
T errifying weather.
E erie sounds form gusty winds that blow.
R unning into drifts of falling snow.
Morgan White, Grade 5
Gaithersburg Elementary School, MD

My House
My house is kind of small,
I wish it was a mall.
Then I would have a ball.

It would be so big,
but I wouldn't be able to dig.
That would be such a swig.

I could get another cat,
how about that.
I would get him a mat,
and even a hat.
But he wouldn't get fat.

But I like my house now,
it wouldn't fit a cow.
Thank goodness it's not a plow.
Trinity Gilbert, Grade 4
Courthouse Road Elementary School, VA

Volleyball Game
As the sweat runs down my head
I hear the pounding of the ball
As it releases from the other person's hand
Bump, set, and I get outside for my attack
I kill it to the ground.
Now it is my turn to serve
I get into my spot
Bounce, bounce, bounce
I toss it high and I hit it as hard as I can
It goes over and never comes back
We win the game!
Kenley Cook, Grade 5
John Bassett Moore School, DE

Protector and Teacher
Dragon
Quick
Fierce
Ferocious
Intelligent
Has small black wings
Breaths electric blue fire
Fights storms
Protects humans and
Teaches other dragons to fly.
Sydney Charette, Grade 5
St Mary School, RI

War
Bombs are roaring loudly
Guns are firing faster
Bullets are whipping past my ears
Trucks are driving past slowly
Many are leaving, faster and faster
They have left me behind
I have been captured by the enemy
An explosion is in the distance
My friends are back for me
We have won the war
Ian Garner, Grade 5
Mary Walter Elementary School, VA

Gracie
I have a dog named Gracie,
My mom thinks she's fat and lazy.
When she tries to seize a ball,
All she does is stumble and fall.
She likes to snooze both night and day,
But when she wakes she likes to play.
She is my friend and she will always be,
I love her and she loves me.
She is the greatest pet,
And she has inspired me to be a vet.
Marlee Dodson, Grade 5
Lightfoot Elementary School, VA

Spring
The sun is warm the air is fresh
It's Spring I guess
The grass is turning green,
Children playing in the fields can be seen
Tree buds are in sight
Old flowers turn bright
People at parks on benches sit
While others exercise to stay fit
Birds chirp a beautiful song
As the days turn long
Old man winter is not to fear
The arrival of spring is finally here!
Hunter Anderson, Grade 5
Mary Walter Elementary School, VA

the rose
dew drops
glistening sequins
on petals

the rose

protected
by thorns
a princess in
a castle

the rose
Samantha Lewis, Grade 6
St Brigid School, ME

Life
In life you'll
fall down a couple flights of stairs
slowly climb your way back up
you'll make a lot of lemonade,
too much to handle
you'll get kicked and slapped,
but you get back up and keep going
with God in your heart
and in your spirit
God will get you through it
you just have to believe.
Katy Baldock, Grade 6
Monelison Middle School, VA

Bear
Bear is a wonderful dog,
Except when he laps spilled eggnog.
He loves to chase squirrels,
When they run, he will twirl.
Sometimes he gets out,
So loudly Dad shouts.
Bear barks at strangers, even girls.
Sierra Hopkins, Grade 4
Gaithersburg Elementary School, MD

Inferno
Dragon
Green, shiny, ferocious, crazy
Uses his fiery breath
Burns down the town
Destroys everything in his path
Victor Paiz, Grade 5
St Mary School, RI

Cinquain
Cinquain
So confusing
Makes my brain twirl so fast
Syllables bouncing here and there
Don't like
Gina Lynch, Grade 4
Waller Mill Fine Arts Magnet School, VA

Moon Love
The moon is a big ball of light,
always glowing,
endlessly gleaming,
forever sparkling,
just like my love for you.
Marie Granger, Grade 6
Monelison Middle School, VA

Track
T errific
R unning
A ctivity
C alorie
K iller
Gardner Blanks, Grade 6
Monelison Middle School, VA

Morgan Freeman
Morgan Freeman
Successful, rich,
Acting, smiling, singing,
Played in many movies,
Hard worker.
Jillian Toomey, Grade 5
St Clement Mary Hofbauer School, MD

Perfect Pouncing Panther*
A very fast panther through the forest runs,
Found on the runway next to Air Force One.
I drive off the runway and into the big sky.
I fly over California on the Fourth of July.
Cody Hartman, Grade 6
St Clement Mary Hofbauer School, MD
*Inspired by William J. Smith

Saltie
Long and slender
The croc is an easy bender.
More green than a pine on top,
And a very bright green on bottom that's splattered like slop.
With very sharp claws
And very sharp teeth embedded in the jaws,
Together they make a killing machine.

With a tail that gracefully glides,
And repeatedly moves side-to-side,
It helps it quickly dive.
It hisses like a rattle snake,
Although its tail doesn't shake.
And when you hear a deep bellow,
Do not act very mellow.

With teeth at are made to bite,
They use those to deathly fight.
It can hunt very fine,
And can easily cut a fishing line.
When it catches its prey,
The death roll begins to take its toll!
This is the Saltwater Crocodile.
Paul Christenson, Grade 5
Forcey Christian School, MD

My Scary Family
My mom is as skinny as a stick
But she likes rice
My dad is big
But he can dig
They both are happy
But they act like the crazy lady named Bappy
My name is Phylecia

And I know this girl name Chylecia
We both look like twins who been in bins
Phylecia Benjamin, Grade 4
Featherbed Lane Elementary School, MD

God the Almighty
From the birds, fish and the sun's luminous light,
to the stars in the night;
Everything tells its own different story,
and shows God's glory;
Saying that God sent us to be the light,
but even when we are dim he keeps us in his sight;
In a dark place where there is no sound,
God is still all around;
Even though we tend to stray,
God will lead us back to the way;
He is our shepherd He is our King,
That's why to him we'll sing,
Hallelujah and Amen
Camden Pugh, Grade 5
Church of the Redeemer Christian School, MD

A Mighty Hunter
The eagle soars high in the sky,
searching for its prey
soaring down, gracefully in its own unique way.
Charging down with grace,
aiming at its prey,
up in the open space.
It strikes its prey down,
flies away,
its tail flowing like a long gown.
Isaac Wu, Grade 5
Church of the Redeemer Christian School, MD

I See Horses
I see horses tall and small
I see horses black, white, brown, and even yellow
I see horses galloping and cantering in their pasture
I see horses playing games
I see horses jumping bars in the fields
I see horses racing for the blue
I see horses in the winner's circle posing for the cameras
I see horses tired and energetic
I see horses proud and humble
Madison Tyler, Grade 5
Church of the Redeemer Christian School, MD

Football
Football is a very dangerous sport
Because in football you can break a bone
Or a hand or a leg
But the good things are: you get healthy
And you get pads so you can't get a lot of pain
So you won't get hurt in the game.
There are a lot of teams in football
Do you like football?
Josue Garcia, Grade 4
Courthouse Road Elementary School, VA

Oceans, North and South…
The ocean winds, churning the water below.
The ships sailing, swiftly through the ocean.
The animals of the ocean, swimming through the deep.
The deep of the ocean, blacker than night.
Up north, where the polar bears roam,
The seals play jack-in-the-box and the walrus' stay away.
Down south, in the Antarctic Ocean where penguins slide,
Glaciers move from side to side.
Jay Cowan, Grade 5
Blacksburg New School, VA

Do I Hear War?
Do I hear a war or is it thunder?
Do I hear screaming or is it my chair squeaking?
Is the ground rumbling or is it an earthquake?
Do I hear a war or is it my imagination?
Sydney Casterline, Grade 5
John Bassett Moore School, DE

I Am Who I Am
I am how I am I can't
change because that's the
way I am. I am not mean
I am nice and that's the way
I am.
Cinthia Flores, Grade 4
Featherbed Lane Elementary School, MD

Karate
Karate
Fun, exciting
Hitting, kicking, chopping
A really fun sport
Taekwondo
Emily Beck, Grade 5
St Joseph School-Fullerton, MD

Easter
Chocolate
Exciting, fun
Playing, hunting, eating
Eggs are hiding everywhere
Yummy
Jonathan Ellis, Grade 5
St Joseph School-Fullerton, MD

Friends
Friends
Fun, kind
Loving, caring, forgiving
Love to be together
Couple
Anna Montelibano, Grade 5
St Joseph School-Fullerton, MD

My Lizard
Lizard
So cute and cool
He makes me smile a lot
Fun to watch him eat crawling worms
My pet
Ryan Vawter, Grade 4
Waller Mill Fine Arts Magnet School, VA

Mr. Best
There once was a man from the west.
Who thought that he was the best.
He thought he could survive,
but he did not thrive.
And he ended up dead like the rest.
Noah Baumgartner, Grade 6
Monelison Middle School, VA

Kiara
K eeps on shining, even on cloudy days
I t's so, so cool to be me
A funny person who makes people laugh
R ocks all night, parties all day long
A nother sunny day to play
Kiara Cooper, Grade 4
Gaithersburg Elementary School, MD

Goalkeeper
The goalkeeper
On the sideline
After the game
Staring into space
He let in the winning goal
Alex Brown, Grade 5
St Christopher's School, VA

Winter
Winter is over today
Summer is on its way hurray, hurray
Flowers are blooming
Caterpillars are cocooning
The pools will be open someday
Marissa Lesko, Grade 5
St Joseph School-Fullerton, MD

A Funny Bunny
There once was a funny bunny
He loved some delicious honey
His friend's ears
Were covered in tears
So funny bunny gave him money.
Kai McPhee, Grade 4
Hebbville Elementary School, MD

Ghost
I sense a presence of an evil spirit
I hear his commands all through the house
His scary laughter makes me shiver
Things are rapidly moving around
I feel something strange is going to happen
Campbell Brusman, Grade 4
St Christopher's School, VA

Wild Horses
Horses
Very useful
Rolling, running, carrying
Four-legged hoofed animal
Domestic
Brianna Smith, Grade 4
Hebbville Elementary School, MD

Friend
Sasha the dragon
Colorful, sparkling, friendly, athletic
Dances, sings, swims
Loves all food
Likes sliding down her mountain
My friend
Natalia Usenia, Grade 5
St Mary School, RI

Scottish Dragon
Ferocious, undaunted, intense, festive
Green, yellow, blue, red
Fights his evil nemesis
He swims in Loch Ness Lake
Is friends with Nessie
They overcome the evil dragon.
Hannah Flynn, Grade 5
St Mary School, RI

Poetry
P aragraphs from your heart
O pen hearts and minds
E mbracing life and loving nature
T aking moments and expressing them
R eaching deep in emotions
Y our life story
Hunter Gardner, Grade 5
St Christopher's School, VA

Sports
Sports
Fun, energetic
Running, throwing, kicking
Different kinds to do
Hobby
Sarah Coffman, Grade 5
St Joseph School-Fullerton, MD

Ocean
Ocean
Beautiful, calm
Glowing shimmering sparkling
See the sandy beaches
Surf
Abigail Kaiss, Grade 5
St Joseph School-Fullerton, MD

Chocolate
Chocolate
Smooth, sweet
Melting, mouthwatering, good-tasting
A very yummy treat
Candy
Allison Floyd, Grade 5
St Joseph School-Fullerton, MD

Summer

The summer breeze blows
Stars shine brightly in the night
Who lives in that night?

Michelle Foster, Grade 6
Monelison Middle School, VA

Love

I am so in love
I can not live without him
He is my true love

Kelsie Leftwich, Grade 6
Monelison Middle School, VA

Basketball

Basketball is great
running all the way up court
He shoots the ball; SWISH

Chad Bryant, Grade 6
Monelison Middle School, VA

Fall

Fall is coming soon,
The squirrels will gather acorns
And birds will go South

Darrien Aigeldinger, Grade 6
Monelison Middle School, VA

Wrestling

We tackle and tackle
You count the six and stay down
RING! My hand raised high

McKinley Doss, Grade 6
Monelison Middle School, VA

Boykin Spaniels

Boykin Spaniels rock.
When water glistens in fur,
On a hot sunny day.

Hallie Sisk, Grade 6
Floyd T Binns Middle School, VA

Colors

In piles very bright
leaves decorate my front yard
Orange, yellow, red

Brooke-Noelle Judkins, Grade 6
Monelison Middle School, VA

Storm

The sky rumble tumbles
The cloud starts to cry sweet tears
Power out; Night night

Chris A. Brown, Grade 6
Monelison Middle School, VA

Fruit Carnivore

The shadows of the night drop onto
the world of Chiroptera — the order of all bats.
Just waking up from the day, the fruit bat
swoops its oval shaped body around in search of
precious fruits; it sucks up the seeds and gnaws on the other fruits it ponders on.
Vigorously, it flies to other trees in search of more provisions,
its round furry head and body in full flight.

It flies through the night, not making a sound,
only sounds other bats can hear.
Its flexible wings allow it to swerve, swivel, dive, and shift
in search of prey, like it is showing off its grace in flying.
Its shadow of its wings and gleaming teeth cover over the rest,
Tis a megabat.

At day it roosts in places like a barn
Like a horse in a corral.
At night, alive, it prowls for food with gleaming yellow eyes,
Like a wolf howling at the moon.
When it finishes its food, it might ponder for further.
At day it sleeps some more…
Beware the fruit carnivore!!!

Sam Cushman, Grade 5
Forcey Christian School, MD

Blue Is You and Blue Is True

Blue is the color of the sky as bright as it can be.
It's also the taste of sweet blueberries.
Blue is when you go swimming and the water goes through your fingers.
When you fall blue is the color left on your leg.
Blue is the color I wear everyday.
Blue is when you say something true.
The ocean is a place where there is miles and miles of blue to see.
Blue is the marker I draw with.
Blue is the color that makes people feel alive and that they can trust.
That is why blue is the color for you and me.

Kallie Mangum, Grade 4
Immaculate Conception Catholic Regional School, RI

LeBron James

L arry Legend is not as good as the king.
E verybody stands and cheers when he scores.
B allin' wherever he is.
R oar! The crowd goes wild!
O rlando's Dwight Howard can't stop the king's power.
N obody can stop him when he drives through the lane.

J amming like Jordan
A nybody who gets in his way will be flat as if they were a pancake.
M ain attraction of South Beach
E rving "Dr. J" can't dunk like Lebron
S o many people look up to him, MJ even has a poster of LeBron on his wall

Justin Worden, Grade 6
Princeton Elementary School, ME

Valentine's Day
Looks like there is a love note on my bed
Smells like chocolate in a box
Tastes like rich love in one single bite
Sounds like love and joy
Feels like love in my heart!
Anna Collins, Grade 4
Greenville Elementary School, VA

Wags
Oh, Wags I know how you run
And bark and love to eat and
Love to play fetch and sometimes
In the car you get scared but
You make me smile anyways.
Sydney Rolison, Grade 4
Greenville Elementary School, VA

Happiness
Looks like a meadow of flowers
Smells like a fruity perfume
Feels like a soft cloud
Tastes like mint chocolate chip ice cream
Sounds like children laughing
Madison Ruiz, Grade 4
Greenville Elementary School, VA

Cat
Cat
Soft fur
Purring, sleeping, meowing
Napping all day
Kitten
Caitlyn Hewitt, Grade 4
Greenville Elementary School, VA

Graveyard
Graveyard
Bone chilling
Haunting, scaring, crying
Bringing back past memories
Cemetery
Dayne Dye, Grade 4
Greenville Elementary School, VA

The Graveyard
Stone graves
Wind blowing
Fresh earth
My salty tears
Lost loves
Ryan Roeber, Grade 4
Greenville Elementary School, VA

Petal Phases
Glory for majestic Flower in bloom,
But days are now colder,
Flower will soon meet its doom,
It cannot forever get older and older.

But days are now colder,
In the chill Autumn days Flower cringes,
It cannot forever get older and older,
It falls steadily and waits for spring.

In the chill Autumn days, Flower cringes,
Winter is on his way,
It falls steadily and waits for spring,
Flower can't wait another day.

Winter is on his way,
The chill is here, and long gone,
Flower can't wait another day,
Now summer has left with a yawn.

The chill is here, and long gone,
Flower will soon meet its doom,
Now summer has left with a yawn,
Glory for majestic Flower in bloom.
Sreya Vangara, Grade 6
Roberto W Clemente Middle School, MD

Life Is Not a Game
Video games are fun
Only if I won!!!
Black Ops is cool
Even when I lose and
Can't be played at school.

Modern Warfare Three
Keeps me very busy
To the TV!!!

The reason I love these games
Is that I never die.
I can come tomorrow and still be alive.

Unfortunately, real life is not a game
To be played
Like these video games.
Can't hit replay and live another day.

That's why our Savior
Came from heaven
To save the day.
So we get to play with him someday.
Terry "T.J." Ford, Grade 6
Salem School, MD

Raccoon Raccoon
Raccoon!
Raccoon!
You have a mask!
What is your task?
Are you a funny guy?
What do you buy?
Do you like to shop,
Or do you like to hop?
Do you like to eat feet,
Or do you like to eat meat?
I like to shop and I
Like to hop!
How about you?
Emily Libby, Grade 4
Greater Portland Christian School, ME

The Sun in My Mouth
I taste it
Warm, buttery, soft
My taste buds are on vacation
From peanut butter and jelly
The outside, smooth
The interior, juicy
The color, like the sun
Warming up my mouth
Just one more scoop,
Maybe two or three?
Until the pot of corn is
Empty
Adrienne Willard, Grade 6
St Brigid School, ME

The Doctor's Visit
The doctor came in
No smile on his face.
"I have bad news,
Don't let it get to your faith.
Look at this site
It's in your right leg
It's a large tumor,
But it's not to dread.
You'll go through chemo,
You may get a little sick,
But please trust me.
You'll get through this."
Skylar Harler, Grade 6
Monelison Middle School, VA

Churchie
Churchie
Is the fattest
Cat you will ever see.
He is a very lazy one.
Oh, Church!
Thomas Archer Jr., Grade 6
Monelison Middle School, VA

How to Make Tender Loving Care

How to cook up love for someone
Is very important to know
So here, right now
You, I will show

Sprinkle
Sprinkle love
Sprinkle tenderness in the air
Just to show that you care

Pour
Pour hope
Pour love from your heart
That could even be the start

Stir
Stir in your friends
Stir your family in there too
Just because they love you

And you love them too.
Lisa Curtis, Grade 6
Princeton Elementary School, ME

My Dog Toby

My dog's name is Toby.
He's sweet and he's kind.
He is very special.
I'm so glad that he's mine.
Yes, he's a big dog,
you think that he'll bite.
But he is friendly,
Toby's all right.
He used to be a stray,
alone on the street.
Scared and cold,
he had nothing to eat.
Some people helped him,
along the way.
And we found him at the SPCA!
Toby and I are best friends;
It's amazing how much time we spend.
Now you know,
why Toby is special to me.
And if you were to meet him,
you would agree.
Taina Cunion, Grade 4
St Thomas Aquinas School, MD

The Strangest Dream

Last night I had the strangest dream.
It woke me from my sleep
I was wearing a bunch of shaving cream.
It woke me up in a big leap.
Bernard Lanier, Grade 4
Hebbville Elementary School, MD

Rocky Road

Dragon
Black
Sharp teeth
Short claws
Heroic
Saves people from the raining rocks
Walks, runs, and flies
Diego Harrington, Grade 5
St Mary School, RI

Big Red

Dragon
Big, red, scaly, funny
His mountain is red, like his body
Brings humor to all
Likes having fun with people
Plays video games
Fun, silly, strong, kindhearted
Matthew Pietrunti, Grade 5
St Mary School, RI

Love and Hate

Love
Peaceful, beautiful
Caring, calming, understanding
Good, happy, bad, angry
Disliking, discouraging, scaring
Hurtful, cold
Hate
Alejandra Drevyanko, Grade 6
St John Neumann Academy, VA

Soccer

Soccer is like kicking the planets,
Reaching for the stars,
Believing in yourself.
In soccer you can score many goals,
You have to dodge people to get around.
It is mostly about having fun.
Madeline Goldstein, Grade 4
Boonsboro Elementary School, MD

Lemurs

Fast, soft
Running, hopping, climbing
They are very awesome
Hooray!
Brandon Mann, Grade 4
St John Neumann Academy, VA

Virginia

In all Virginia
Dogwoods blooming sweet flowers
Spring has come at last.
Harrison Stewart, Grade 4
Greenville Elementary School, VA

Recycling Starts with You

Don't dump on the Earth,
It's wasteful and mean.
Try to recycle,
So it'll be clean.

Scrap metal and soda cans,
Are not for the trash.
Recycle it all,
And make some cash.

Done with that game?
Don't throw it away.
Give it to a friend,
Make somebody's day.

Magazines and paper,
Bottles and milk jugs too,
Put them in the proper bins,
Recycling starts with you.
Jacob Henry, Grade 4
St. Clement Mary Hofbauer School, MD

What Is Poetry?

A way of escaping life
Entering our own world
Where everything is perfect

A way to express our feelings
An explanation of ourselves.
Writing who we really are

Our creativity written on paper
A new story told
Maybe the ending untold
Having us stop and think:
Why?

Everything on our mind
An extension to our hearts
Written as
Poetry
Grace Maloney, Grade 6
St Brigid School, ME

teddy

teddy
it means happy, nice, cool
it is the number 10
it is like the sky in the morning
it is the vacation to the beach
it is the memory of Dad
who taught me how to hunt and fish
my name is teddy
it means nice
Teddy Shelton, Grade 6
Hardin Reynolds Memorial School, VA

Ocean

I feel cold sand.
The sand is a whitish color.
I saw a horseshoe crab, a blue crab, and a gray stingray.
I heard the waves splashing on the shore.
I tasted sand that had blown on my food; crunching in my mouth.

Trevor Woolbright, Grade 5
Rosemont Forest Elementary School, VA

The World Is a Machine

The world is a machine
There are no extra parts
There are no missing parts
So go on and find your hidden part and show it to the world
So they can see your great part that you have in you.

Mia Hall, Grade 4
Courthouse Road Elementary School, VA

The Beach

The beach has water as clear as the sky
Its sand is sometimes as rough as sandpaper
With beach balls as colorful as the rainbow,
The beach stands out like a blazing hot day in June.

Anna Sharpe, Grade 4
Riderwood Elementary School, MD

Apple

The apple is red as a rose.
It is crunchy as a chocolate walnut bar.
The apple stands out like a stop sign.
With a stem like a branch, it is the best fruit.

Teddy Koronios, Grade 4
Riderwood Elementary School, MD

Chester the Kitten

Chester's brown spots are as rare as a heat wave in winter.
His brown eyes are as brown as smooth dark chocolate.
With ears as pink as a flamingo.
As soft as a bunny.

Jack Johnson, Grade 4
Riderwood Elementary School, MD

The Octopus

The octopus is as purple as a dollar store flamingo.
It eats like it's starved.
With fish skeletons scattered in his tank like a graveyard.
At night in his tank, the fish's ghosts dance like they're hooked.

Brandon Trageser, Grade 4
Riderwood Elementary School, MD

The Dalmatian

The Dalmatian has black spots like coal
Its body is like white paper
With a tongue as pink as a flamingo.
The Dalmatian stands out like snow in summer.

Rachel Young, Grade 4
Riderwood Elementary School, MD

Flower

If I was a pretty flower, I would be a magnificent rose,
I would be purple in color
and sensitive to the nose.
I will open slowly in the day,
during the month of May.
I would quietly close at night,
because of no sunlight.
My smell will be so sweet,
My petals will be so neat.
If I start to droop in the hot heat,
Please water me because that would be so sweet.

Brandy Sullivan, Grade 5
Lightfoot Elementary School, VA

The Battle of Sweden and America

When the Vikings go to war, they go insane.
The enemy must feel great pain.
The sword of my enemy drops and falls to the ground.
Then the weak enemy falls down.
When I run into battle, I go extremely crazy.
My enemies are so consistently lazy.
When I slaughter my dangerous enemies,
It brings out the best of me.
Could it be? We won the battle,
Please don't tattle.

Chase Staub, Grade 5
Lightfoot Elementary School, VA

My Dog Tike

I love my dog Tike; when he jumps he looks like a dove,
He is the best dog I have ever had, and he is the dog I love.
When he tries to fight me, I don't let him bite me,
Then he sits on top of my head, and I cannot see.
Tike is tiny and hyper and likes to run,
He likes to scamper in the big, bright sun.
He things that he is big, bad, and tough,
But when I play with him, he doesn't play that rough.
When Tike sneezes, I say bless you my dear friend,
I will love my dog Tike until the very end.

Jayquan Towles, Grade 5
Lightfoot Elementary School, VA

My Cat Speedy

My cat Speedy is very divine,
When he climbs up a tree, he gets stuck on a vine!
When he was a kitten, he was very nice,
But when he was a frisky teenager, he chocked on a dice!
As he got more brazen, he would try to scratch the clock,
And he would get risky and run in a geese flock.
One day we were trying to find the remote,
That's when that stubborn cat got into the tote.
When we first got him, he was scared of hogs,
But as he got older, he became scared of dogs.

Corey Tolbert, Grade 5
Lightfoot Elementary School, VA

Nature

Splashing drop at sea,
white clouds are like cotton balls,
soft breezes through trees.
Malcolm Robinson, Grade 6
Floyd T Binns Middle School, VA

The Rain

Clear and soft water
drips on trees and flower buds
beautiful new life.
Antanaya Harris, Grade 6
Floyd T Binns Middle School, VA

Icicles

Gleaming in the light
Shining and melting lightly
Falling to the ground
Olivia Conte, Grade 4
Greenville Elementary School, VA

Sunset

Fading with the sun
Mixing colors through the sky
Beauty of the night
Morgan Malinow, Grade 4
Greenville Elementary School, VA

Stream

Silver, luscious stream
Always flowing, never stops
Playful yet serene
Maddie Green, Grade 4
Greenville Elementary School, VA

Winter

Winter is pretty
Snow fell on my window sill
So soft, so quiet
Yazareth Ramirez, Grade 6
Monelison Middle School, VA

Sun

The bright sun shines on
The glistening waves.
Pure, clear, and open.
Kelsey Corbett, Grade 6
Immaculate Heart of Mary School, MD

Frog

You let me touch you
Your gold-gilt eyes and smooth skin
On the shower wall
Maggie Colangelo, Grade 6
Eagle Ridge Middle School, VA

Misty May-Treanor

Misty May was eight in her first volleyball tournament, that's where it begins
Misty May is now the most successful female player ever with 107 tournament wins

Volleyball has been valuable to Misty all throughout her life
She triumphs in tournaments even when she's in strife

She played volleyball while in college at Long Beach State
Misty was the captain of the first undefeated NCAA team in 1998

Now Misty and her partner, Kerri Walsh, are on the U.S. Women's Volleyball Team
Training together every day, working hard like dogs to get to the extreme

Three Summer Olympics for Misty in 2000, 2004, and 2008
In '04 and '08 she played with Kerri, they dominated, that's something you can't debate

Against tough teams from Brazil and China, two gold medals were won
Oh Yeah! — The only team to repeat in volleyball but trust me they aren't done

Like peanut butter and jelly, Misty and Kerri are back together again
Training for the 2012 Summer Olympics in London, their persistent passion never ends

Being a part of "The greatest beach volleyball team of all time"
Going for the Olympic gold again is what Misty has in mind
Caroline Pasquariello, Grade 6
Most Blessed Sacrament Catholic School, MD

Soaring Falcon

I love to hover by the mountain peaks,
And wait for an appetizing dinner to eat.
I admire my extended and powerful wings.
I see myself as an aggressive and royal king.
I prefer to swoop up a slimy fish from an active lake,
Then to be chased by a famished cat looking for an enjoyable juicy steak.
I always wanted to glide through the expanded corn field,
I will be unrestricted with nothing in my way like a glistering shield.
I enjoy sleeping during the gloomy night and hunt when it is blazing and sunny,
I love floating through the sky and chasing a fluffy, baby bunny.
Tyler Singer, Grade 5
Lightfoot Elementary School, VA

What Is in My Attic Full of Memories?

What is in my attic full of memories?
My Dad's aged trophies sit in a box
My old baby crib that my Mom used to rock
My Mom's old dolls that brought childhood fun
My camping items that faded in the sun
My Dad's trombone that he played in good old school
My dusty kitchen toy which totally ruled
My Mom's lunch box she used when she was six
My holiday decorations are quite an appropriate mix
At Christmas we put out my Dad's fabulous trains
My Mom's college books which helped her clever brain
My baby clothes and shoes that I wore as I held my Mom's apron string
And boxes and bundles and bunches of things!!!
Carissa Gabbard, Grade 6
Most Blessed Sacrament Catholic School, MD

Pandas

Pandas are cute and cuddly.
I have never seen one named Dudley!

They are very nice and very sweet.
They also love to eat!

They munch and munch and crunch and crunch,
because they eat bamboo for lunch!

They play and play.
They play all day!

Pandas are black and white.
I think their fur coats are very tight.

Pandas can be very fat.
They are not skinny as cats!

My cute and cuddly big friend,
Well, to him it is almost the end.

Well, his species no longer can exist.
He may go away in the mist.

So if you love nature,
always remember, PANDAS ARE ENDANGERED!

Vani Parthiban, Grade 4
MOT Charter School, DE

Hiccups

Hiccups, hiccups! I have the hiccups
Put water in my cup
And drank it all up
But still I have the hiccups!

Hiccups, hiccups! I tried holding my breath instead
But it didn't work, unlike everyone said
And still I have the hiccups!

Hiccups, hiccups! My mom suggested peanut butter
But every time I eat peanut butter
It makes me sputter
I dislike peanut butter
And every time I hear the word
It makes me shudder
And still I have the hiccups!

Hiccups, hiccups! They say that sugar makes hiccups stop
So I had an ice cream sundae with a cherry on top
I ate and ate 'till my buttons popped
But again and again I said "Hiccup!"

So I hiccupped and hiccupped and hiccupped all day
'Till I hiccupped and hiccupped my hiccups away!

Jessica Kilmer, Grade 5
Union Mill Elementary School, VA

Branches

There is a time when the trees grow high
And the seasons go by
But when people let you down
The trees start to brown
Soon, there are not enough trees left for your town
And your empty soul starts to cry

Inside you've turned hollow,
You gave up on leading, so now you follow
Once your leaves turn yellow
Months of being covered in snow
Then you'll have time to grow
Just follow the big white arrow

Don't wait
Or procrastinate
You know who you are
You know you can go far
You're a shooting star
And it's your time to fascinate

Emily Cook, Grade 6
William Henry Middle School, DE

Space

Eight planets around sun
On an axis revolving
Different planets
Nebulae are clouds of stars
The stars move faster than speeding cars
Our galaxy is a tight bound
Planet X has not yet been found
Exoplanets are not ours
But they do orbit a star
Mercury is close to the sun
While Venus is crispier than a bun
Earth is our home
Mars is the god of war
Jupiter has a solid core
Saturn has spectacular rings
Uranus is tipped on its side
Neptune is covered with blue dye
Eight planets around sun
On an axis revolving
Different planets

Rachel Hexamer and Skylar Dalton, Grade 5
John Bassett Moore School, DE

The Surrender

The Civil War, a bloody war
The Confederates gray, the Union blue
They died and died until one guy
Decided what he had to do
The surrender at Appomattox Court House would be
To Ulysses S. Grant from Robert E. Lee.

Cole Trani, Grade 4
Waller Mill Fine Arts Magnet School, VA

Runaway

It tastes like freedom on the tip of my tongue.
It feels like a sting on my back.
It smells like tobacco everywhere.
I hear shooting all day.
I run off into the woods.
I'm free.
Freedom!!!

Omari Lee, Grade 4
Waller Mill Fine Arts Magnet School, VA

America

A merica's people are loyal.
M illions of people died for our freedom.
E xcellently, our people fought for us.
R emarkable, is a word for America.
I ndependence is very important to us.
C ivil rights play a large part in our government.
A merica is AMAZING!!!

Allyson Shrewsberry, Grade 5
Connor Consolidated School, ME

My Grandpa's Backyard

The greatest place is where family is.
With small palm trees enclosing it.
The cookouts smell like greasy, delicious food.
People feel as if there is a heater burning over them.
The pool is as blue as the bright sky
And makes me desperate to swim in it.
My favorite place is my grandpa's backyard.

Jesenia Morales, Grade 6
Wyman Elementary School, RI

Believe

B e thankful for what you have
E arn what you get
L ive life like the end of the world is tomorrow
I ntelligence is perfection
E ncourage yourself to do different things
V olunteer for different activities
E mbrace yourself in many ways

Ashlynn Moss, Grade 6
Monelison Middle School, VA

I Am a Dog

I am a cocker spaniel, cute and fury
I am a poodle, fancy and expensive
I am a pit bull, mean and rough
I am a jack russell terrier, playful and energetic
I am a chihuahua, skinny as a stick
I am a dog but different types of dogs

Shaniya Williams, Grade 4
Featherbed Lane Elementary School, MD

Butterflies

As the butterfly flutters in the air it glistens like the sun
it likes to fly all day long it blends in and has fun
and in the end of the day
it rests the night away

Sierra DeBenedictis, Grade 5
John Bassett Moore School, DE

Bunnies

The bunny's fur is as soft as a warm blanket
Its tail is like a fluffy cloud
With a pink nose like a flamingo
The bunny stands out like a surprise on a spring day

Lindsey Schlossenberg, Grade 4
Riderwood Elementary School, MD

The Tornado

A tornado has the power of a bull.
The sound as shrill as noise at Disney World.
With speeds enough to pick you up and throw you far away,
Stands out like someone giving away gold for free.

Gavin Franklin, Grade 4
Riderwood Elementary School, MD

Steve

I have a turtle
His name is Steve

I found him in the woods
Thrashing in the leaves

It was unusually warm
For a winter's day

So Steve went out
And decided to play

I picked him up
He was very small

A bit bigger
Than a bouncy ball

He lives in a tank
And sleeps underwater

He also sunbathes
To keep body temperature

Steve is my pet
And I love him so

My family does too
And I will never let him go!

Sydney Wyant, Grade 5
Mary Walter Elementary School, VA

Monkeys
Playful, fluffy
Swinging, jumping, screeching.
Gorillas, orangutans, chimps, macaques,
Hugging, caring, loving,
Babies, families.
Nidia Lara, Grade 5
Gaithersburg Elementary School, MD

The Monkeys
Monkeys
Aggressive mammals
Jumping, climbing, swinging
Happy, loving, friendly, kind
Animals
Olayemi Omirin, Grade 4
Hebbville Elementary School, MD

Bats
Bats are scary
They come out at night
Some are helpful
But some give you a fright
Rashawn Nelson, Grade 4
Hebbville Elementary School, MD

The Smart Monkey
The monkey likes to read
It also got an A in his work
It likes to work a lot
And likes to say "I'm smart."
Daniel Awogbesan, Grade 4
Hebbville Elementary School, MD

Autumn
Apples are gathered to make apple cider.
Under the leaves is a great place for hiders.
Trees are colorful, beautifully bright.
Unbelievable how there's less sunlight.
Jade Keyser, Grade 4
Hebbville Elementary School, MD

The Little Star
Oh oh little Star why do you twinkle Star?
I want to know I want to know now.
Please can you tell me.
I twinkle in the moon light of the night.
Trinity Edozie, Grade 5
Courthouse Road Elementary School, VA

My Friends
My friends bring joy to my life
I wish I could see them every day
They're the love and happiness in my life
I love them in every single way
Taylor Jones, Grade 6
Magnolia Elementary School, MD

Paradise
Summer of 2011, sunny and bright
Desire for sea water fills my mind
As I look out my car window
And leave my Virginia home behind
Stepping out, ocean air fills my lungs
Wind plays with my hair
As I watch the water
I don't have a care
Sand tickles my toes
Sun tans the soul
Water washes away my worries
Catching a fish is my goal
Seafood fills the cravings
With steamed crab and juicy shrimp
But when it comes to slimy oysters
I am a wimp
All of a sudden, my paradise ends
My heart fills with tears
As commitments drive me away
But the ocean still calms my fears
Caroline Anderson, Grade 6
St John Neumann Academy, VA

This Is Courage
Courage
Is what makes us
What divides us
What drives us

It is what stops us
Creates news
Demands more

It creates blame
Brings shame
Shows in schools

Determines the cool
Divides the weak
Pours out like a leak

It is what makes us
What divides us
This is courage
Kyonna Dandridge, Grade 6
Hardin Reynolds Memorial School, VA

Birthdays
There's a special day, it's true
And it's made just for you!
It's not a time to hit the ground,
Birthdays come all year round.
Come on, now. You're getting old
And there are stories to be told.
Maya Hopkins, Grade 4
Gaithersburg Elementary School, MD

Fire
I can feel your heat,
you burn tall,
you spread wide.
Your might knows no bounds.

The only battle you lose
is with the sea,
lake or stream.
You cannot fight them,
only tiptoe around
and hope not to get hurt.

They rain on your parade,
and storm on your summer break.

Your massive size,
overwhelming power,
and great strength,
do not help in the end,
you just fizzle out.

Compared to the sea's size,
and the lakes strength,
you are nothing.

You know from experience,
your time has come.
You are fading fast,
no matter how hard you fight.
You rest as ashes,
until a new flame is born.
Dylan Lomax, Grade 6
Tilghman Elementary School, MD

Rainbow of Scales
Make a wish upon a fish,
A bunch of rainbow scales,
An oval for a body,
A triangle for a tail.

It darts through the water,
Silent, smooth, and sleek,
Looking for little tidbits,
And tasty plants to eat.

Like a wave of Jell-O
Going through your fingers,
It swims through the ocean,
As it lingers…

Make a wish upon a fish,
A bunch of rainbow scales,
And oval for a body,
A triangle for a tail.
Jade Thompson, Grade 5
Forcey Christian School, MD

Carousel

prancing ponies
up and down
spinning round and round

polished poles
don't touch the ground
spinning round and round

bright lights
on a crown
spinning round and round

merry music
laughing sounds
spinning round and round

Rachel Matthews, Grade 5
Church of the Redeemer Christian School, MD

Life Is Like a Butterfly

Life is like a butterfly.
You fly peacefully until you stop where you're needed
Elegantly, beautifully
Letting the wind take you wherever it blows you.

Landing only when needed
When swatted you fly right back up
Avoiding obstacles Earth throws at you
Hiding solemnly from prey.

Flying home after a long day
Freely, sweetly
Only to stop to avoid harm
Cautiously.
Life is like a butterfly.

Clinton Phinney, Grade 6
Massabesic Middle School, ME

Roller Coasters

Roller coasters
Roller coasters
Roller coasters
Loopy roller coasters
Fast, hilly roller coasters
Insane, scary, watery roller coasters
Weird roller coasters
Safety roller coasters
Learning, fancy, Scooby-Doo roller coasters
Awesome, bad, Nemo roller coasters
Backwards roller coasters, too
Underground roller coasters
High roller coasters
Don't forget chocolate roller coasters
Last of all, best of all, I like Viking roller coasters

Drew Robinson, Grade 4
Greenville Elementary School, VA

Me, Myself, and I

Well, it's just me, myself and I
I just can't deny
this is what it looks like in my eyes,
I feel I'm about to cry

I am a dove with a group of crows
And when one passes the others go.
I am a homeless person asking for change,
But when they say no, it stars to rain

I just want to be surrounded by people
Who adore just me
And want to sit and talk with me

I know I'm cute, I know I'm cool
But when it comes to work; I'm hot in school
My biggest phobia of all — being alone
My biggest wish is going home

I can sit at a table and I can be alone
But when I move over,
They just want to go

Now y'all know it's just me, myself, and I
Is there a reason why
It's just me, myself, and I?

Afeovomeh Garba, Grade 6
Magnolia Elementary School, MD

Some People Talk

People talk
Lips smacking
And never stopping
Words flowing like a brook
That won't stay

It is not in the nature of words to stop flowing
Though I keep my mouth closed because I find
Words are sacred
There are some who find it hard
To shut up.

They smack, smack, smack their lips
And hardly ever come up for air
Long enough to listen to the world
They talk about small things, like weather
They talk about big things, like politics
They talk about others
They gossip and giggle
Their obscene sniggers
Rising like smoke
They never listen
And never learn

Brenda Hayes, Grade 6
Orchard House School, VA

Animal Alphabet

A pes are aggressive
C ats like to meow and
E lephants like to train their babies,
G iraffes eat dark green leaves,
I guanas like to hang on rocks,
K angaroos are known to jump,
M acaws have a colorful cast.
O striches have long necks,
Q uails are types of birds with flecks.
S nakes can slither, too.
U nicorns are different horses, who knew?
W hales are mammals in the sea,
Y aks are big and quite furry,

B aboons are so cute,
D ogs are fun, too.
F alcons fly up high,
H ippos love to play in mud, and I wonder why.
J aguars run so fast,
L ions like to roar and
N arwhals live around igloos,
P enguins like to play on ice,
R abbits like to hop around,
T igers can be white or orange,
V esper sparrows are tiny birds,
X -ray animal bones to learn more,
Z ebras have black and white springs,

And now I know more than before!

Katye Vasquez, Grade 5
Gaithersburg Elementary School, MD

The Hug-Bug

If you go underground, way underground, you'll find the place where the Hug-Bug is found,
He'll hug you and bug you until you can't rest because, oh because, he thinks you're the best.
He looks like a kid and smells like one too; the only problem is, he's bigger than you,
You'll shake and you'll shiver because he's so tall; so much that you'll run into a wall.
But the Hug-Bug won't hurt you 'cause he's a nice kid,
And when he leaves you, you'll be sorry he did.

Hannah Underwood, Grade 5
H M Pearson Elementary School, VA

Dr. Martin Luther King, Jr.Living the Legacy: We Are All Part of His Dream

I would change the world by making it caring and kind. Dr. Martin Luther King was brave. He was a hero because he united us together. He loved his family and friends. Martin was respectful and peaceful toward others and encouraged them to do the same to have a wonderful life. Martin was helpful to others who needed his help and care. He was persistent so his dream wouldn't go away. He was a very independent man who inspired others to join him and come together to make his dream come true. I think of Martin Luther King as my biggest role model because he united us all. Now we go to the same schools, shop at the same stores, and get paid for jobs evenly. Martin Luther King's dream came true and now we are together forever.

Nidia Lara, Grade 5
Gaithersburg Elementary School, MD

Precious Hands

These precious hands that hold me. They are there when I have nightmares and need to be rocked slowly. They're the ones that grip me tightly when I have fears of monsters under my bed. They clap for me when I achieved my goals and set my bar sky high and succeeded. Every morning they pull my hair in a tight ponytail. They sign my school papers when I need them to. These hands are so important to me. These precious hands keep me going. They'll drive me to the end. These precious hands I speak of belong to you.

Morgan White, Grade 6
Paul L Dunbar Middle School for Innovation, VA

Spring Is Coming!

Singing birds like a song,
Perfect days with no more wind
Running outside
Playing soccer in the field
Going to the park
It's an awesome time of year
No more bad weather because spring is here!

Luis Gonzalez, Grade 4
Gaithersburg Elementary School, MD

Friends

F riendships can last forever, no matter what
R espect each other and your teacher
I t's good to be kind to one another, as you would want to be treated
E verything is possible, so never give up
N ever with for something that is not worth fighting for
D on't keep secrets from one another
S hare with your friends, and they will share with you

Jessica Flores, Grade 4
Gaithersburg Elementary School, MD

Pandas

Pandas are so cute
I love their colors and fur
They are very soft
Taylor Hunley, Grade 6
Floyd T Binns Middle School, VA

Breeze

Trees dance in the wind
a cooling breeze whistles by,
while birds sing a tune.
Coen King, Grade 6
Floyd T Binns Middle School, VA

Turkey

Turkeys say gobble,
They walk in the woods at dusk,
Beautiful feathers.
Taylor Franklin, Grade 6
Floyd T Binns Middle School, VA

Fire

The fire burns fast
It burns the trash quietly
Embers die slowly
Leekwai Scott, Grade 6
Floyd T Binns Middle School, VA

The Wind

The wind blows in trees.
The wind quickly weaves in leaves.
The gust is so soft.
Mikey Carpenter, Grade 6
Floyd T Binns Middle School, VA

Birds

I open the door,
I see birds fly in the sky,
They are headed south.
Alyssa Bowles, Grade 6
Floyd T Binns Middle School, VA

Nature

I walk through the woods
Birds chirping and bears roaring
It's nature singing.
Jacob Suter, Grade 6
Floyd T Binns Middle School, VA

Tornados

Feel the wind twirling
like a whirlpool in the sea
spinning really fast.
David Magiera, Grade 6
Floyd T Binns Middle School, VA

Disneyland

As I'm walking by the doughboy stand.
White misty powder surrounds my face
As if I were a plane soaring through the clouds.
I look up to see the biggest ride,
And there I see people screaming as if there were no tomorrow.
People are taking photos with Mickey Mouse
While the other Mickey is in the bright parade.
Cinderella's castle is drowned with colors.
A lot of people are just standing there
Like millions of penguins huddled up
Enjoying the unbelievable atmosphere.
I walk by the Jurassic Park water ride,
And I can smell the water that smells as if I'm in a tropical rainforest.
I can also hear the robotic dinosaurs roaring and repeating
Their same movement in the water.
As I'm on the Looney Tunes ride, I think I'm almost getting hit by a train,
But it is just another drop
That gives me butterflies in my stomach.
The atmosphere makes me feel
As if I'm actually in that place.
Wow, Disneyland is a magical place!
Tommy McMullen, Grade 6
Wyman Elementary School, RI

Beenie Teenie Greenie

I think green is the best color of all. It is a lizard in a forest on a rainy day.
Green is slime crawling down your hand.
Green is a wreath on Christmas Day.
This is the color of swaying bushes on a bright summer day.
Green is the color of Mom's yummy broccoli and peas.
Green is the color of little visitors from space.
Green is the horrible stench of trash and garbage.
Green is the color of gremlins or monsters.
Green is a frog in a wet, wet, pond.
BLAH! BLAH! Green is when you're sick.
Green is when you want revenge and you're jealous.
Green is Saint Patrick's Day with green shamrocks and leprechauns.
Chirp! Chirp! Green is a cricket chirping all night.
SCORE!!! Green is when the home team scores a touchdown.
OWIE! Don't get pricked by the prickly prickle cactus.
Green is a caterpillar peacefully squirming across a tree.
Green is a scaly dinosaur.
Green is the biggest tree in the whole wide world.
Green is an elf in a winter wonderland.
Green is when you're camping in a tent.
Green is the most amazing color of all.
Brad Hutchison, Grade 4
Immaculate Conception Catholic Regional School, RI

The Calico Cat

A calico cat's fur is as fluffy as a baby bunny in the spring.
Its beautiful coat of orange and black is as pretty as butterfly's wings.
With its pink nose as pink as bubblegum and ears as delicate as a flower.
They really are wonderful things.
Hanley Francomano, Grade 4
Riderwood Elementary School, MD

Bald Eagle

I see you soaring through the sky,
While I eat delicious blueberry pie.
It's not pie that makes my day,
It's seeing you fly all through the month of May.
Through the pasture and in some hay,
I like when you swoop down and get your prey,
You swoop down and make the wind go past,
Right through my eyelash because you go so fast.
Your prey can't hide because you have a special eye,
You give me whiplash and make me sigh.

Caleb Young, Grade 5
Lightfoot Elementary School, VA

Summer

It's fun to play,
All sorts of games.
And the sun is so bright,
It gives the Earth light.
You can play pretend
With some friends.
In the summer school is out,
You can go out with friends and roam about.
This is why it is time,
To play all day.

Isaiah Clifton, Grade 4
Cedar Bluff Elementary School, VA

My Dog Sophie

My dog Sophie is a German Shepherd and extremely playful,
And I think she's the queen of everything and very beautiful.
She is my favorite dog in the whole wide world,
She is a lovely animal, and her hair is always curled.
Sophie is out excitedly playing in the mud;
She's constantly out in the sun and is always my bud.
Sophie is there when someone is down in the dumps,
And she always makes someone jump.
Sophie perpetually likes to play when she's happy,
Sophie does not like to entertain when she's all sappy.

Alex Ragle, Grade 5
Lightfoot Elementary School, VA

My Future

My future,
I am so scared to face it
My future is gong to be as bright as the light,
Or it will be dim like the summer night?

My future, I write
My future, I decide
But, later it will be
    History
In time

Hersona Abraham, Grade 6
Magnolia Elementary School, MD

The Lion Who Liked Sports

The lion played a round of soccer.
Then he frowned because they lost.
He tried again after he ate bread.
While he was playing he tripped over thread.
He felt very sad but he felt bad for his teammates.
He was just having a bad day.

Eric Bingham, Grade 4
Courthouse Road Elementary School, VA

Summertime

Summer is almost here!
Listen to the children cheer!
Sunglasses, flip flops, ice cream, I can't wait!
Get to sleep in late!
The last day of school is near!

Caitlyn Warfield, Grade 5
St Joseph School-Fullerton, MD

The Giraffe

The giraffe's neck is as tall as a long tall tree
Its long tongue is as long as a four year old's body
With brown spots like chocolate frosting,
The giraffe stands out like dirt,
Flying up in the air during a horse race.

Emily Guzzo, Grade 4
Riderwood Elementary School, MD

What the World Needs

P eople become friends with everyone
E verybody is grateful for everything they get
A ll wars end and everyone is happy
C ops don't have to do dangerous jobs as much
E nemies become nice to everyone and help others

Jeremy Bradley, Grade 6
Floyd T Binns Middle School, VA

Fruit

Fruit is good and juicy.
It helps me refresh my mind.
When I eat it, makes me feel like my day is fine.
Fruit comes in different shapes, sizes, and color.
It doesn't matter because it is the best thing ever.

Sierra Gray, Grade 5
Rosemont Forest Elementary School, VA

The Difference Between Hoping and Believing

You hope something will come,
You believe in what is here.
You know you believe in it.
You think about what to hope for.
I am believing and hoping in God.

Meigs Helms, Grade 5
St John Neumann Academy, VA

I Really Do Love Pandas

Pandas are so cute
but they don't really move
and they don't really hoot.
But, I really do love pandas!

They're as quiet as a bunny,
which seems kind of funny.
They usually eat bamboo
but sometimes they just chew.
But, I really do love pandas!

A tree is a panda's bed
but sometimes they hit their head
and then go back to bed again.
But, I really do love pandas!

Jenna Malone, Grade 5
John Bassett Moore School, DE

The Holocaust

What she saw over the fence
What she saw was very tense
No one laughing, no one smiling
And my Dad was inside filing.
I saw the flowers in my hand

When I saw the marching band.
They were in their suits holding guns
No one was having fun.
A lot people got taken away
It was the Nazis some say
Trying to hide away from them
I would feel stupid if I was them.
Taking people because of their religion
I guess that was Hitler's vision.

Erin Snyder, Grade 5
Wm Winchester Elementary School, MD

Sister, Sisters

You're sticky like glue
Tight like knots
You shop til you drop
You love each other,
Through sunshine and rain
You're sisters

There is a four letter word that defines you
Starts with an "L," ends with an "E"
Do you know what word it may be?

Sometimes you fight
You may hate each other
But you'll always be there for one another
Sisters, sisters forever

Janneh Freeman, Grade 6
Magnolia Elementary School, MD

Earth Needs Help!!!

Get out and work for Earth's success;
You'll probably get interviewed by the press.
The bag not to use is plastic;
One thing you can use is a basket.

Help by recycling bottles and cans;
You might have lots of fans.
Want fame?
Join the Earth Game!!!

Jacquelyn Cook, Grade 5
Eastport Elementary School, ME

Dew Drops

Crystal clear bubbles
Lie upon the leaves

They magnify the mysteries,
Through the moisture you can see
Bright white veins on the green

They sparkle, glitter, and glisten
Shiny dewdrops are the life of the leaves.

Kinsey Kidder, Grade 5
Mary Walter Elementary School, VA

Free Verse

The sun is like a spark of fire,
But then there is the moon.
It shines in the night,
So everyone can enjoy.
Then there are the stars,
That gleam and sparkle.
The stars shine and light up the night,
So people can watch them in awe.

Madison Peckham, Grade 6
Monelison Middle School, VA

Dragon's Destiny

Renlik the dragon
Small but fiery
Brave
Determined
Kind
Has a shy side
Is a fiery crimson red
Finding his destiny

Kateri Bajer, Grade 5
St Mary School, RI

Spring

The trees are budding
The flowers come out
The blue jays are back
The robins give a shout

Michael Berg, Grade 5
St Joseph School-Fullerton, MD

My Class

Happy, encouraging
Helping, smiling, laughing
My very best friends
Awesome!

Matthew Christian, Grade 4
St John Neumann Academy, VA

My Dog Huntzie

He is as black as the dark night sky.
He has a beard as gray as a stormy cloud.
With his eyes as brown as the dirt.
He stands out like a clock on a bare wall.

Brier Ziegler, Grade 4
Riderwood Elementary School, MD

The Pig

The pig is as dirty as dirt.
It can be as pink as strawberry ice cream.
With a tail as twisty as curly fries.
The pig is as sweet as a piece of candy.

Maren H., Grade 4
Riderwood Elementary School, MD

A Peacock

A peacock is as unique as the Bahamas Sea,
It's as beautiful as a beach during a sunset,
With a blue body as a summer sky,
it's as special as your birthday.

Abbey Walsh, Grade 4
Riderwood Elementary School, MD

Me!

I'm an awesome guy
I like to have lots of fun
So party with me

Shaun Daniel, Grade 6
Monelison Middle School, VA

Eyes

Sparkling blue eyes shine
They're the portal to the mind
Window of the soul

Niraly Patel, Grade 6
Monelison Middle School, VA

Dirt Bikes

Dirt bikes go so fast
A powerful engine roars
Race a dirt bike now!

Andrew Brunner, Grade 6
Monelison Middle School, VA

Lions

They are great beasts,
Surviving in the wild.
They snore, they roar,
In their dens.

Lions are searching beasts who hunt,
All day for prey.
While at night, their cubs
Love to play.

They are the kings of the jungle,
They rule with pride.
Like a conductor,
Other animals follow their stride.

Mike Bedford, Grade 5
Tilghman Elementary School, MD

I Miss You Bompie

I miss you from the earth I live on
I miss you more than the stars in heaven
I love you father of my father, my grandpa
My granna loved you so very dearly
Why did you have to leave her?
I miss you father of my father
My dearly loved one
I miss you so very much
Father of my father
So very close you were to me
Father of my father
I miss you and I love you
My dear grandfather, Bompie

Carrie White, Grade 5
Home School, ME

The Beach

People bathing
Waves rolling in
Salty ocean air
Salty ocean water
Warm, hot sand

Isabella Heffel, Grade 4
Greenville Elementary School, VA

Dandelion

O look! What a dandy lion
Roaring with the wind.

Swaying back and forth
With its opponent knowing
It would win.

Towering above the grass
And protecting its yard,
Is that yellow dandy lion.

Faith Sacre, Grade 4
Greater Portland Christian School, ME

My Family

I have one brother named Edgar
My dad is really tall
My mom likes to play tennis
My brother likes to play with cars
I like to watch TV

Nelson Rivera, Grade 4
Courthouse Road Elementary School, VA

Sweet Puppy

I'm a girl, yes
I like puppies
They can make you smile
But one thing that blows my mind
They are so kind.

Takira K. Oaks, Grade 4
Featherbed Lane Elementary School, MD

The Mean Bunny

The mean bunny
He sat on my head
He ate my chocolate bar
I loved that chocolate bar so much
It looked so good

Lauren Schutrum, Grade 4
Courthouse Road Elementary School, VA

The Moon

There once was a moon during the night
That could be seen so very bright
When the sun came out
People woke with a shout
And then there was a very bright light.

Isaac Ogallo, Grade 4
Hebbville Elementary School, MD

Pizza

P izza is good to eat.
I love the way it tastes.
Z ucchini is nasty on pizza.
Z ealous is how I feel about eating pizza.
A ll pizza is good with meat.

Kahvontey Woodbury, Grade 5
Gaithersburg Elementary School, MD

My Wish for Our World

Peace
Awesome, wonderful
Loving, caring, smiling
My wish for our world
Happiness

Ashley Egertson, Grade 6
Floyd T Binns Middle School, VA

Clean Revolution

Our environment is full of pollution.
What can be the solution?
But to work together,
For a clean revolution.

Let us clean our garbage,
Pile them up nicely.
Separate all the trash,
Recycle them wisely.

It may take more work,
It may take more time.
But in the end,
The Earth will be fine.

Let us think about this,
And do what we need to do.
To make the air cleaner,
For me and for you.

Archangel Deguzman, Grade 4
St Clement Mary Hofbauer School, MD

Trail of My Tears

The trail of tears
Or some call
Torture.
The pain it felt
Walking and walking
Until you die.
If you're lucky,
You will
Survive.
The white men drove
My people off
The land
The thousand mile walk was
Your worst nightmare
So scary, it's
Scarring.
The trail is full
Of my bloody
Tears.

Connor Ruff, Grade 5
Rosemont Forest Elementary School, VA

Turtles

All turtles have a shell.
And no turtle can ring a bell.
Every turtle is a reptile.
When I see one, it makes me smile.
Turtles move pretty slow.
Come on, turtle, *go, go go!*
Turtles, also, can't drive cars.
Are there turtles living on Mars?

Alex Pates, Grade 4
Gaithersburg Elementary School, MD

What Friends Are For
Laughing as loud as we can
While eating ice cream on the porch
Riding bikes all day
Under the warm sun, burning like a torch,
That's what friends are for.

Glued to the screen
On cold, rainy days
Quickly pressing buttons with our thumbs
Because we can't go out to play,
That's what friends are for.

In the backyard or at the park
Screaming, "Go deep for a pass,"
Having fun all the time
Whether shooting "three's" or playing tag,
That's what friends are for.
Javier Love, Grade 6
Magnolia Elementary School, MD

Shadow
In the dawn of the day,
It pops up at your feet,
Fully grown.
It follows you wherever you go.

At noon it has shrunk to its smallest.
Ending three inches away from your feet.
Barely noticed.

It copies my every move,
An alien in disguise.
Until dusk it grows bigger and bigger,
Morphing into sight.

As night comes it is gone,
From the earth until the next,
Day is born.
Cian McCue, Grade 5
Tilghman Elementary School, MD

I Am Beautiful
I am beautiful in many ways
That's why I am here today
I am beautiful because of my intelligence
And my personality
Because I'm not fake, I'm reality
I am beautiful; the way I dress or the
Sloppy, improper grammar words I text
I am beautiful because I'm weird
And the ways I scream of fear
I am beautiful because I'm me
And no one can change that
I'm beautiful
Kiasia Thomas, Grade 5
Rosemont Forest Elementary School, VA

My Life
My life is no smaller
Than a piece
Of dust
It is just waiting and
Looking for something
To happen.
Am I a nothing?
A nothing to be an anything?
Why do I feel
This pain?
Are my feelings in the
Way of my life?
Let go of the past.
I need to keep moving;
To live.
Sara Rodriguez, Grade 5
Rosemont Forest Elementary School, VA

At the Beach
Waves smash onto the sand
Like thunder on a cloudy sky.
The beautiful blue ocean
Travels on forever.
Splash!
Cold water covers me
As a wave crashes at my feet.
The salty water smell
Fills me with delight.
Nothing is better
Than sitting in my favorite beach chair,
Eating a cold ice cream,
Warm sand surrounding my feet,
All on a perfect summer day.
Haley Vest, Grade 6
Trinity School, MD

Harriet Tubman
H ad a dream
A bolitionist
R an like the wind
R ocks
I think she is awesome
E ast was not the direction she was heading
T he abolitionists called her Moses

T he slave owners did not like her
U p in attics a lot when hiding
B lack sky when she was awake
M aryland is where she was born
A great fighter
N orth was her way to freedom
Shelby Warren, Grade 4
Waller Mill Fine Arts Magnet School, VA

Blue
Blue is the color of the sky
Blue is blueberry pie

Blue Ridge Mountains
Gurgling fountains

The color of a Smurf
The water where we surf

A blue moon
A sad tune

A Blue Jay
Hydrangeas in May

Blue fills up every day
Connor Dunlop, Grade 5
Blacksburg New School, VA

Waterfalls
As I peer over the balcony,
I notice that some are
gentle and small,
making quiet drips and drops.
Others are strong, huge, majestic,
and roar like lions,
but all are clear, cold, and foamy,
where the water turns to mist
with a loud splash.

Below,
I touch the water with my hand,
and it isn't enticing enough to pull me in,
but it feels cool and fresh,
reminding me of a spring rain.
Seth Gregory, Grade 6
Trinity School, MD

Civil War
The cannons had fired,
More soldiers were hired
For the Civil War.

Smoke would go by
When the bullets would fly
Then the soldiers would lay on the floor.

The slaves were free
When Robert E. Lee
Surrendered to the Union.

"Oh my" Lee did chant
When he saw little ole Grant
But for now it's a big reunion.
Isaiah Schmit, Grade 4
Waller Mill Fine Arts Magnet School, VA

The Field Mouse

A little field mouse scampers
into the secluded, lush green valley:
he skitters toward the tiny, shady tree
as fragile as my mother's hand painted china.
The mouse gathers bitter acorns,
laps the fresh river water,
and licks the bland grass.

The wind whistles and shrieks
ruffling the mouse's velvet fur,
and rustling the plush grass.

He dashes back to his oak tree
with bark as rough as a bull's skin.
The peppery smell of autumn warns that winter is coming.
So the mouse must get back to work —
With haste.

Ellie Heffernan, Grade 6
Trinity School, MD

When I Look at the Sky

When I sit on the beach,
I'll think of your cane thumping against the sand.
When I sing a song,
I'll remember your voice, so beautiful, singing with me at Mass.
When I look at the sky,
I'll remember your eyes, always so bright and full of faith.
When I pick a flower,
I'll remember the floral scent of your perfume.
When I laugh,
I'll hear you laughing with me.
When I see a cloud,
I'll think of you standing at the gates of
Heaven, rejoicing in the grace of God and
I'll know someday I'll be standing there with you, and
We'll be laughing and hugging, because we'll know
That we never need to be separated again.

Sidney Wollmuth, Grade 6
River Bend Middle School, VA

Wild Horses

They're beautiful, wild, and free,
Everything we wish we could be.
They run, gallop, and play as they please,
While their beautiful mane and tail flow through the breeze.
They are extremely gorgeous and not at all restless,
And their sorrowful worries are pointless.
The parents, they sleep all day.
While the little ones frolic and play.
They live on the island of Chincoteague,
We watch and ponder how they came to be so free.
Horses, they inspire me each day,
They remind me to be healthy and happy
while shining all the way.

Mikayla Kzinowek, Grade 5
Lightfoot Elementary School, VA

Blue

Blue is a wave that splashes on your feet.
Blue is a blue jay flying across the horizon.
Blue is a raindrop that splashes on the roof.
Blue is the feeling when you get cold.
It is a sunset on a hot summer night.
Look up look down look all around there will
Always be something that is blue.
Blue is the color of my eye glass case.
Blue is a sunset.
Blue is the sky.
Blue is the color of ink
Blue is the purest color of all.

Steven Sardella, Grade 4
Immaculate Conception Catholic Regional School, RI

Blue Blue oh Blue

Blue is the color of a wave crashing down on your toes.
Blue can be the color of a yo-yo or a race car.
Blue is the color of blue jays chirping all day.
Blue can be the color of people playing croquet.
Blue is the color of angels singing for you.
Blue is the color of things that I like to do.
Blue is the color of the bright blue sky.
Blue can be the color of a new marker.
Or a big tear dripping down your cheek.
Or even a new pair of jeans.
Blue may be beautiful or sad but you should love it all.
That's why blue is my favorite color.

Stephen Walsh, Grade 4
Immaculate Conception Catholic Regional School, RI

I Spy (Nature)

Listen to those magnificent birds—
Chirppity-chirp that's what I heard
See those two young squirrels, they're chasing each other
Hey look there is their mother
Have you noticed what she found?
She's holding acorns that were lying on the ground
Look over there! I found a bunny
The way it hops seem so funny
Look right there! I see a crow
It's peeking at our neighbor's scarecrow that wears a bow
Thank God for all He has made
Thank Him throughout your day

John Adjani-Aldrin, Grade 5
Church of the Redeemer Christian School, MD

A Worldwide Wish

My worldwide wish would have to be peace for all eternity
Another thing I think is keen
Is helping others even when they appear to be mean
Also we need to try to help alike
And really try hard not to fight
That is what I have to say would be my worldwide wish today

Theangela Johnson, Grade 6
Floyd T Binns Middle School, VA

Searching

I'm a little ant,
So small and round.
You walk around me every day.
When it rains I hide.
The queen ant died and I have no sisters.
I'm wandering around trying to find my mister.
I want someone who is long and lean.
I hope my dream comes true.
My mister, my mister I won't stop looking for you.

Alexis Jackson, Grade 6
Monelison Middle School, VA

It's More Than Just a Game

When it was my turn to bat, I was nervous as can be.
I thought to myself, this is easy as can be.
I stared at the pitcher, he threw my favorite pitch.
I raised my elbow and swung for the fence.
I hit the ball with a bam, Hooray! Grand Slam!
As I rounded third, I saw my team at home plate.
They were waiting to say, "You're great!"
Even though I'd love the fame,
It's more than just a game.

Cole Cline, Grade 4
Tazewell Elementary School, VA

Mittens

I once had a kitten,
His name was Mittens.
We let him out one day but
He walked away.
4 years later there was a sway in the trees
And we looked up.
And there was a big black cat
With a golden collar.
Engraved in the collar was the name Mittens.

Owen Sanborn, Grade 4
Greater Portland Christian School, ME

Summer

S un is hot and shining down
U nder an umbrella we sit on the beach, looking for shade
M aking sandcastles at the water's edge
M oving in the water, playing in the waves
E ating yummy foods like ice cream and watermelon
R unning across hot sand, burning our feet

Ruth Benavides, Grade 4
Gaithersburg Elementary School, MD

Spring

You can taste the sprinkling water coming from the sky
You can see the beautiful maturing flowers
You can smell the dew among the grass
You can touch the silk, soft, fragile petals
You can hear the birds low, quiet hums

Kara Nicole White, Grade 5
Church of the Redeemer Christian School, MD

Best Friend

Of course she's a girl
Best friend in the world
She makes me smile
More than a while
She's my best friend and you know it
Yes, I'm trying to express it and show it.

You think girls are icky and maybe even sticky
But they are not
Cupid says everyone will be shot
And you'll be in love
Thinking about doves
Everyone show some LOVE!!

Dwayne Harrison, Grade 6
Magnolia Elementary School, MD

Summer Work

This summer work is giving me grief.
When it is done it will be a relief.
So much to do, I have a ton.
I have no idea when I'll be done.
Math, poem, postcards, and journal.
All my hard work is eternal.
When will the hard work ever stop?
I'll keep working until I drop.
All I like to do is play on my iTouch.
With work my mom says, "There's never too much."
Now you know how my summer went.
Now I know what I'll give up for Lent.

Jeb Wickham, Grade 4
St. Christopher's School, VA

Earth

Earth is a happy
And dangerous place
You don't know
What's going to happen these days
Every day you wake up and see the sunshine
And the next morning your grandma dies and
You say why?
There is sorrow everywhere
Even downstairs
But happiness too
So it's a clueless world,
What are you going to do?

Travis Kennedy, Grade 6
Magnolia Elementary School, MD

Nightmare

I woke up to the moon only to find the sun;
as a voice screams inside my head but I can't make out a sound;
I breathed in heavy gulps of air as a shiver goes down my spine;
Questions, answers just one, What gave me such a scare?
I looked around the room in relief it was only a nightmare

Chloe Bort, Grade 6
Paul L Dunbar Middle School for Innovation, VA

About Me

M ichael is my name,
I saac Wu is my best friend,
C an run fast,
H ave a brother, and 2 sisters,
A m athletic,
E njoy singing,
L egos are my favorite hobby.

D o like to play football,
A m part Russian and German,
V iolins are one of my favorite instruments,
I like to read,
D o like to eat macaroni and cheese.

D o enjoy playing games on computer,
R eading the Bible makes me feel safe,
E xercise a lot,
S wimming is one of my favorite sports,
S cience is my favorite subject,
L ove God most of all,
E njoy traveling,
R ight-handed.

Michael Dressler, Grade 5
Church of the Redeemer Christian School, MD

My Life

My life is very busy;
It's like I live in the city.
When my brother is racing,
You'll always find me pacing.
I'm always on the go;
It's like I'm moving from head to toe.
When I play sports,
My brother watches me dribble down the court.
My life is busy — this is true,
Is your life busy, too?

Madison Greenlaw, Grade 5
Eastport Elementary School, ME

Civil War

The Civil War broke out in 1861
Everyone stood ready with a gun.
They fought for what they thought was right
It was a long four year fight.
He won the first battle, let's give Stonewall a cheer!
Bullets flew around him, but he did not fear.
There was a person named Robert E. Lee
He led the Confederate army.
He couldn't fight against his home state
So he went with the Confederates.
He lost the war which was no more
Ulysses didn't make him turn over his sword.
The Civil War had started in 1861
By 1865, the North Union had won.

Carter Law, Grade 4
Waller Mill Fine Arts Magnet School, VA

My Vision of the World

We drive through the streets with cellphones in hands
We ignore those folks walking around
They look at us with sorrow and distress
Snickering in disgust we continue to let them die
We jog across the roads wearing headphones
Music makes life energetic and fun
Traffic light signals green yellow and red
While our favorite bands give us no chance
A few little girls are out selling treats
Cheerleading for a cause or a pause
They have reasons for a better world
We turn them back as we don't believe in the future
Lights turned yellow, we "Go Green"
Earth and her kids have to survive
Let us sow the seeds of love and compassion
Grow the beautiful trees of fruits, shade and life
Paint the world with color, spread the fragrance of love
I sing for you, my vision of the world

Mahima Sindhu, Grade 6
Jack Jouett Middle School, VA

The Brook

I sit on the tree-bridge with my friend.
It's rough, and the bark scrapes my hands,
But I don't mind.
On the banks of the stream sprout wild flowers,
Reaching up to the sunlight from the oak tree's shade.
A cool breeze rustles the leaves.
The birds sing their joyful song.
Beneath us are jagged rocks,
Homes for snails, snakes, and leeches.
Water spills over the edge of the waterfalls behind us.
A steady splash echoes through the trees.
Water rushes by.
It's pretty, shallow, and full of rocks.
Sunlight glistens on the water.
Rays strew onto the moist earth.
Trees, that have grown for many years,
Stand straight, proudly, and strong,
Like soldiers guarding my brook.

Sophia Carter, Grade 6
Wyman Elementary School, RI

Fenway Park

Baseball is a spectacular game.
What even makes it better is the baseball park.
The park's astonishing smells permeate the air.
The juicy hot dogs and hamburgers are especially irresistible.
The park's luscious grass waves in the wind as if it's saying, "Hello!"
Fans cheer wildly as their favorite player
Bangs a homerun out of the park.
The dirt looks like brown snow, undisturbed and powdery.
Players strut onto the field confidently and looking relaxed.
Fenway Park is the most glorious ballpark in the world!

Matthew Woods, Grade 6
Wyman Elementary School, RI

I Hate It

It is horrible,
I hate it,
I want to turn it around,
But I back away,
Every time I am about to confront it,
It makes me cry,
Like the smell of a rainy day,
I hate it,
I hate it like murky, salty water,
Or a gloomy, cloudy morning,
Weeping or my dog crying,
I hate it,
I hate it,
I hate it,
I hate it,
I cry in a corner,
Hoping something will change,
And I run away.
I hate it.

Tomas Moser, Grade 6
McLean School of Maryland, MD

Fifth Grade

Being in fifth grade is rough;
I try and try, but it is tough.
When you get there you will see,
But sometimes it is fun — believe me!

Math is what I like best,
I don't like getting things wrong on my test.
But when you do get it right,
You feel like you're in the limelight.

Reading is not easy;
It makes me feel queasy.
When I finally read aloud,
I am very, very proud.

So the next time you think of school,
And you feel scared, or you feel cool;
Think about life in a different way,
Homework first, and then play.

Roxanna MacGregor, Grade 5
Eastport Elementary School, ME

The Lonely Leaf

The fragile scarlet leaf,
blown from its home
on a tall tree,
feels scared as it
tumbles to the ground,
wondering where it will land,
dreaming about reuniting with friends
in a safe leaf pile.

Olivia DiMeo, Grade 6
Trinity School, MD

Summer Breeze

Carrying the sweet scents,
Of flowers in full bloom
I feel the warm sunshine
Filling me with the good feeling
Of summer

Lifting the birds up,
While they sing
Sweet, sweet summer breeze
You comfort me

Letting me know,
Summer is truly…
Here

Erica Eubank, Grade 6
Monelison Middle School, VA

Matchbox Cars

Matchbox cars all over the floor,
Matchbox cars near the door.

Matchbox cars in neat rows,
Matchbox cars between my toes.

Matchbox cars over my head,
Matchbox cars in his bed.

Kobie's cars are everywhere
Sometimes I think they're in my hair.

Little cars for little hands,
Too bad, I'm not a Matchbox fan.

Abbie Talmoud, Grade 6
Adelphi Elementary School, MD

Love, Me

I love you because you're awesome,
I love you because you care,
I love you because you love me,
I love you because you're there.

It's funny how you see right through me,
It's funny how you know,
It's funny how you care so much,
It's funny how you love me so.

I hope you can see the love I have for you,
I hope you see how much I care,
I hope you see how awesome you are,
I hope you'll always be there.

Symone Brooks, Grade 5
Brookewood School, MD

Trail of Bloody Tears

I am sad and depressed
In a lonely shell of a body
I have to keep moving to live my life
I don't want to give up
I will not be a quitter
I must still keep moving
My blood and my tears are on the ground
But my life depends on moving forward
I will live
My family is the strength
I have to keep going

Cori Riddick-White, Grade 5
Rosemont Forest Elementary School, VA

McKayla

McKayla
Nice, funny, crazy, loving, awesome
Daughter of Darrell and LeAnn
Lover of cheerleading, shopping, and eating
Who feels ecstatic when on roller-coasters
Awesome when shopping
Proud when cheering
Who gives love, care, and hugs
Who fears clowns, bugs, and snakes
Who lives in Virginia
Holmes

McKayla Holmes, Grade 5
H M Pearson Elementary School, VA

Stars

Star, star of the night
Wonderful light
So, so bright

Countless numbers
In the clear, dark sky
Rolling way past by

Twinkle, twinkle the night away
Especially during the blooming of May
Like a line, a ray

Inaya Andrews, Grade 6
Magnolia Elementary School, MD

Look at Me

Look at me
you might think
that you can't see
me, but I will
look into your eyes
and say "Here I am"
look at me, if you
look at me you see a
person, a great person.

Travis Whittington, Grade 4
Featherbed Lane Elementary School, MD

Computers Every Day

I use the computer every day.
Do you?
You use it for research.
I use it for play.
You do it for important things.
I do it for happiness every day.

Alexandra Neaves, Grade 4
Courthouse Road Elementary School, VA

Music

Sometimes it's soothing
Sometimes it's bruising
Sometimes it's loud
Sometimes it's in front of a crowd
This is one of my best
Now it's time for me to rest.

Marquette Crew Jr., Grade 4
Waller Mill Fine Arts Magnet School, VA

Yellow

Yellow is the color of the rising sun
Blue is the color of joy and fun
Green is the color of my moldy food
Red is the color when I'm in a bad mood
Brown is the color of my hamburger bun
Orange is the color of the falling sun.

Blake Douglas, Grade 5
St Christopher's School, VA

Apple Pie

Pie, Pie, I prefer apple.
Sweet, sugary, cinnamon slices,
with warmth waiting in every bite.
The liquid apple leaps across my tongue,
As delightful as a summer breeze,
As comforting as a blanket.

Kieran McKinnon, Grade 6
Trinity School, MD

Sports

S occer is my favorite sport.
P laying soccer in the middle of the field.
O nly winning the game makes me happy.
R unning after the ball is hard.
T eamwork makes goals happen.
S coring big to win the game.

Christopher Rosales, Grade 4
Gaithersburg Elementary School, MD

Swimming

I love to swim in the pool
It is really cool
I like to do it after school
Even with my pet dog, Jewel

Tai Stewart, Grade 4
Hebbville Elementary School, MD

Hi But Not Bye

I just came to say hi
But not good-bye
I love you so
But now it's time to go
Bye and hi are not to say I
I love you much
Cause we really have a touch
I just came to say hi
But not good-bye

Kaylin Harper, Grade 4
Featherbed Lane Elementary School, MD

Friends

Me and you
will always be together
we are always laughing and giggling
we are stuck like glue
but that's what friends are supposed to do
You got my back I got yours
That is what we are here for
We are everlasting friends
We are together through thick and thin

Amber Foster, Grade 6
Hardin Reynolds Memorial School, VA

Mystery Man

He made me get off the phone
This little twerp won't leave me alone
His voice is hot
His hands are cold
His personality is very bold
Who is this guy?
Let's look and see
You never know
It could be me

Kelby Campbell, Grade 6
Monelison Middle School, VA

Halloween

Scary Halloween nights
People yell in a fright
Ghosts scream
"Don't eat ice cream!"
And I don't stay up at night

Sheridan Hightower, Grade 4
Hebbville Elementary School, MD

Summer

S un comes out and we still have fun
U nhappy winter goes back down
M ay be hot, but it still beats cold
M r. Sun, please shine on me
E veryone at school knows you're cool
R emember, everyone the sun loves you…

Lisa-Ann Aryee, Grade 4
Gaithersburg Elementary School, MD

Alexis

A is for athletic
L is for lovable
E is for energetic
X is for extreme
I is for independent
S is for smart

Alexis Lawrence, Grade 4
Featherbed Lane Elementary School, MD

The Wind

The wind comes
on little dog feet.
It sits quietly
over countries and cities,
on silent bridges,
and then keeps moving on.

Jasmine Crawley, Grade 6
Monelison Middle School, VA

Friend

F aithful
R eliable
I nspirational
E ndless
N ice
D elightful

Bethany Tracey, Grade 5
Rosemont Forest Elementary School, VA

School Oh School

School oh school,
you drive me crazy!
School oh school,
you last too long!
School oh school,
you must be 50 hours long!

Haley Kerhart, Grade 4
Courthouse Road Elementary School, VA

Tigers

T igers hunt at night
I ntelligent hiding skills
G rowl like thunder
E at over thirty animals a year
R ely on their coat to camouflage
S trike from only a few yards away

Renee Stubbs, Grade 4
Connor Consolidated School, ME

Sushi

Great food
Eating, enjoying, tasting
Great food when hungry
Fish

Troy Pittman Jr., Grade 4
Hebbville Elementary School, MD

Dainty Pink
Pink is the color you see in your dreams,
A pink dolphin floating down a stream.
Pink is the horizon spread across the sky, I wonder why.
Pink is a smile on your face!
Pink is a wild goose-chase!
Pink is a butterfly, flying high in the sky!
Pink is what a flower girl throws out at a wedding.
Pink is the color you feel when there's no doubt in your mind.
Pink is the color of a flamingo.
Pink is the color that pops out on the rainbow.
Pink is the color of a dance called "The Tango."

Sofia DiGregorio, Grade 4
Immaculate Conception Catholic Regional School, RI

Football
I am a girl, but I love the exciting game of football,
I'd rather be outside than playing with a stupid doll,
When I put on my helmet and pads,
I love to hear the yells from all the dads,
I run across the field and tackle the quarterback hard,
I hope you don't get smooshed like a flat, small card.
Football is the toughest and hardest sport I know,
While playing I hope I don't break my little, pinky toe.
When I run across the grass, it flies in my face,
A loss can taste like failure and disgrace,
Wherever my dignity has gone; I can find no trace.

Alyssa Murphy, Grade 5
Lightfoot Elementary School, VA

Snow
Tiny snowflakes fly around,
Blankets of snow touch the ground.

Little squeals of little kids,
They rub their eyes and open the lids,

They eat their breakfast and get ready to go,
They get bundled up and say, "I love snow!"

They finally get outside and make a snowman,
They chant, they sing, "Let it snow again!"

Devin Rooney, Grade 6
St John Neumann Academy, VA

James
james
it means weird, happy, thankful
it is the number 911
it is like the sunset on a warm summer evening
it is the vacation to California
it is the memory of dad
who taught me how to fish
my name is james
it means weird

James Lane, Grade 6
Hardin Reynolds Memorial School, VA

I Wish
I wish I lived in a tree;
There it would be so perfect for me.
I wish I had a pair of wings;
And a bluebird that sings.
I wish I had an orange ape;
For every trick I'd give him a grape.
I wish I had a little brown kitty;
That had a cute face and looks awfully pretty.
I wish and I wish, but nothing's happened so far;
Maybe I should try wishing upon a star.

Sarah Bartlett, Grade 4
Eastport Elementary School, ME

My Blue Scarf with Yellow Polka Dots
My blue scarf with yellow polka dots where are you?
Up or down, side to side
Where can you be my blue scarf with yellow polka dots?
Could you have been under the bed?
Where are you blue scarf with yellow polka dots?
I miss you up and down, side to side where could you be?
Please come to me blue scarf with yellow polka dots
I miss you blue scarf with yellow polka dots
I want to see you under my neck soft and calm

Hiba Fatima, Grade 4
Courthouse Road Elementary School, VA

The Little House on the Hill
A lady named Jill
A husband named Phil
They were moving to a new house on the hill.
A dog came along
His name was Chill
When they came into the house
There was a friendly guest mouse
They all lived together on the house on the hill
So make sure you come to the hills.

Christina Hunt, Grade 4
Courthouse Road Elementary School, VA

Spring
S unshine escapes the clouds
P eaceful birds flutter their wings
R ainbows in the sky after rainfall
I rises, tulips, and daffodils start to grow
N ow it's time for the cherry trees to bloom
G od's creation makes the world complete

Kristina Allen, Grade 5
Church of the Redeemer Christian School, MD

The Moon
Moon moon why do you only come out at night?
Please tell me please tell me why.
And your little friends stars.
Oh moon now I know why you come out at night.

Caroline Slick, Grade 4
Courthouse Road Elementary School, VA

The Grand Canyon

G od's Creation
R ocky
A wesome
N ever want to leave
D angerous

C olorado River
A mazing sight
N ice hiking spot
Y ou'll be blown away
O n top of the world
N ational Park

Nolan Macek, Grade 5
Church of the Redeemer Christian School, MD

Echo Lake

Arriving to the lake, everything is silent.
If you make a noise, everyone will hear you.
Taking a dip is freezing at first.
When I adjust to the cold, I never want to get out.
The crickets start to get quieter when people arrive.
The view is beautiful.
I notice the orange dots on the ledge.
I realize that they are people.
When people arrive, the quietness disappears.
I never want to get out, but the temperature gets colder.
The sun starts to set, and the people leave.
And now the silence is back again.

Scotty Campbell, Grade 6
Wyman Elementary School, RI

Life

I am life. I can be sweet but I can be cruel.
Air I eat and I can eat yours up or I can act like I'm full…

Bitter sweet I can be.
Or I can be nice and really sweet!

I can walk up to you and squash you like a bug.
Or I can help you out and give you a hug!

I am life strong and pretty
I am life mean and petty

TyJae Pittman, Grade 4
Featherbed Lane Elementary School, MD

Trail of Tears

I walk with fears and with my ears, I hear tears.
I eat with sadness, but my mind is full of madness.
I hear people crying as I'm dying.
My feet have scratches and I need patches.
My hair is dry, as I cry.
In vain inside on the inside;
On the outside, I'm beautiful.

Shymeek Dixon, Grade 5
Rosemont Forest Elementary School, VA

Crystal Clear

Isn't it all so crystal clear?
I wake up in the morning.
I put my pants on my head.
My shirt on my legs.
Isn't it all so crystal clear?
I put my shoes on my hands.
I put my socks on my ears.
I carpool to school.
I ride outside the car.
Isn't it all so crystal clear.
So I'm at school.
My teacher asks for my homework.
I say I'm doing it now.
She says why?
Aren't we supposed to be doing it now?
I had to go to the principal's office.
I got in big trouble.
Not just because I was wearing my pants on my head.
Why doesn't anybody get my way?
Isn't IT ALL SO CRYSTAL CLEAR!

Zoye Williams, Grade 4
Courthouse Road Elementary School, VA

A Fire Inside

Red, orange, yellow, are words that come to mind.
You can feel this over somebody.
Or about anything.
You can feel it in your stomach.
It builds up inside you.
Eventually you can't hold it in.
You burst out with it.
Your firsts clench up.
And soon you have no control.
Face gets red.
And revenge can come to mind.
It feels like the time you got punched in the stomach.
And you want to punch back.
All your organs turn to lava.
Your head feels as if it blows up as big as it can get.
Getting redder and redder.
And you're about to explode.
But then someone is there to calm you down.
Hoping to keep you under control.

Jared Postal, Grade 6
McLean School of Maryland, MD

My Journey to Freedom

I run down the risky road
Not knowing of what I hold
Running in the dark night; running with all my might
I follow the star that holds the light to accomplish my journey
I see my destination, the joy in my heart
I know I've finished
I know I succeeded in my journey to freedom

Jeremiah Brown, Grade 5
Rosemont Forest Elementary School, VA

My Outside and My Inside Self

My outside self and my inside self
Are more different than you think

My outside self has big fluffy hair
Big glasses so I can see better when I blink
Strong skinny long arms
Tall enough to sit in the back and let others in the front
Long legs that make it hard to stretch
And not very good at football when it comes to punt

My inside self is different
As you can see

An awesome swimmer
Speeding inside of me
Dirty blond hair
As handsome as can be
Jumping with joy
As he wins the swimming competition inside of me
                    Mody Kutkut, Grade 5
                    Blacksburg New School, VA

Disneyland

On the morning in November, 2010
Mom, Dad, me and Nan
Hopped on a plane to Disneyland
Looking out the window, looking at the land.

We arrived in Florida
We got our bags and hopped in the car
We went to the hotel
The pool had a big bar.

We went to Disneyland
We saw Mickey, and Minnie, and Goofy too
We saw a ballerina with a tutu.
We went into a haunted house and the ghost said "Boo."

We got to eat hot dogs
With mustard, and ketchup, and bread
Then the parade came through
With stuff flying everywhere, and beads too.
                    Makenzie Henderson, Grade 6
                    St John Neumann Academy, VA

Volcanoes

Low patches of naupaka bushes line the monster.
A few tangled hau trees try to taunt her.
The pahoehoe lava slides down so easily,
while the a'a doesn't go as breezily.
It gives no sign; no sign of threat,
But leaving immediately is a safe bet.
It can destroy everything in a blink of an eye,
But to her it's only a stretch, a yawn, a sigh.
                    Sydney Jones, Grade 5
                    Lightfoot Elementary School, VA

I Don't Care?

When all is gone away
Me?
I'm never okay
People look at me with pity
All my love is all drained away
So I'm different
Do I deserve all these tears?
You have no idea what I've been through; no one is here
You glance upon my face
As you receive a fake smile
While my faded eyes are filled with tears
I take all the insults
They are the thoughts in my head
My best friend, a tissue
Wiping the tears from my face
I may say I don't care and walk away
But just don't stand there
Help me
Save me
Make me
Okay.

                    Isatu Fofanah, Grade 6
                    Orange Hunt Elementary School, VA

The Crusades

The Crusades were bloody wars
To protect what their enemy was coming for.
Massacres were as common as traitors
Fathers, brothers, sons, and neighbors
Were proud to fight against the raiders.

Once there were many toddlers
Who dreamt to be knights
They grew up to be knights who fought for their rights.
Knights were so loyal
That they would die for their soil.
And die they did to honor those who were dead.

Anger arose throughout the war
And lies were told to all in war.
Fighting for God was not what some knights were there for
More land! More power! More riches! They screamed
Killing those who did not believe
And demanded that they leave.
The Crusades were dreadful times
Which lasted a long time.
                    Maximo Edwin Tello Thompson, Grade 5
                    Church of the Redeemer Christian School, MD

Henry David Thoreau

Henry David Thoreau's record at school is not great
But he graduated from Harvard around 1838
He lived in Massachusetts most of his life
He never married so he had no wife
                    William Cadogan, Grade 6
                    Immaculate Heart of Mary School, MD

A Storm of Perspective

Thunder's the reaction to the lightning that breaks;
Thinking ahead of time is all it takes.

The thunder pauses before he shouts;
He knows what he's saying when he lets it out.

Triggers brew feelings of anger in the clouds;
Thunder feels embarrassed when he shares them aloud.

The sky's melancholy is expressed through its tears;
Then it spreads to the harbors and piers.

Victory brags within the Sun's gleam,
And there's also happiness mixed in the beam.

But the Moon keeps his feelings inside and maintained;
He protects them with his heart and his brain.

John Mills, Grade 5
Eastport Elementary School, ME

Ocean

In the ocean, the mighty swordfish want to fight.
In the ocean, dolphins play by daylight.

In the ocean, the hungry sharks search for their prey.
In the ocean, starfish are lazy all day.

In the ocean, the massive whales yell out hello.
In the ocean, a tang is bright yellow.

In the ocean, a swift marlin swims so fast.
In the ocean, a sailfish makes a wild dash.

In the ocean, vibrant coral feed on small shrimp.
In the ocean, a blowfish looks like a blimp.

In the ocean, a school of mahi mahi is a beautiful green.
In the ocean, please let's keep it clean.

Sophia Bandorick, Grade 6
Most Blessed Sacrament Catholic School, MD

Memories

My feet ache,
My bones are about to break,
My mother left me,
The memories of her keep me going,
They don't give us food,
I miss you too much,
I can't go on,
These final words are for you,
You have taken care of me all these years,
But now my adventure begins,
I think my adventure is going to end like yours,
I'll see you soon.

Lyndsay Doptis, Grade 5
Rosemont Forest Elementary School, VA

Bubbles

Bubbles, Bubbles 1 2 3
through that bubble I see me!
Blow em' Pop em', Blow some more
do they have em' at the store?
So many bubbles it's bubbles galore!
They come in different sizes and shapes
Even colors too!
Now you know why I love Bubbles
I'll write again soon!

Sienna Barnett, Grade 6
Paul L Dunbar Middle School for Innovation, VA

Sunshine

Sunshine, gentle on my face
Sunshine, gentle, kind
Sunshine, traveling through endless miles of space
Sunshine, forever on my mind

Sunshine warms the gentle Earth
Sunshine warms the seven seas
Sunshine chases sorrows, welcomes happiness
Sunshine does its very best to please

Kathlee Diaz, Grade 6
Magnolia Elementary School, MD

Blue

Blue is the ocean waves hitting my toes, splish splash.
Blue is nature calling your name.
Blue is cotton candy going in my mouth.
When I feel blue, I can smell soup downstairs.
Blue is the color when I feel embarrassed inside.
Blue is the color of our school community.
Blue is the thing you see when you go on a cruise ship.
Blue is the feeling of getting dressed in the morning.
Blue is the feeling of joy!

Robert Smith, Grade 4
Immaculate Conception Catholic Regional School, RI

Green

Green, green, nature's color scheme
It can take you to a place you could only dream
You see plants everywhere
They make you want to be gentle and care
Look outside, a big green scene

Molly Williams, Grade 5
St Joseph School-Fullerton, MD

Marines

The Marines fight for the American flag
They use different grenades from stunt to mag
Keeping evil from knocking at everyone's door
Using shotguns, snipers, oh bullets galore!
Saving thousands of lives almost every day
America is my country and that statement will stay!

Justin Tabron, Grade 4
Waller Mill Fine Arts Magnet School, VA

Sugar Glider: Fur Ball of the Night
It darts through the night
Skittering on branches as it lands.
The creature bounds on a eucalyptus tree.
The Sugar Glider sucks the sweet nectar.
It feeds on sticky sap.
It munches on crunchy bugs.
The Sugar Glider plays its heart out
Until dawn comes out for the day.
Gray, white, and black is what you see
With sap stains here and there.
A furry bundle of adventure.
It glides with grace.
Using flaps of skin for help.
It uses its tail like a rudder.
A tool to steer it through the night.
Screeching in alarm when an intruder comes,
Hissing in astonishment,
It zooms up trees.
It's delighted to steal sweet sap from trees.
The Sugar Glider drifts and bounds on trees.
That Amazing Wonder!
JD Wharton, Grade 5
Forcey Christian School, MD

The Little, Quaint Circle
A soft, slender breeze laps my face like a dog,
as the birds twitter and cheep
in the great oak tree.

Pink, red, and green
surround me with joy
in that little quaint circle
around Mary's statue in our school yard.

My tired legs are frail, glass vases,
waiting to be put down,
so I sit on the cool wood bench to relax.

The sky is a clear blue;
there are no clouds to block its delight.
Its friend, the sun, shines, with
might and majesty.

On this splendid morning,
that little quaint circle,
is where best to experience spring.
Jon Pejo, Grade 6
Trinity School, MD

Night Light
There's no need for a night light
When there's going to be a night light tonight
The moon gives us a good night light
So we can sleep well tonight
Diana Orozco-Garcia, Grade 4
Featherbed Lane Elementary School, MD

Portrait of a Tasmanian Devil
In a scavenger's life in a distant world
It awakens at night, famished and curled.
It crawls out of its home.
Her fur shines like chrome.
With a pouch, many wonders, and a coat of black,
She always looks for a carnivorous snack.

She screeches, crawls, and screams
And that is not all, it seems.
Her name comes from her sound that's fierce.
It just might make your ears pierce.
You might be afraid of its guttural growl,
Yet it might be more afraid of an owl.

Like a great contender, pound for pound
She has the most powerful bite around.
She can be aggressive and sometimes fight
And shall try to win with all her might.
Once she is victorious she earns her meal
From a maniacal rage and nerves of steel.
Ariel Edinbugh, Grade 5
Forcey Christian School, MD

Crush
I have a little secret.
It's becoming hard to keep it.
None of it is bad.
I've had a crush on a guy named Chad.
We're opposites from what can be seen.
He's strong but may look lean.
I'm fat and lazy.
Plus, I think he thinks I'm crazy.
I only see him in band.
I sit next to him and sometimes I wish he would hold my hand.
He's awesome and I'm not the best.
He's like the gold in a little wooden chest.
Every time of the day I tend to be smart.
But when he's around my brain seems to get tart.
I wish I could keep it to myself,
and remain still like a book on a shelf.
But yet I want to proclaim my crush for him,
though I can see he has or had a thing for a girl name Kim.
Oh how envious I am of she.
Why does it have to be he?
Sarah Dean, Grade 6
Independence Middle School, VA

If I Were a Booger
If I were a booger, they would pluck me around.
So far, so far, even to the playground.
If I were a booger, I wouldn't say a peep.
Not one peep or I might fall asleep.
A booger, a booger ewww! they might say.
But when I am around, I will never go away!
Simone Smith, Grade 4
Featherbed Lane Elementary School, MD

Mistake

The snake hissed at me
I meant to hiss back at him,
I mooed like a cow!
Christopher McCormick, Grade 5
St Christopher's School, VA

Nick Markakis

Nick Markakis rocks
He is number twenty-one
He's a right fielder
Alex Garing, Grade 5
St Joseph School-Fullerton, MD

Springtime

In spring the deer roam
The flowers will bloom brightly
Animals come out
Madison Warren, Grade 5
St Joseph School-Fullerton, MD

My Pet

I adored my pet.
She went to hamster heaven.
My heart has a void.
Kylee Zetterman, Grade 5
Connor Consolidated School, ME

Bears

Bears are eating fish
On top of a waterfall
He finally gets one
Jacob Porter, Grade 4
St John Neumann Academy, VA

The Moon

It shimmers at night,
makes the ebony sky bright,
and beams all around.
Julie Plante, Grade 6
Wyman Elementary School, RI

Sun

I am bright yellow
You need me to brighten paths
God created me.
Logan Gardner, Grade 6
Monelison Middle School, VA

Cat

A cat
is like a hissing engine
as it's breaking down.
Beth Kidd, Grade 6
Monelison Middle School, VA

Ocean

The ocean is lively one day, calm another.
You can hear the gulls, and waves crashing upon the rip—rap.
The sight of the beautiful sun, resting on the water,
As it shimmers, is quite a sight.
The sun is setting down, walking away, preparing for another day.

The ocean is now awake, the fury of the waves,
Destroying houses, and eating the land.
You can hear the thunder roar, and the lightning strike, at the trees.
The rain is pitter-pattering, on the water and sounds like rocks colliding.

Slowly a hurricane loses power, by hitting land.
It calms down, turning back into this amazing water.
The ocean is like life, one day it's alive, then slowly it dies down.
Respect its beauty, and always be bewildered, by its cycles.
Jasmine Robinson, Grade 6
Tilghman Elementary School, MD

Things in the Dugout

Players anxiously ready to play
With blue helmets on their heads
One by one going to hit at the plate
Sweaty from sprinting
Sticky gum under the bench
Salty sunflower seeds stuck on the sandy slab of cement
The ping ping ping of a composite bat
The cloudless blue sky
The bright ultraviolet sun
The clank clank clank of heavy bags full of bats, gloves and a helmet
The screams of overjoyed players after a scorching home run
Oh how I feel rancor when I'm not playing baseball!
Christian Harrington, Grade 6
Most Blessed Sacrament Catholic School, MD

I'm Here

When you feel a frown coming with the sudden urge to break down.
When you fall to your knees and think "Why now?"
When you cry and tears fall, they won't hit the ground, I'm catching them all.
I'm here with you no matter what, don't pick up that razor, don't make a cut.
I'm here singing you a song when negative thoughts are coming, singing a melody with you,
spreading happiness and smiles through my guitar strumming.
I'm here with you through everything, through anything. I'm here.
Roxanne Quimen, Grade 6
Paul L Dunbar Middle School for Innovation, VA

Musical

M any types of music — classical, rock, pop, and rap are but a few
U kuleles can be considered classical instruments
S axophone is a classical or jazz instrument
I nstruments are hard to learn how to play, but it can be fun
C larinets are woodwinds, another classical instrument
A n accordion is a jazz instrument
L ater on, if you try your best, you can become good on an instrument.
Jonathan Nick Works, Grade 4
Gaithersburg Elementary School, MD

Sunflower

I am sometimes asked,
What is beauty?
I think it's sitting on my porch
On a spring afternoon,
Where I can see my mom's under maintained lawn,
Dominated by wild sunflowers.
My mom hates sunflowers and weeds,
But I adore them.
They show a wild spirit I never had,
Destroying all the greenery.
The sunflowers are somewhat loyal, though,
As they always point toward the sun.
The soft rustling of their oval petals,
The crushing of salty sunflower seeds,
Under my teeth.
That is beauty to me.

Gustav Gulmert, Grade 6
Trinity School, MD

My Dog Rex

My dog Rex likes to chill with a bat,
Also his best friend is Speedy the cat.
Rex likes those adorable poodle dogs,
But despises those weird, wild hogs.
Rex is my genuine friend and considerably the best,
He is truly better than all of the rest.
My dog Rex is greatly frisky,
Once he ran in front of a car, and that was risky.
My dog Rex is extremely hilarious,
But he doesn't like the green vegetable asparagus.
Rex is beautiful inside and out,
His love is something that I would never doubt.
Rex sometimes acts like a ferocious hungry bear,
And sometimes he makes me sad
Because he doesn't seem to care.
I love my dog Rex!

De'Atryse Dickerson, Grade 5
Lightfoot Elementary School, VA

Nature

A bird flying above me
B eside a glittering pond
C rickets chirping, how lovely
D ragonflies buzzing with glee
E xcited, they dance over my head
F rogs leap in and out of the wet pond
G oats stomping in from the mountainside
H elicopters and airplanes are nowhere in sight
I lie in the swaying grass
J ust as a fawn in his first spring
K nowing only the world around him
L osing all track of time
M y senses strengthen, surrounded by
N ature.

Morgan Rizzo, Grade 6
Home School, VA

Secretariat

Fastest horse ever known,
No racer has beaten him, whether fast or slow.

He made himself known through all racing history,
How he did it is still a mystery.

His timing was amazing, a lap ahead of the rest,
This horse is still the best.

Secretariat is his name,
This horse always loved to be part of the game.

Catherine Sheen, Grade 6
St John Neumann Academy, VA

Cool Spring

C old things are gone, like ice.
O utside, there is no more snow.
O ur city feels better, warmer.
L ife in spring is more than a dream.

S uper great is how I feel.
P eople cheer up because the weather is so much better.
R ight now is the very beginning of spring.
I t's time to sing of sunshine and happiness.
N othing is better than this.
G oing outside now to have some fun!

Isaac Cedillos, Grade 4
Gaithersburg Elementary School, MD

A Very Wonderful Place

The world as I see it is full of green meadows
Horses, unicorns, and Pegusi play
Nickering with joy, grateful for the day
Luscious green clover to make their mouths slobber
Water trickles down the side of a mountain
Only to find itself in a pool on the ground
Clear blue skies full of hidden stars, soon to be shown
A deep dark purple sets its tone
Soon to be dark they lay down to sleep
When they wake up, it's a brand new day and they're ready to play
Once more

Jessica Montgomery, Grade 6
Floyd T Binns Middle School, VA

Tulips

I spy a garden with a profusion of pink tulips.
Their soft, silky, and smooth petals
bob and rustle in the light breeze,
giving off a delicate smell
as sweet as cotton candy.
All too soon these petals will drift
away into a brisk cold day,
but don't worry the tulips will be back next year
to share their sweet blossoms.

Emily Parrott, Grade 6
Trinity School, MD

Speckled Snow

Snow snow
the wind blows.
See the rocks far below.
As the blue sky flows above.
Sit on rocks
here we go.
Under the tree
and on the rocks.
Dream dream day dream!
Enjoy this day out on snow.
Have a picnic even though there's snow.
We had a nice day out on rocks
but now it is time to go
Say bye to the sight the wonderful sight.

Gianfranco Messina, Grade 4
Immaculate Conception Catholic Regional School, RI

Spring in the Garden

Walking barefoot on the soft grass,
Every flower too elegant to pass.
Sunflowers holding their heads up high,
As bees are busily rushing by.

Roses with petals of velvet; smooth and soft,
While hanging baskets of morning glories are aloft.
Lavender blossoms release their fragrant perfume.
And flowering vines weave themselves on a grassy loom.

Irises holding their head up with pride,
While the light breeze makes lilies sway side to side.
The tulips displaying their petal cups, so colorful,
With daffodils and carnations looking to beautiful.

Nicole Luengo, Grade 5
Church of the Redeemer Christian School, MD

Lake Norman

Lake Norman is so fun, you can tan in the sun.
There is no school, you can swim in the pool.
You can ride in a boat, or you can float.
It's the vacation spot to be, there are many sights to see.
Don't forget to bring your fishing pole, having fun is the main goal.
You can play volleyball, make sure you are not too small.
You can walk on the pier, it is so fun here;
I hate to leave.

Aleah Holmes, Grade 4
Cedar Bluff Elementary School, VA

Water

Sounds like the ocean that I hear in a shell.
Looks like the mirror floating in the well.
Tastes like heaven running down my throat.
Feels like the surface on which stands a boat.
Smells like the shower that I take every morning.
But when you have an overflow, this is your last warning!

Paul Marcuson, Grade 4
Waller Mill Fine Arts Magnet School, VA

The Life of a Lion

She lurks through the tall grass
To attack her helpless prey.
She descends in a glorious chase
Through the bush, through the trees.
She strikes the pitiful sick or young.
The carcass is feasted upon by all.
She lies and rests for the next hunt or death.

The lion cubs play.
The mischief comes in bundles.
They attach to their mother,
They push through the crowds to get attention.
They touch, groom, and rub to bond.
The cubs play friskily as friend or foe.
They bite, claw, and smack to come out on top.

The Alpha male is feared by all.
The others cower away when he comes.
His roar can be heard by the entire herd.
His black mane means, "Keep your distance" to the males.
He prowls the Savannas for foes.
Lions are one big family that have teamwork as their lives.

Rylan Crosby, Grade 5
Forcey Christian School, MD

My Family

They might be crazy and annoying, but I love them.
They help me out when I am down.
They are the best thing that happened to me.
They are like my best friend who always stands by.
They are my shoulder to lean on.

People let you down but FAMILY is there.
Family is something to appreciate and never forget.
I will never regret having them in my life.
They always stand by…"Family!"

Adaeze Akaoma, Grade 6
Magnolia Elementary School, MD

My Dream

I was five years old when I started to play,
And I loved it so much I still play today.
I love that cold that comes with fall,
I'm back in my helmet and cleats after all.
It's bumping heads and talking trash,
The smell of mud, dirt and grass,
the sound of clashing football pads.
The quarterback gets all the glory,
But he's only part of the story.
In football, teamwork is the key,
For the backs, linemen, receivers, and the safety.
It takes a lot to be part of the team,
A lot of heart, time, sweat and blood.
But football is my dream.

Kaleb Shreve, Grade 5
Cedar Bluff Elementary School, VA

My Wordly Wishes

My wish for the world is for the waters to teem,
With every water creature in every stream.
My wish for the world is for the night,
With every star twinkling bursting with light.
My wish for the world is for no more fear,
With everyone grinning from ear to ear.
My wish for the world is for good decisions,
No more hurting no more collisions.
My wish for the world is for a long, long life,
To live it happily without any strife.
My wish for the world is for green grassy hills,
Where animals can graze and eat their fills.
My wish for the world is for no more pollution,
This would be a very great world solution.
My wish for the world I think would be great,
With a lot more love, and a lot less hate.

Gabi Saunders, Grade 6
Floyd T Binns Middle School, VA

Penguins

P enguins are funny birds, dressed in black and white;
   Who are unable to take flight.
E very penguin waddles around in the snow,
   But when they jump into the icy water,
   You won't believe how fast they go.
N ests are built by male penguins, with lots of rocks;
   Then protected by both parents against other flocks.
G athering fish and other seafood with their hooked bill,
   Is how all penguins get their fill.
U nderwater they use their wings to swim like a torpedo,
   But they look like a funny fish wearing a tuxedo.
I love the penguins webbed feet,
   And how they walk is really neat.
N ever underestimate what penguins can do.
   And I don't believe they belong in a zoo.
S eeing how penguins love to play, makes me want to play all day.

Sara Rinehardt, Grade 5
Cedar Bluff Elementary School, VA

Report Cards

Report cards are coming soon
I am probably doomed
I hope I get no bad grades
If I do, I am going to tell my teacher
Please give me all A's
If you don't, it will not be okay
What if I get in trouble?
Would I still be able to play with my guinea pig?
Would I still be able to watch TV?
What if my sister says, "That's terrible!"
You need to get all A's or at least get some B's too
Well, oh no, what will I do?
Oh report cards, oh report cards,
What will I do?

Jordan Clark, Grade 4
Courthouse Road Elementary School, VA

Christmas Eve

Outside I see the footprints,
   Where others walked by.
It is completely white out,
   Except for the tracks.

Inside I smell cookies in the oven,
And a gingerbread candle burning.
I enter the living room,
Following the scent of Christmas pine.

It is a sweet smell,
And it reminds me of the place we got our tree.
I hear the song Jingle Bells on the radio,
And presents getting wrapped behind my parent's door.

My parents finally come out,
And stack the big presents on the bottom,
   And the tiny ones on top.
They resemble two skyscrapers,
   On either side of the tree.

One side is mine,
   The other my sister's.
My mother says "time to go to bed."
But, how with Santa on his way?

Savannah Stewart, Grade 5
Tilghman Elementary School, MD

Arlington

All of the white little stones
Lined up perfectly

American soldiers lay in peace under the grass
Listening to Taps played for another
One that's going to be laid with the others

Arlington National Cemetery
Where soldiers who did not hesitate
To die for their country lie

Unfortunately, every day a new stone is put in
Grieving families kneeling
Saying a prayer

Everybody in the cemetery feeling pain
The same pain thousands of other families felt

Every time you hear 21 guns
You'll know
Another hero brought home to us

Soldiers
Proud to be on this piece of sacred property
Arlington

Emily Haley, Grade 6
St Brigid School, ME

Chicken Wings

Chicken wings
Chicken wings
What a treat!
So warm and scrumptious,
You're delicious to eat!

chicken wings
Chicken wings
What a treat!
Covered in hot sauce,
Feel the heat!
Jennifer Uzor, Grade 6
Magnolia Elementary School, MD

Stars

Stars are bright
Like a shining knight.
Across the moon
And across the sky,
We see stars glimmering
Only at night.
When we go to sleep
They are a twinkling sight.
When we wake in the morning we
Don't see them but I
Can imagine that they are with me.
Erika Velasquez, Grade 5
Gaithersburg Elementary School, MD

The Best

I'm the best
Better than the rest
I'll put on a show
That will surely glow
I'm mostly right
And I love the limelight
It's what I'm about
And I'll shout it out
I'm the best
The best of the best
Well at least in my world
Tosin Idowu, Grade 4
Featherbed Lane Elementary School, MD

Poetry

I can't decide which to do
A cinquain, concrete, or haiku
A limerick poem, diamante too
There are so many that I can choose
I don't have to win or loose
Poems aren't ever failures
There's no reason to get paler
Poetry is for me.
I can write anything!
Savanna Holzshu, Grade 4
Waller Mill Fine Arts Magnet School, VA

Birthdays

Hope
A wonderful day
Presents
Prizes
Yearly celebration
Beliefs
I love cake!
Restaurants for dinner
Tons of people one day of birth
Happy birthday
Don't eat too much cake!
Absolutely uplifting
Yes, I love my birthday!
Emily Fisher, Grade 5
H M Pearson Elementary School, VA

Poetry

Poetry,
Poetry,
It's a great thing.
Sometimes it might make you sing,
Most of the time it makes me smile,
Even if it takes a while.
I like it some
I like it a lot
Even if it's about a spot.
Poetry,
Poetry,
It's a great thing
Even if it makes you sing.
Ben Hatch, Grade 4
Greater Portland Christian School, ME

My Dad

You're always there to help
no matter what life brings
to laugh with me to be proud of
me and share all the happy things

But even more importantly
you're there when plans go
wrong to help me work things
out when disappointments come
along and so I want to
thank you Dad and tell you
lovingly you are the best
thing life has given to me!
Jayda Jackson, Grade 4
Featherbed Lane Elementary School, MD

The Bell

Ring! Ring! Oops you're late
Ringing dinging bell I hate
Once again…I'm late.
Tyler Crank, Grade 6
Monelison Middle School, VA

Saving Ocean Life

The ocean is so vast,
One of life's mysteries.
Keep dumping trash in it,
And it will be history.

Coral, sharks, fish, and dolphins,
Even the lovely stingray,
Protect them and their environment,
SO they live to see another day.

Lobster, crabs, and shrimp,
Are all used for food.
If you keep polluting the ocean,
They will be in a bad mood.

Every living thing,
Depends on the ocean to survive.
Let's all do our part,
Keep hope alive.
Khara Truelove, Grade 4
St Clement Mary Hofbauer School, MD

Green Fan

We need to clean it up.
Come on, let's go.
We have to do it NOW!
Skip your TV show.

Look and see the beauty of it,
Clean water and fresh air.
Get on the ball and move.
Treat Mother Earth with care.

We need to recycle.
It's all in the plan.
Our world needs our help.
Because it's dirty, man!

We're going to get it done.
Use a recycling can.
The junk, just throw it out.
Become a GREEN fan!
Grace Whaley, Grade 4
St Clement Mary Hofbauer School, MD

Baby Dragon

Covered in a coat of yellow stars
Small wings
Shy
Peaceful
Tries to fly, but just not yet,
Stays by her mother's side
Makes friends with other dragons
She may be small, but she can do it all!
Bethany Glynn, Grade 5
St Mary School, RI

Yellow

Yellow is a bright smile on a kid.
Yellow is pasta boiling in water.
Yellow is the bright hot sun in the summer.
Yellow is a bee buzzing in your ear.
Yellow is a balloon (pop). Or maybe a lemon.
Yellow is a bird chirping in a nest.
Yellow is a huge bow on a gift.
Yellow is a banana in a bowl.
Yellow is a sticky note or maybe a marker.
Yellow is a star shining above you at night
Yellow is a French fry.
Yellow is a show off no doubt about that.
Imagine living without it.

Simone Pimental, Grade 4
Immaculate Conception Catholic Regional School, RI

Spring

The sun shines, the deer graze
rivers flow with birds singing.
The clouds are fluffy like
cotton candy. There is a meadow
where rabbits hop in the tall
grass and foxes run around and play.

Then it starts to rain, the deer run
for shelter. The birds stop singing and
fly to their nest. The cotton candy clouds
turn dark, the rabbits in the meadow run to
their den, so do the foxes that were playing.
Now everything is quiet as it rains.

Hannah Huffman, Grade 6
Hardin Reynolds Memorial School, VA

Football

F avorite players in the club, I have several.
O ver the years, there have been 44 Super Bowls.
O ver the years, many different teams have won.
T reat others with respect, on your team and on mine.
B e kind to one another, on and off the playing field.
A ll football games are played mainly in the fall.
L iking both watching and playing football
L ucky to play such an awesome sport.

Eduardo Reyes, Grade 4
Gaithersburg Elementary School, MD

Superstar

I want to know what it's like
To be a superstar.
The fans, the fun, the fame, the friends, the concerts.
Meeting other famous people,
And becoming an overnight sensation.
My friends think so, too.

So, maybe we can find a talent competition…

Hannah Damanka, Grade 5
Gaithersburg Elementary School, MD

PMS

What's wrong with me?
Just listen and see
I'm always more angry and never less
My feelings are a total mess.

I always scream and yell for no reason at all
All this screaming makes my heart want to fall
My mom says to just take a chill pill
But I just look at her and want time to stand still.

I did research and it says it happens to women from east to west
And guess what?
It's nothing but PMS!

Ramlah Bethea, Grade 6
Magnolia Elementary School, MD

The Beauty of Spring

Flowers are in bloom, and in the sky is the moon,
Shining bright for all to see,
Really that is spring to me.
I wish that spring could never end
For spring is a postcard I will not send
So…what is spring to you? Pollen, flowers, cows going moo?
Seeds are sprouting, looking at you.
So answer this question,
Tell me the truth,
What does spring mean to you?

And that is the beauty of spring.
Happy spring!

Alexandra Haggerty, Grade 4
Walsingham Academy Lower School, VA

Majestic Power

Dragon
Intelligent, ferocious, powerful, majestic.
His fights on the battlefield are epic.
With destruction and power he will wipe out all foes.
Knowledge is power.
There's nothing he doesn't know
Gray, black, green, red.
When this beast roars, you'll feel a pounding in your head.

William Tuttle, Grade 5
St Mary School, RI

Family Reunion

Having the time of my life
Skylight showing sparkly stars
Children running around playing

Barbecue steaming with hot dogs and burgers
Mothers gossiping, fathers talking
What do I call these people
My family

Dieynabou Diallo, Grade 6
Magnolia Elementary School, MD

Giselle
G reat girl
I ncredible star
S ometimes she's shy
E ncouraging person
L oving child
L ikes to play soccer
E nergy inside and out
Giselle Zapana, Grade 4
Gaithersburg Elementary School, MD

Dog/Cat
Dog
Energetic, hyper
Barking, sniffing, wagging
Hair, sharp teeth, claws, stripes
Napping, sleeping, strolling
Sleepy, lazy
Cat
Wes Featherstone, Grade 5
St Christopher's School, VA

Light
Light
bright, joyful
shining, comfortable, saving
warm, favorable, sinister, forlorn
frightening, alarming, distressing
sad, lonesome
Darkness
Hannah Harr, Grade 6
Immaculate Heart of Mary School, MD

Fear
Your heart is pounding fast
Something makes you get scared
You're in the dark place
You turn the corner and
There's nothing there at all
It is all in your head
Or is it?
Jeffrey Ramos, Grade 6
Magnolia Elementary School, MD

Happy and Sad
Happy
Smile, giggle
Laughing, clapping, snapping
Fun, pleasure, sorrow, unhappy
Crying, whining, uncomfortable
Frown, moan
Sad
Jordan Walters, Grade 4
Hebbville Elementary School, MD

Friends
Friends are like sisters
They go through good times and bad
They have lots of fun
Cecelia Goodman, Grade 6
Monelison Middle School, VA

Michelle
Michelle is funny
She is my best friend always
I love her to death
Kelsy Mays, Grade 6
Monelison Middle School, VA

Great Depression
On the streets, homeless
Starvation spreading quickly
Children with no clothes
Allysa Franklin, Grade 6
Monelison Middle School, VA

Nature
Spring flowers bloom soft
Animals' sweet beauty sings
Water splashing, wave
Tessa Smith, Grade 6
Monelison Middle School, VA

Storm
Winds blow fast and hard
Water rises way too high
And the clouds darken
Russell Crist, Grade 6
Monelison Middle School, VA

Messy Mix Up
Oh no! My makeup
Messy colors all mixed up
Now I look like YUCK!
Malaysia Haythe, Grade 6
Monelison Middle School, VA

Peaceful Nature
Peaceful birds lay on
a tree; gentle chirping fills
the air; what beauty
Salona Copper-Luckey, Grade 6
Monelison Middle School, VA

Football
Blue! Forty-two! Go!
Says the quarterback loudly
Fling! Goes the football
Cameron Sprouse, Grade 6
Monelison Middle School, VA

Animals
I love all kinds of animals.
That is, if they are nice to me.
I have two animals in my house.
Of course, I wish that it was three.
There are so many animals in this world.
I hope that they are sweet.
I really love helping animals.
There are so many I'd like to meet.
Isabella Lemm, Grade 4
Waller Mill Fine Arts Magnet School, VA

They Bicker, Bicker and Bright
My parents always bicker
And I always be bothered
My dad says one thing
And my mom says another thing
But when they are not bickering
They're so bright
Sometimes when they bicker
They always be right
Aaliyah Robinson, Grade 4
Featherbed Lane Elementary School, MD

Feelings
Happy
Cheerful, excited
Singing, laughing, jumping
Quiet, bored, awful, loud
Screaming, stomping, slouching
Unhappy, mad
Angry
Brooklyn Gardner, Grade 5
Eastport Elementary School, ME

The Wonders of the World
Earth
Beautiful, wonderful
Growing, revolving, singing
Planet, world, shelter, safety
Protecting, covering, relaxing
Comfortable, warm
Home
Molly Luckinbill, Grade 6
Floyd T Binns Middle School, VA

The Future
The future is ahead
Thoughts in my head.
What is coming next?
I can feel it coming.
How many, how much?
How many days, how many months?
All I can do is just wait.
Olivia Wharton, Grade 5
St John Neumann Academy, VA

Soccer
Soccer means a lot to me,
It will never let me be.
But that is what I like,
Soccer is just my type.
The ball seems to tell me,
That it will stay with me
And never go away.
I could play all day.
I like soccer, and soccer likes me.
Ava Veith, Grade 4
Waller Mill Fine Arts Magnet School, VA

My Dog
Lilly is silly
She runs all around
Like a baby deer
She runs after her tennis ball
As fast as the wind
I can't beat her to it
You shake her treats
She's there in a heartbeat
Lilly loves others like her brothers
Emily Hartman, Grade 5
St Joseph School-Fullerton, MD

Rainbows and Blueberries
Dragon
Clumsy
Hilarious
Blue green eyes
Rainbow colors
Blue green feet
Red and green striped wings
Blueberry pie is what he eats
Yum!
Zoe Frusher, Grade 5
St Mary School, RI

Guitar
Guitar
Fun, challenging
Strumming, playing, creating
I love making music!
Instrument
Olivia Wassman, Grade 6
Immaculate Heart of Mary School, MD

Sunset
S ight-seeing beautiful sky
U nder the sun hides the gentle moon
N ever will you feel alone
S un is almost ready to set
E nds the brilliant light of day
T ill tomorrow brings another golden sky
Fabianna Herrera, Grade 4
Gaithersburg Elementary School, MD

Shining Star
The shiny golden lights of the dancing stars
Shine upon our faces
While we gaze
Up at their
Untarnished beauty.

As they continue to waltz through the sky,
We feel ourselves
Drifting off
To slumber.
Mia Grove, Grade 6
Trinity School, MD

Blue Berry Friends Words
Blue berry
friends is the word.
Everybody what up.
Everyone clap clap.
Say hello and bye
that word everyone.
Asking my name and that
How it works.
It's call blue berry friends,
for blue bell!
Jade Harris, Grade 4
Featherbed Lane Elementary School, MD

Dreaming
One day I'll
be as strong
as you I'll keep
my head high and
dream just like
I will never stop
even if I have to
I wanna grow up
and be just like
you I love you.
Dwayne Holley, Grade 4
Featherbed Lane Elementary School, MD

King Cobra
K ind of snake
I t's not good to get close to a snake
N ever keep a snake as a pet
G etting bitten by a snake is dangerous

C obras are poisonous snakes
O n trees is where you can find snakes
B oas are HUGE snakes
R ats are a snake's favorite food
A snake could sneak in your house
Egardo Merino, Grade 4
Gaithersburg Elementary School, MD

A Lump of Red
A cardinal, red feathers in a lump,
The bird appears as a bright red bump.
A fire with red, orange, and brown.
A building on fire, not burning down.

The cardinal has good sight;
As she is awaiting for food on her flight.
The cardinal, soaring through the air,
Passes the galloping mare.

At noon the cardinal devours bugs,
All kinds of insects and many slugs.
Later she find a maple tree, she has sap,
For a tasty snack,

In the evening the cardinal flies,
And to the tree she glides.
At night the cardinal settles down for a rest,
Sitting on the tree with its bright red crest.

A cardinal, red, orange, yellow, and brown,
It is easy to spot when you have found.
A cardinal, red feathers in a lump,
The bird appears as a bright red bump.
Annabelle Treadon, Grade 5
Forcey Christian School, MD

The Farmer Down the Block
The farmer down the block
helped the grocery store stay in stock.
But that was about to change,
his life would soon rearrange.

The cowgirl up the hill
always helped those who were ill.
And when a huge storm came,
everyone else became lame.

The cowgirl went to tell
the Word of God to make them well.
The message did just that,
and in return she got a hat.

The angels in Heaven rejoice.
More have heard God's truthful voice.
No other religion is true;
we've been saved, me and you.

The farmer down the block
now keeps the Bible bookstore in stock.
Yes, this is his new work
where fellow Christians lurk.
Daniel Mullins, Grade 4
Tazewell Elementary School, VA

Summer
I feel breeze on swings
Snow cones are so wonderful
We go to the pool
Janae Lewis-Brown, Grade 6
Monelison Middle School, VA

Spring
Rainbows, flowers grow
Peaceful, animals in spring
Chirping birds sing low
Madison Monark, Grade 6
Monelison Middle School, VA

Softball
Softball is a sport
You don't have to be perfect
You just need to try
Haley Garner, Grade 6
Monelison Middle School, VA

Spring
Listen as birds sing
As the wind blows peacefully
Spring is almost here
Bailey Ferguson, Grade 6
Monelison Middle School, VA

Best Friends
Best friends will be yours
Always in eternity
They are things you keep
Chiann Meng, Grade 6
Monelison Middle School, VA

Flowers
Flowers colorful
They bring my allergies too
But bees love them so
Cierra Richerson, Grade 6
Monelison Middle School, VA

Fire
Sparks lick up from me
Wait I shall soon dance for you
I'm a great fire!
Joey Ledingham, Grade 6
Monelison Middle School, VA

The Owl
Hoo! Hoo! The owl goes
in the dark, quiet, night breeze.
Its eyes shine brightly.
Dakoda Williams, Grade 6
Monelison Middle School, VA

Me
I am a pen, I am used to interpret.
I can extend and retract my feelings at will.
The ink of my thoughts fills nearly 70 percent of my capacity.
I am smooth and sleek classic yet ever-changing, neutral and creative.
I am used to carry on stories and biographies.
I am the approval of creativity and the tool of inspiration.
Montana Taylor, Grade 4
Featherbed Lane Elementary School, MD

School
S o many kids learning about amazing things
C ommunities working together to help students earn Certificates of Success
H elping people learn that hitting is not allowed
O nly schools can help you learn, using objects such as rulers and protractors
O n school grounds there is no bullying allowed, only you can be the best that you can be
L etting everyone learn no matter who they are, by listening to the teacher
Frederick Aaron Schwartz, Grade 4
Gaithersburg Elementary School, MD

The Spirit World
An eerie image of trees, lanterns, and drapes
Whispers, singing, crying, and laughing
The smell of rotting leaves, decayed animals and the profound smell of rosemary
Dull, moist, and sweet air
Ghostly hands touching my skin and the cold breeze of silence
Trystan Manahan, Grade 4
Greenville Elementary School, VA

A Perfect Day
A perfect day is when,
all is fine in the air,
nobody is screaming or upset.

A perfect day is when,
the sun is shining,
and all is wonderful,
with friends and family,
as you hang out with one another.

A perfect day is when,
everybody is having a thrilling time,
with one another,
during a friendly game of wiffle ball.

A perfect day is when,
everybody is having a spectacular time,
with one another,
as friends and family do,
on magnificent days.
Coby Wilson, Grade 6
Tilghman Elementary School, MD

Life
I wonder what it would be like,
If I could flip
The pages of Life,
Back and forth,
To the past
And the future…
I could take back
All my words,
And prevent something
From happening.
But one thing I know
For sure…
It would certainly
Eliminate
The mixture of
Sorrow, fear,
And mysteries,
Which would turn
Our lives into
A WORLD OF BOREDOM.
Faeza Ashraf, Grade 6
Calvert School, MD

Love
Love could be spoken or,
Love could be broken,
Love is like a perfect dime,
When it goes through your time,
Love is like an apple falling from the tree,
'Cause when one apple drops,
The other one flees.
Leilani Kabigting, Grade 5
Rosemont Forest Elementary School, VA

Flowers
F ull blossoms in the trees
L ovely cool petal breeze
O utside it's sunny weather
W ind's blowing small bird feathers
E veryone is out there
R ain cools down the air
S pring is finally here!
Maya Walker, Grade 4
Gaithersburg Elementary School, MD

Teacher
T hey teach
E ven when they're tired
A teacher teaches math
C an give us homework
H as a classroom
E ven teaches in the afternoon
R eally likes us
Jaylen Cook, Grade 4
Featherbed Lane Elementary School, MD

Seeing My Dad
Visiting my dad every other weekend is hard
My trip starts with happiness
It ends with heartache
His face shows joy; then pain
This hurts me, too
As he leaves
His aching face wants to stay with me
Jessica Littel, Grade 5
Rosemont Forest Elementary School, VA

Spring and Summer
Spring
Cool, wet
Raining, blooming, blossoming
Flowers, school, fun, play
Swimming, playing, hiking
Warm, dry
Summer
Sara Rodriguez, Grade 4
Greenville Elementary School, VA

London Eye
L ooking over the Thames River
O h, look I can see the Tower of London
N ever know when you get down
D own on the ground then up
O ver the city then down
N ot one bad sight

E verything glows at night
Y ou can even see the Westminster Abbey
E ven the gift shop is far away
Oliver Sabo, Grade 4
St Christopher's School, VA

Adventure
A wesome
D aring
V ast
E xciting
N ew
T rue
U nder
R eal
E nchanting
Mikayla De Atley, Grade 6
Floyd T Binns Middle School, VA

The Guy That Murdered Me
I turned around and saw
the guy that murdered me
he started talking to my ghost
and said, "Look, you see.

I didn't mean to harm you
no, not in any way
but when I took you out of your fish tank,
your life slipped away."
Hannah Massie, Grade 6
Monelison Middle School, VA

Love
I love you from my heart
I love you when we look at the sea
Because that is when
We make it fun
And I thank you for that
Markia Dates, Grade 4
Featherbed Lane Elementary School, MD

God
God is tremendously great.
He loves kids who are only eight.

God has fun living up there,
There's lots of food and tons of air!
Anna Shewchuk, Grade 4
St John Neumann Academy, VA

Life
My time is ticking,
I will hit the ground running,
Life to the fullest.
Mady Sale, Grade 6
Monelison Middle School, VA

Flowers
Flowers are blooming
Letting free a hidden scent
For the world to share
Tijesunimi Borode, Grade 4
Hebbville Elementary School, MD

Index